Richard Peters

RICHARD PETERS
Portrait by John Wollaston in the Academy of Fine Arts, Philadelphia

Richard Peters
Provincial Secretary and Cleric
1704–1776

Hubertis Cummings
with a Foreword by Paul A. W. Wallace

Mechanicsburg, PA USA

Published by Sunbury Press, Inc.
Mechanicsburg, PA USA

www.sunburypress.com

Copyright © 1944, 2024 by Hubertis Cummings.
Cover Copyright © 2024 by Sunbury Press, Inc.

Sunbury Press supports copyright. Copyright fuels creativity, encourages diverse voices, promotes free speech, and creates a vibrant culture. Thank you for buying an authorized edition of this book and for complying with copyright laws. Except for the quotation of short passages for the purpose of criticism and review, no part of this publication may be reproduced, scanned, or distributed in any form without permission. You are supporting writers and allowing Sunbury Press to continue to publish books for every reader. For information contact Sunbury Press, Inc., Subsidiary Rights Dept., PO Box 548, Boiling Springs, PA 17007 USA or legal@sunburypress.com.

For information about special discounts for bulk purchases, please contact Sunbury Press Orders Dept. at (855) 338-8359 or orders@sunburypress.com.

To request one of our authors for speaking engagements or book signings, please contact Sunbury Press Publicity Dept. at publicity@sunburypress.com.

FIRST SUNBURY PRESS EDITION: January 2024

Set in Adobe Garamond Pro | Interior design by Crystal Devine | Cover by Lawrence Knorr based on the painting by John Wollaston in the Academy of Fine Arts, Philadelphia, colorized by Alice Buchman | Edited by Lawrence Knorr.

Publisher's Cataloging-in-Publication Data
Names: Cummings, Hubertis, author | Wallace, Paul A. W., foreword.
Title: Richard Peters : provincial secretary and cleric 1704–1776 / Hubertis Cummings.
Description: First trade paperback edition. | Mechanicsburg, PA : Sunbury Press, 2024.
Summary: Richard Peters was one of the most important officials in colonial Pennsylvania, involved in all matters of the Penns and the founding of many institutions.
Identifiers: ISBN : 979-8-88819-124-4 (paperback).
Subjects: BIOGRAPHY & AUTOBIOGRAPHY / Religious | HISTORY / United States / Colonial Period (1600-1775) | HISTORY / United States / State & Local / Middle Atlantic.

Product of the United States of America
0 1 1 2 3 5 8 13 21 34 55

For the Love of Books!

Contents

Foreword *by Paul A. W. Wallace* — vii

I.	Refracted Vista	1
II.	Departure from Grace	7
III.	Aspirations of a Cleric	10
IV.	Inches of Earth	24
V.	For the Good of Souls	31
VI.	Stone Wall at Fulham	46
VII.	Gossip and Politics	54
VIII.	Chagrin and Some Business	65
IX.	More Business and Some Beatitude	76
X.	Little Less Than Treason	86
XI.	Cabins and Academy	106
XII.	Promise of Beulah	121
XIII.	Foretastes of Battle	142
XIV.	Aftermath of Defeat	156
XV.	Moods in a Province	170
XVI.	Peace and War	186
XVII.	Recovery of Function	196
XVIII.	Riot and Respite	210
XIX.	Last Excursion	227
XX.	Sans Dieu Rien	244
XXI.	After Indian Summer	258

Acknowledgments — 265
Sources — 266
Index — 269
About the Author — 277

Foreword

Pennsylvania was well served by its Secretary, the Reverend Richard Peters, during the middle years of the eighteenth century. Modern readers desiring to know something of the history of the colony during the generation preceding the Revolutionary War will find themselves no less well served by the Reverend Richard and his present biographer, Dr. Cummings.

Richard Peters saw, as no other man of his time did, the whole of Pennsylvania. He had an energetic, inquiring mind, and he was, for many years, established in official positions that gave him the means of satisfying his curiosity. As Secretary of the Land Office, Secretary and Clerk of the Provincial Council, Rector of Christ Church, Philadelphia, and President of the Board of Trustees of the College of Pennsylvania, he devoted himself to mastering the details of Pennsylvania's expanding life, economic, political, religious, and educational. His office was the clearinghouse for the province's most important business, and whenever possible, Mr. Secretary Peters himself took an active part in the conduct of affairs.

He watched with admiration the rapid growth of Philadelphia and was the friend or associate of the men who made the city great: William Allen, Ben Franklin, James Logan, and Andrew Hamilton.

He helped to survey the disputed boundary between Pennsylvania and Maryland. He served with distinction at the Lancaster Conference of 1744, which made firm the chain of friendship between the Six Nations and the English colonies. He observed closely the thwarting, by popular movement, of the manorial system administered by the Penns from across the sea. In 1755, he offered General Braddock advice, which that irascible gentleman would have done well to take. At Easton, he met the Delaware "King," Teedyuscung, and then supervised the treaty in 1758 that brought peace to Pennsylvania after years of Indian war. He assisted General Forbes in the campaign that cleared the Ohio Valley for the English. He attended the signing of the treaty at Fort

Stanwix in the Mohawk Valley. He met George Washington, and he lived to hear the Liberty Bell ring in Philadelphia.

If the reader of this biography finds himself watching the history of Pennsylvania through the Secretary's office window, he will at the same time be ever mindful of the Reverend Richard himself. The man had individuality and is interesting even when we do not admire him. His ingenious threading of the labyrinth of colonial church politics, his snobbery, his careful eye for self-interest while attending to the good of the province he loved, and his combining "of the ways of grace and business" afford material for comedy. Yet with all his veneer of eighteenth-century cleverness, we see in him at times warm-hearted impulsiveness, much gaiety, and even candor, which give complexity to his character and draw us to him.

In the present volume, Dr. Cummings succeeds in bringing Richard Peters alive for us and in letting us see the growing colony as it mirrored itself in the Secretary's acutely perceptive mind. For the author to have accomplished this without either minimizing the history or magnifying the man is an artistic achievement of unusual distinction.

Paul A. W. Wallace
Lebanon Valley College
March 1944

I
Refracted Vista

One of the celebrities of his age in Pennsylvania, William White, was born in the old capital city of that province on the Delaware during the closing year of King George's War. He was schooled in the College of Philadelphia, pursuing subjects of divinity as well as the classics, and sometime after his graduation in 1765, was posted overseas to be ordained in London into the clergy of the Church of England. On his return to America in the early 1770s, he took place amid a number of assistant ministers to the Reverend Richard Peters, Rector of the United Churches of Christ and St. Peter's, in the parish of his birth. Subsequently, he functioned as chaplain to the Continental Congress, sitting in Philadelphia during occasional years of the struggle for American Independence. Upon the conclusion of that war, his gifts of moderation, piety, and organizing labor all having borne a timely and wholesome spiritual fruit, he was consecrated at the hands of the Archbishops of Canterbury and York and of the Bishops of Bath and Wells and Peterborough, to be a bishop in the new Protestant Episcopal Church of America. Later, from the years of his own greatest usefulness and eminence, when in himself he had become the fruition of almost a century of Churchmen's dreaming of having a proper head for the American Colonial Church, he could look back both to schooldays during which Mr. Secretary Peters was a trustee of the Academy and College of Philadelphia and to ministerial days when, in processional and recessional at Christ Church, he attended the Reverend Dr. Richard Peters, his gracious and immediate ecclesiastical superior.

Preceding William White by some three or four years at the Academy and College was another boy, less happily and less circumspectly born, who also throve in learning and industry and was more directly guided by the Secretary to the Province of Pennsylvania, whose namesake and nephew he was. Sprig of the Secretary's brother William Peters, the older youth knew early that he gathered more credit to himself as his uncle's ward than as his father's

American heir. Moreover, much as Governor Denny might fulminate at his too-constant companionship with his guardian and mentor, the second Richard Peters adhered close to his good-natured relative and friend. His opportunism was fostered no less than his capabilities by the all-provident Secretary, and he, too, waxed in citizenship and merit. He studied law, was admitted to the bar in Philadelphia, became Register of the Admiralty, a commissioner in the negotiations of the treaty of Fort Stanwix with the Indians in 1768, a captain of a company of Associators on the approach of the Revolution, Secretary to the Board of War serving American Congress, member of the Assembly and the Senate when Pennsylvania had become an independent commonwealth, and for crowning laurel, Judge of the United States District Court in Philadelphia. In the quarter-century of his own highest distinctions, he could recall his Uncle Richard's pleasure in 1762 at being able in that year to resume actively his sacred calling of priest and to add the rectorship of Christ Church to his lay duties as a member of the Council of the Province. He could remember, too, when he chose the arrangements for the old cleric's burial in 1776 in the sanctuary where, during the last fourteen years of his life, his pious guardian officiated at the pulpit and altar.

In brief, Bishop White and Judge Peters had good reason for intimate acquaintance with the career of their common sponsor and benefactor. Both men were luminaries of the culture of an eighteenth-century commonwealth. Both were witnessed in a signal fashion to the birth in their native city of a great new nation. Both might have been expected to retain many a memorable image of a life that had been a prime expression of all that preceded that revolution in the American experience out of which their successes had been carved. Yet neither Bishop nor Judge had really much to say when a late eighteenth-century or early nineteenth-century memorialist approached him on the subject of the once wide ruling ecclesiastic and secretary. Lack of time rather than of will in each may have been the cause. But the annotator who consulted them and whose rude scrawls are today preserved in the Department of the Archives of Pennsylvania in the modern city of Harrisburg gathered little from his aides that was exact and less that was revealing with regard to a man who a few brief decades before had been as lively a spirit as Philadelphia had ever prospered in its midst. To read the four-page scribble of that unidentifiable memorialist is to conclude with what celerity the wind passes over the life of a man and how quickly he is gone.

Yet hasty conclusions are no proper index to the flourishing that the flower of a field may have had in its heyday of bloom. In one of his sanctimonious moods, the older Richard Peters might have admitted the validity of the Psalmist's text even with application to himself. In richer moments, he would have smiled at its inapplicability. He would have accepted benignly enough some of his memorialist's omissions and most of the inclusions he would have approved. But he would never have found the man's affirmations wholly adequate, and he would have remembered clearly, could he have seen the fellow's script, how different really had been his flowering. For Richard Peters, in his lifetime, had joined in his personality the candor of Alice's Cheshire Cat with the grave reserve and insight of the Sphinx. Governor William Denny excepted in the trying years of 1756–58, he had never knowingly smiled himself into the disfavor of any man, and to the end of his days, in sunshine or rain, amid litigants, controversialists, politicians, patriots, proprietaries, deputy governors, Indian chiefs, statesmen, revolutionaries, Churchmen, Moravians, Presbyterians, Lutherans, merchants, attorneys-general, and chief justices, he had steadily kept it his business to please. One thing can be depended on: the earlier effervescent Mr. Peters in the Pennsylvania Land Office or the State House office of the Secretary to the Province would never have refused his interest to the scribbler who, two decades after his death, put down in ink his mitigated encomiums.

Let those lauds stand here, then, for what they would have been worth to the inspirer of their subject—to a character seldom given to showing his own hand fully:

> Of the reverend Richard Peters, I should be glad to furnish more ample memorials than I have been able to obtain. From his nephew, my worthy & excellent friend Judge Peters, I have received answers to some of my enquiries, but he regrets the destruction of many of his papers during the revolutionary disturbances. Bishop White also kindly lent his assistance.
>
> Richard Peters was born at Liverpool about the year 1704. His father was an eminent member of the profession of the law & for this occupation his second son, the subject of this memoir, was originally intended. His education was conducted in the best manner then in use among people of rank and fortune. Westminster School always in high repute, Leyden, the resort of much of the learning of that time & finally, the University of Oxford contributed in succession to the formation of the elegant and profound scholar that he proved to be. His own inclinations led him to prefer divinity to law and after the choice was finally made by him he pursued his theological studies with a great ardor & effect.

On the death of his father the family estate devolved on the eldest son William, the father of our Judge Peters, and Richard was, of course, obliged to exert his talents for his own support.

With this view he emigrated to America but the exact time of his arrival here is not ascertained.

It appears, however, that he was in the exercise of clerical functions in 1736. The Episcopal colonists were at that time so dependent on the Bishop of London that his consent was necessary even for the appointment of an assistant minister and August 1736 the vestry of Christ Church in this city requesting that the reverend Richard Peters might be appointed assistant to the Rector the rev'd Archibald Cummings. The appointment was made but from a disagreement between the two gentlemen, the union did not continue.

About this time he became engaged in elevated secular employments under the patronage and in Possession of the confidence of Thomas Penn by whom he was appointed Secretary of the Province, Secretary of the Land Office, & his principal agent & commissioner of property. Although the scene of action was comparatively narrow yet the relative importance of those offices at that time was great.

The population of Penna. about this period began to increase more rapidly than before. The conduct of the political interests and the Proprietaries required to be conducted in liberal and judicious principles. The interests of the Proprietaries sometimes appeared to be likely to come into conflict with those of the people. It required constant care and sound judgment to preserve the harmony which in fact was necessary for both.

Similar offices in a great empire would not have required superior talents than those which were requisite here on a reduced scale & if Mr. Peters skillfully steered the bark thro the shoals his merit was as if he had had the management of a greater enterprise.

A. He continued in these employments after the return of Mr. Penn to Europe in 1741 till a late period when his infirmities compelled him to relinquish active business and he retired with the full acknowledgement on the part of his honorable friends of his faithful and meritorious services for about 20 years when he relinquished them on being appointed Rector of the United Episcopal churches of this city in which station he continued until September 1775 when on account of his increasing infirmities, he resigned it.

In 1771 he received from the University of Oxford the degree of Doctor of Divinity and the only matter of surprise in this transaction is that it should have been delayed so long for no one perhaps was ever better entitled to this distinction. His theological erudition was accurate, extensive & profound. His opinions were what that Church denominates orthodox—always liberal but towards the close of his life tending to what is termed evangelical.

[At this point, the manuscript interlines excisions with the text which it adopts—excisions really as pertinent as its accepted contents: "and he retained to the last that fondness for the Greek and Roman Classicks which always characterizes finished scholars." "His theological erudition was inferior to none among us."]

His library contained a collection of the works of the Fathers which, when his sight ("towards the close of his life") became impaired, he delighted to have read to him.

In his disposition, he was charitable and humane the sorrows of the afflicted were never disregarded and when in his power to assist never unrelieved. In domestic habits, he was hospitable, friendly, and polite... [Through this last unfinished paragraph, a great X is drawn, as though to suggest its inadequacy as statement or some necessary substitution of praise more relevant and dignified.]

The old Secretary and Clergyman would have interpreted phrases and clauses in this belated quasi-obituary notice rather more objectively than men today would interpret them. But the two aspects of his smile would both have been engaged in his estimation. The Cheshire Cat side would have liked "people of rank and fortune," "the elegant and profound scholar," "elevated secular employments," "Similar offices in a great empire would not have required superior talents," "theological erudition," "domestic habits ... hospitable, friendly, and polite." The Sphinx side would have been serenely cryptic toward "With this view, he emigrated to America," "so dependent on the Bishop of London," "from a disagreement between the two gentlemen," "the harmony .which in fact was necessary to both," "but towards the close of his life tending to what is termed evangelical." There would have been pleasure for both sides in "orthodox" and "liberal," the latter one, dared it have raised its eyebrows with its smile, would have asked why an X should have been superimposed upon Richard Peters' disposition as it was described in the final paragraph. Neither side would have challenged any inaccuracy which redounded to the credit of the subject of the memoir. An error in a date or two would have been a mere peccadillo; a misconstrued motive was hardly to be troubled about.

But whatever might have been the manner of smiles conjectured of the dead in 1800, whether Bishop William White could have told a good tale of his one-time superior or the District Court Judge a full narrative of his uncle—Richard Peters did live and have a story. If many of his papers were destroyed "during the revolutionary disturbances," enough thousands of them were left to round out the spaces of a vivid, busy life and to send full beams of light into the shadowy annals of a forgotten but wide-boundaried province. An earl of Derby, an offended clergyman, a proprietor of Pennsylvania with his henchmen and his enemies, Indian interpreters and Indian traders, dissenting preachers, a British general, a line of lieutenant governors, a statesman and world celebrity whose statesmanship remained unrecognized by him, two acclaimed heroes of the French and Indian Wars, fractious Presbyterians and obstinate Quakers, a pair of celebrated surveyors, and a cluster of admiring clerical *proteges* and assistants—these were not all crowded into his secretarial and ecclesiastic memories to make his mortal experience seem an empty one. More profound scholars may have lived in the eighteenth century, millions of truer saints and thousands of more honest men. Only an occasional Chesterfield or a Fielding, a Voltaire or a Beaumarchais, a Franklin or a Benedict Arnold could have been more animate than he in that epoch of alacrity. Indeed, it was not too of ten that the salt of human nature lost savor in that double-functioned priest and layman while he basked—rather than shone-in the offices of church and government.

II

Departure from Grace

Miss Esther Peters, daughter of Ralph Peters, barrister and sometime Town Clerk of Liverpool, was not one to take lightly either her conscience or that of others. The honor of a Christian and the happiness that came only through the preservation of one's immortal soul in ways of duty were the constant subjects of her study—as of many another eighteenth-century English gentlewoman.

Into young womanhood, she lived in sweet and simple faith and found all things well. Her father was a successful man, able to provide for his family, both the townhouse in Liverpool and his country place Platbridge, to have his daughters trained in the accomplishments of young ladies, including reading and writing, to meet the expenses of his sons at the noted public schools, at Oxford, and the Temple. Esther grew up in full belief that the advantages of education that her brothers and sisters shared made easier for them the path of good and the means to divine approval of their lives.

She was almost come of age before the first interruptions broke upon her quiet counsel. Her father had become strangely silent about her second brother, Richard. All talk of the youth in the family circle grew guarded while obvious care troubled the eyes and brow of Ralph Peters. Something had happened at Westminster College. Almost within the shadow of the Abbey, where so many of the old kings and queens of England lay buried, Richard had erred in some fashion. Could he have been spending money too lavishly, his sister wondered? Could he have been drinking to excess? Had he not been giving the proper attention to his studies? Indeed, the sudden plans for having Richard sent over the Channel to attend lectures in Leyden were all rather unaccountable until her mother tearfully explained that they were a way of saving Richard.

Gradually Esther came to know that amiable, sanguine Dicky had had to be rescued from a life of obloquy. A serving maid at Westminster, an impossible and vulgar person—in brief, nothing more than a creature—had ensnared her brother. Before he realized his mistake, Dicky had been lured into what his relatives chose to term a "Fleet" marriage. The best means of preserving Ralph Peters' son from a life of ignominy thereafter was to launch him in a new environment, and Esther's parents had combined to deliver the culprit from the instrument of his disgrace. Divorce was impossible in English law without cause in adultery, but the courts were not known to oblige young gentlemen to live with low-born wives to whom they had impulsively plighted solemn troth. Such procedure would have been quite too unfair to poor Dicky, who had been wantonly betrayed-snared, in fact, by a wench ere he was even well along in his teens. Esther approved the step, which was to ensure her brother his deserved opportunity of a moral life.

And, indeed, all seemed to work out for the best. Richard had several happy years at Leyden, deepening his knowledge of history, natural philosophy, and languages. Then, without demur on his return to England, a ruddy-cheeked youth cheerful as the day was long, he fell in with his father's plans and took up residence at the Inner Temple to study the law. His older brother William, who had preceded him there, soon sang praises of his junior's progress, and Richard's mentor and friend, Mr. Bootle, could speak as well of him. In fact, that legal gentleman spoke so well of the young man that, to Esther's delight, presently Dicky had won his father's permission to discontinue the law for what he maintained he had wished from early boyhood: to read for the ministry in the Church of England. His sister was very happy to witness the work of Grace in him. A year later, she was very proud when he was made a deacon by the Bishop of Winchester in 1730, still more proud when he was ordained a priest at Chelsea, and certainly elated when, after some further study of theology at Wadham College, Oxford, the influential and benignant Mr. Bootle had the twenty-eight-year-old ecclesiastic collated to Lathom Chapel. All the family rejoiced that the abyss into which Richard had been plunged years before at Westminster School was now so remote from that donative in the parish of Ormskirk in Lancashire which the generous benefactor at the Temple had procured for his disciple in the law. Caprice, it seemed, was not to dominate the life of a favorite son and brother.

Yet chance, Esther Peters was subsequently prone to admit, had as much to do with the next years of the cleric at Lathom as wise and impartial Providence. His service in Lancashire brought the affable Richard Peters into favor with the tenth Earl of Derby, resident nearby in his palace of Knowsley, and that genial nobleman, possessed of certain near relatives who bore his family name of Stanley but could not inherit his estates and title, soon found a pleasant commission for the young ecclesiast. This was to escort the Earl's two youthful kinsmen to

Holland and enter them at the University of Leyden. Then, on his return from placing Charles Stanley and his brother on the Continent, the Reverend Mr. Peters was, to his own very great relief, informed by a number of associates from older days that the nondescript partner of his "Fleet" wedlock had died-that he was free. It was a moment of opportunity, and Richard, to the delight of his own family and the satisfaction of the Earl, paid punctual suit to the sister of the two charges whom he had just taken to their schooling.

He paid it so effectually that his lordship James Stanley's charming female ward had become Richard Peters' bride and the mother of an unborn child before the serving girl of Westminster suddenly made a reappearance, an apparition not so dreadful for her own shame but notoriously material as a witness to the fact that a clergyman of the Church of England had committed bigamy. The blow fell like a thunderbolt on all. The daughters of Ralph Peters in Liverpool shuddered at the tragedy of a sister-in-law whom they loved and at the resumption of the infelicities that dogged their luckless brother. Mr. Ralph Peters was again in a quandary. Much was necessary in the way of virtue. Richard and the lady of his choice must cease living together. The Earl must look to his kinswoman, Mistress Stanley, to her own newly clouded name. Refuge must be found for a curate whose honor in his native country was now doubly stained. The boy just out of Westminster had been preserved, so his family had thought, by removal over the Channel. A more distant harborage was imperative for the man who might no longer, with credit to it or with comfort to the Earl at Knowsley, hold the benefice of Lathom. One of His Majesty's provinces overseas would be the best asylum for the unfortunate. Pennsylvania, it was believed, was a place of opportunity for able men. The Venerable Society for the Propagation of the Gospel in Foreign Parts was known to have several prospering missions there.

III

Aspirations of a Cleric

In the autumn of 1734, then, the displanted Curate of Lathom took leave of his father Ralph Peters, of his brother William, of his mother, and of Esther and his other sisters, and sailed for Philadelphia. Before his embarkation, he promised all the family he would omit no cautions in the future. The sin he had committed with his second consort bore so ugly a name that he dared not further offend her conscience or his own with any form of promise. God might have mercy on them both! For his own soul's sake, he was resolved. He would make another new start in the New World. America was a place of beginnings. There was a church of Christ in the city on the Delaware. In Andrew Hamilton, formerly of Accomac, Virginia, but now of Bristol and Philadelphia, he might find a friend, for Richard's mother had been a Preeson, and her kinswoman-in-law, Anne Brown, widow of Joseph Preeson, had taken the Scotsman for her second husband when he was making his way in the more southern province. Any connection with a lawyer of prominence in the city of the Penns might be helpful.

Yet, tried in the fires of his century as he had been, Richard did not plunge into his future without scruples on the associations of his past. With some eagerness, he scanned the first letters from home that reached him at the house of the Friend and Provincial Councillor, Clement Plumsted, to whose consideration Andrew Hamilton had been prompt to turn him.

One came early from his brother William. It commented on their joy back in Liverpool to hear of Dicky's safe arrival. It tried to inspire the displaced priest with praise for his excellent qualifications for "making a handsome progress in the law." It warned him that legal practice was incompatible with such a disposition for gaiety and company as Richard—if he would pardon his brother for remarking—had always seemed to show. It informed him that a month or so earlier, Charles Stanley had come home from Leyden to attend his sister and very briefly that the lady's child had been born, just lived to be christened, and died. In fact, a parenthesis consisting of one word sufficed the legalistic William to indicate that the infant whom Richard had begotten had been named Esther, receiving the appellation of an aunt that was no aunt, of a woman whose love of duty had kept her true in her friendship to a lady who was a mother but not a wife.

Richard's thoughts were prayerful for a time. He was glad for the christening of the child. He could not long repine that she had escaped so soon the sorrows and sins of the mortal human state.

But it was true that William Peters had a deeper sense of Richard's temperament than his sisters possessed. Affection, mirth, and society appealed more to the exiled clergyman than apprehension and remorse. Serenity, he believed, was one of the first marks of a Christian, and without effort, he remained of good cheer. He lost no great time, therefore brooding on his unintended misdemeanors. Instead, he entered with zest into his new experience, forgetting the counsel of his sisters on the fulfillment of duty to remember the cautions of his brother: not to avow principles or show attachment to any party that might prejudice him in his affairs. Second nature helped him to keep his open and sanguine countenance level with the shrewdness of his judgment. If Richard Peters, at thirty-one, did not know life, at least he knew men, and he knew as well how to make his way among them. He chose no more to make his friends unwisely, and almost immediately, his ease of manner had endeared him to Philadelphia. It was well that in his first months in Pennsylvania, he could be sponsored by both a member of the Council in Friend Plumsted and the Speaker of the Assembly in Mr. Hamilton. Determined to fit in, he guarded his advantage shrewdly.

A brief interval and his acceptance was so great that he had friends in religion and government alike. The Reverend Mr. Archibald Cummings, Rector of Christ Church and Commissary of the Bishop of London, was attracted to his cheerful and pious behavior and, to the pleasure of the unfortunate but genial exile, invited him to be his assistant, to read prayers and preach sermons for him on alternate Sundays. That privilege kept Richard within the priestly circle that he had chosen for himself, his residence with Clement Plumsted, at the same time offering him close touch with political affairs. Not much later, at the side of James Logan, he was to find occasion to attend country Quaker Meetings, where he wore his hat slouching and kept his face as mute as any. Presently, in considerable esteem with the freer elements in the congregation of Christ Church, he had also been introduced to the attention of staid Thomas Penn, an active figure in the Proprietary Family and for the decade in Philadelphia serving their interests in the colony, which their father had founded. With churchman and dissenter, he felt alike at home. He had followed strictly upon his brother's counsel and joined no party. He was once more on a fair way to success among men of established good sense and fortune. For a year and a half, his sermons afforded delight to many who worshiped in Christ Church, and the preacher entered into full enjoyment of his new experience.

But the idyl was not always to be an uninterrupted one. Mr. Cummings grew apprehensive when gossip, beginning to permeate from England upon the subject of Mr. Peters' mischances and behavior there, was made the more significant by the charm which his priest had for the more restless elements in the parish. The good Rector could see that Richard Peters was much in the company of persons fairly nondescript. Moreover, Archibald Cummings cherished inward convictions that the Church of England could never meet with solid encouragement in the province until the Proprietaries of Pennsylvania should deliver the government of it over to the Crown. He was well aware that the Penns if they gave friendship to his church, expected friendship back from pulpit and parish, and he knew that Andrew Hamilton, with whom his assistant had grown into a familiar, now served in the Proprietary interest. Suddenly, in the spring and summer of 1737, the clerical teapot in Philadelphia boiled into a tempest.

Scandalmongering began, laymen divided from laymen, rector from assistant, and laity from clergy. Not for a quarter century had the members of Christ Church known such perplexity or such excitement. Old memories revived, new insinuations began, and honest Churchmen shook their heads, recalling the old breach in the bitter congregational quarrel of 1714–15. Some folk muttered that Peter Evans was up to his old tricks. Others ventured that Richard Peters was very likely only another Francis Phillips and hoped that the aging sheriff would be as effective in saving the parish with the riddance of Peters as he had been in the old day in rescuing it from Phillips. Some argued that the church would have fewer troubles in Philadelphia were only a bishop installed in America to exercise punctual authority over rectors and missionaries. What if they were to have another affair of a dissipated, impudent priest like Francis Phillips, who, in insane and drunken Charles Gookin's governorship, had boasted of lying with wives of the most respectable gentlemen in the parish, been defended in letters to the Bishop of London witnessed by the Governor himself, and only got rid of a year and a half after he had perpetrated his mendacity? Would there be a new experience of embarrassment for unblemished Christian ladies, of suspicions and fears among faithful husbands, from some new set of lies? Fortunately, Proprietor Thomas Penn was neither a Gookin nor a member of

Mr. Cummings' present parish. He would exercise no baneful influence from the center of the sanctuary. Still, eyes were best kept on Andrew Hamilton lest his young friend from England carry things with too high a hand in the interest of Proprietary circles. Better not have some instrument of the Penns or of the Quakers beginning to dominate the counsels of the Philadelphia parish of the Church of England. Peter Evans was right to object to an assistant who was wriggling "himself into the affections of the multitude" and of that part of the congregation who had been "generally bred dissenters." That was no pleasant story—if there were any truth in it—of the charwoman at Westminster who turned up as Mr. Peters' first wife when he had been married to his second in Liverpool. If Andrew Hamilton did not like Mr. Cummings, it was hardly a civil way to try to spite the good Rector by foisting a man of Peters' reputation into his pulpit every other Sunday. What a brazen lot of folk Stephen Vidal, Joseph Shippen, the two Ouches, and Evan Morgan were to go with other rabble like themselves into a tavern, represent themselves as churchwardens and write to London challenging the Bishop's authority and ask in whose diocese Philadelphia properly lay?

But not only gossip, queries, and defamation raged. Once the apologists for the assistant whom Archibald Cummings now wished to dismiss had got their presumptions off to England, properly constituted vestrymen and churchwardens, convened in a more circumspect place than a tavern, posted memorials of their own to the Bishop overseas. Skillful pens addressed themselves, too, to the Secretary of the Venerable Society on the dangers inhering in a wriggler. Moreover, while letters flowed to distant ecclesiastical authorities, the energy of clerical dispute continued in the City of Brotherly Love. The breach between rector and minister became sharp, and to add sauce to the excitement of parishioners, while the tenure of Mr. Peters remained in question, Mr. Cummings and his quasi-assistant did verbal battle on alternate Sundays before the congregation, censuring the doctrines held, or not held, by one and the other.

Time elapsed. The decision of Edmund, Bishop of London, was not to be hurried. In his palace at Fulham, he must weigh all the epistolary argument thrusting itself on him. A letter came from Jeremiah Langhorne, Justice in the Supreme Court of Pennsylvania, which told with candor the story of Richard's unfortunate experience at Westminster College, of his associations with relatives of the Earl of Derby, of the young man's assurance of the death of his menial wife, of the new contract with Miss Stanley (which Langhorne dated "Christmas twelve month," as though it had occurred in December 1734, the Judge's letter being despatched in May 1736), of the astonishing reappearance of the Westminster woman, and of the young clergyman's coming "voluntarily" to America with the consent of his "wife," by which the apologist meant the Earl's kinswoman.

Then, in September 1736, Bishop Gibson, having read the appeal from the old jurist, responded tenderly. He signified his belief in the innocence of Mr. Peters. He regretted the man's blunder in the hapless second marriage. Upon conditions, he indicated his approval of the young priest's remaining in Christ Church. The unfortunate must not cohabit again with his second choice in wedlock. He must take great care "to behave so" and not, through any disregard to that injunction, "give any uneasiness to Mr. Cummings." Should Mr. Peters err in that respect, the Bishop would have to revoke his consent. In fact, despite its kindly tone, sanction in the answer to Langhome's apology was distinctly qualified.

Having found its way into Richard Peters' hands, however, it inspired rather than mollified or prohibited. The assistant felt befriended by the Justice and vindicated, as it were, by my Lord at Fulham and held to his pulpit on the Sundays for which he had been engaged.

But evidently, Mr. Cummings' uneasiness, for one reason or another, did not diminish. In fact, in June 1737, the Rector of Christ Church decided to add the support of printer's ink to the power of words spoken in the pulpit. He published in clear set type his animadversions on the principles preached by his curate. Promptly thereupon, his adjunct and adversary, fortified with what he chose to interpret as the Bishop's favor to him, rallied to his defense with two sermons and punctual printing of the same with the aid of a jobber who called himself B. Franklin. In brief, Mr. Cummings, having exposed to an incredulous world the schisms discernible in Richard Peters' tenets, the victim of that flagrant procedure, chose to have all Philadelphia readers know the fervent demonstrations of his orthodoxy and guileless character which he had delivered on the last two occasions of his preaching in July. To his sermons, he added a preface almost as long as the disquisitions themselves, in which he had the satisfaction of reviewing all Mr. Cummings' misconduct toward himself and exhibiting for what it was the ambiguity of that gentleman's correspondence with the Bishop. Neatly, he dealt with his superior's eagerness to get him on into Maryland for the restoring of his spirit when he had among his papers a letter from Fulham explicitly assenting to his being retained as an assistant to the Rector of Christ's Church. The pleasure of that invented confutation was almost as great as the enjoyment he had known at Leyden when he wrote lampoons on the pedantries of lecturers. But wisely, he refrained from excess of satire, choosing to depend on the polish of his sermons for the proof of his innocence and the soundness of his theology. Better to make men see that he was neither attacking Mr. Cummings nor protecting himself, better to have his readers aware that those worthy parishioners who had approved Mr. Peters at Christ's Church were free from every stigma in themselves, generous, affectionate, and true. Well to make Philadelphians know that he regretted Mr. Cummings' error in publishing the "too warm" sermons attacking him more than any injury done to himself. How, indeed, could he answer with satisfaction another who had aimed shafts to show "the danger of breaking Christian unity" except by preaching the theme of love?

Proudly, then, he printed his moderate rejoinders. The text of his first, "But God is faithful, who will not suffer you to be tempted above that you are able," had it been read aspersively, might have applied all too relevantly to the preacher's recent past, but his divisions of it into three parts tended to bring out more particularly God's right to demand of all the utmost of their powers in his service and to elucidate what is required of men in the Christian religion. In brief, rather than inflaming people with a zeal for the unity of the Church, Richard Peters advocated the "acquisition of a religious, charitable, and good frame of mind, which was to be obtained by reducing into practice the rules of the Gospel and setting Christ before us as a pattern." The second sermon, under the text, "Be not overcome of evil, but overcome evil with good," likewise exhorted its hearers and its readers to "the improvement of an affectionate and benevolent temper" and by characterizing it as the voice of nature gave threefold dignity to that purpose, the dictate of reason, and the command of God. In essence, the author showed that love is the test of Christ's religion and that "there's not a page of the New Testament but what glows with this affectionate flame." In conclusion, as by an afterthought, the discourse dismissed quite unaffectedly the charges of unsound doctrine and adherence to Popery. Richard Peters could waste no time on such patent nonsense.

That anything of unction clung to his prose, he remained mildly unaware. But that his sermons were of the same stuff as his convictions was certainly evidenced in the pious warmth of a letter that he penned in much the same season to the wife of a new friend:

> I troop off to John Galloway's, there the joy I have to see you stamps such an affectionate kiss that methinks I hear the goodman say, as he did at parting, "What, kiss my wife so before my face?" Dear John, be not offended at my ardor, 'tis sheer gratitude and esteem that has no base

alloy in it, 'tis fully as innocent as that which I am going to give you and Polly and Sammy and Johnny and Josey.—Do, dear lady, kiss them all for me. I never was in a family in my life where I parted with my general civility so soon to take up as tender a regard as if I had been born amongst you, we cannot help loving you in six weeks more than six years acquaintance would produce amongst many others.

For the effusiveness of Richard Peters' manner ran directly into his meditations, and the joy which stamped affectionate kisses image fully upon his mind readily transformed itself into encomiums upon cheerfulness and prudent enjoyment. His predilection for benevolence remained a constant asset with him, and he never found it impossible to discover charity as the conscious motive for his behavior.

Affable to all, he moved on from Mr. Cummings' disfavor into the protection of other men's affections. James Logan chose generously to be a friend advising with him. Even more than that, he wrote a long letter of recommendation of the displanted sermonist to the Proprietor, Thomas Penn, calling that dignitary's notice to the fact that a successor to Robert Charles in the Land Office must presently be appointed and narrating the qualifications of "a person here, one Rd. Peters of Lancashire, who served seven years in the Temple to the Law, studied the Civil Law two years, was bred besides at the University, an ingenious man in all respects." Mr. Peters, he assured Mr. Penn, had from his native honesty and candor disinclined from the practice of the law, taken to the clergyman's gown and been "uncommonly admired" in the pulpit. Now, "offended with the insincerity of his brethren of the Cloth," the man believed he would be happier "in some employment in which he could get a decent living with a good conscience without being obliged either to wrangle at the Bar to gain a cause however unrighteous" or to subject himself to ecclesiastical "forms and rules, with which he was not in himself fully satisfied." Having esteemed Richard Peters' frankness and rated his powers, the eminent Philadelphia Friend also recounted his misfortunes. He deplored the unhappy experience of the fourteen-year-old boy at Westminster School inveigled by a servant maid of the house into marrying her, told of her eventual disappearance and of her hapless young husband's belief she had died, explained that her reappearance had been timed by certain political enemies of Peters' patron, the Earl of Derby, to embarrass that peer and his young friend on account of t e side they had taken in the late elections in England. He remarked simply that by his first wife's turning up, the unfortunate young man "was obliged to change the air."

Mr. Logan asserted that he believed all this history, and although he was convinced of his disinclination to the Law, he assured Mr. Penn that Mr. Peters' skill in that branch, in which he thought he equaled "the best here," would serve in the Land Office in good stead. He regretted that the secretaryship there offered so slight a stipend, scarce a hundred pounds of Pennsylvania money. Something ought to be annexed to it to gain the acceptance of a person of such distinguished parts.

Chiefly, James Logan's counsel prevailed. Thomas Penn was favorably impressed with the native abilities of Archibald Cummings' recent assistant. By October 1737, Richard Peters was ready to slip gracefully into a new service.

The Proprietors of Pennsylvania came forward with a highly satisfying proposal. Through their brother and spokesman, Thomas, the Penns offered Richard Peters the office of Secretary of the Land Office for the Province. His discretion, integrity, and knowledge of civil law had been his sponsors. Now they drew up a commission which in the diction customary among the Friends "authorized thee to receive and take into thy custody all minutes, records and other papers belonging to the Secretary's office," and the unseated clergyman of the Church of England chose in the exigency not to hold aloof. Though emanating from dissenters, the handsome offer came from the highest provincial authority. Mr. Peters accepted with no undue procrastination. Better take such an office, he reasoned, than bring disruption into Christ's church by obstinate holding out for the consideration that Mr. Archibald Cummings had denied him.

At any rate, one month after the formal papers had been drawn, he sat writing a long relation and apology to the Bishop of London, humbly recommending himself to "your Lordship's Benediction and Prayers" and repeating his desire to have "the continuance of your Lordship's Paternal regards extended to

"My Lord,
Your Lordship's
Most dutiful Son
And most obedient Servant."

He begged the Bishop's pardon for the great troubles he had caused him. He lamented the hard charges made by Mr. Cummings and that clergyman's unprecedented manner of publishing them. He decried his temerity in printing his own sermons in rebuttal, thus continuing a debate that should have been laid quietly before His Lordship rather than put so noisily before the world. Yet the discouragements and ill-treatment he had received had been excessive. He had retorted out of too great pain. He was full of contrition that in a country which abounds with all sorts of dissenters—for the moment, he cared not to remember he was entering into the service of such—he should so indiscreetly have contributed to exposing differences within the church in Philadelphia. It really had been best for him to suspend the exercise of his function in the interest of Christian harmony. Now, he had accepted the Proprietor's appointment when clerical appointments were, it seemed, not to be had. Yet he assured his Lordship he had no intention thereby of loosening his filial relation to him and hoped he might be permitted to retain that high honor.

The generous Bishop's ultimate decision was a wise one, being of a sort that in every way commended Mr. Cummings and his friends in Christ Church and, in the interest of harmony in the parish, refrained from the censure of the opponent. It may have been somewhat motivated by the fact that petitioners for the Rector had made it clear that the authority of bishops was as necessary to the Church of England as a monarch was to the kingdom, whereas those who had subscribed themselves in a Philadelphia tavern had bluntly asked the great ecclesiastic whether the Province of Pennsylvania was in his opinion "annexed to any and what diocese" and whether the parish of Christ Church might induct and appoint without application to such authority. But it was quite within the disposition of the assistant to accept the second part of the Lord Bishop of London's action as an apology for his deportment.

Conscience satisfied and cheer retained, the Reverend Mr. Richard Peters turned with diligence to the improvement of those secular gifts with which he had been born.

The Philadelphia to which he had come was a raw town. It could not contain as many as fifteen hundred houses. Taxable folk in it could not number certainly as many as six thousand. But it was a busy place, full of economic opportunity, and beyond its slim environs and the country places which its better-to-do citizens enjoyed just outside in the county were hundreds of thousands of wild acres calling for settlement and tillage. Artisans, tradesmen, lawyers, politicians—all throve in its narrow streets (broad, though, compared to London and English ways) from Water to Sixth, from Vine to Pine. Beyond the Schuylkill, many a prosperous farm was already developed. Further inland along Perkiomen and Tulpehocken and on toward Susquehanna, thousands had begun development. Furs and skins poured into the markets from trappers' and Indians' enterprises in the forests and valleys to the west, wheat, barley, and rye from the farmers. Vessels kept bringing cargo from the West Indies or immigrant passengers from English Bristol and London. Scotch-Irish folk, Palatinate Germans, and Moravians were flowing into the port, keeping both quarantine officials and the Land Office busy. The promotion of a province, not as a mere utopian experiment in religious liberty or political equality, but as a frank means to individual wealth and solid burgher comfort was afoot. Fortune and material respectability appealed alike to Quaker, Presbyterian, Lutheran, and Churchman. Rank and file—for these were both in clear existence in the city, though the process of turning from bond to free, from poverty to esteem, or from secure estate to impecuniousness never disappeared—sought with one will the improvement of their social conditions. Corps of surveyors, shipyards, docks, merchants' shops, printeries, guilds of carpenters, plasterers, and masons enjoyed increasing activity. Every form of earthly pursuit admitted and provided for in the Charter of King Charles II to William Penn and in the early contractual frames of government drawn in the 1680s was in effect. The capital of Pennsylvania was replete in established offices to control the bents of humankind and to challenge the aspirants to fees and commissions—and there were few rules to prohibit a man of spirit from holding as many of these as he could wish to be invested with. Courts of vice-admiralty, of equity, of orphans, of common pleas, of chancery all were in being. Recorders-general, surveyors-general, registers of admiralty, secretaries of the land office, to the Proprietary and the Council, justices of the peace or the common courts, justices of the Supreme Court, chief justices—all were necessary. Officialdom required a numerous staff of clerks. Tradesmen required ample quotas of bondservants and apprentices. Transactions required notaries, scriveners, and agents. Laborers and menials were in demand.

More houses were always built. Christ Church was adding architectural dignity to dignity, devotedly presided over by Dr. John Kearsley, a zealous communicant and liberal contributor. The main structure of the new State House had already risen on Chestnut Street, in the proportions designed for it by free-thinking Andrew Hamilton, who had been as tireless to afford the commonwealth a hall for government as his pious rival Kearsley was to endow religion with a sanctuary. Personal ambitions of this world took minds of Friend and Episcopalian alike off religion to fix them on country houses and estates beyond the denser environs of a city running nine blocks north and south along the Delaware and some eight to ten east and west in the direction of the Schuylkill. Chief Justice James Logan's mansion house of Stenton near Germantown, Mr. Hamilton's Bush Hill to the northwest of the last streets, and Graeme

Park, home of Dr. Thomas Graeme, a score of miles out in Bucks County-these were seats to be envied and emulated by prospering men of affairs. Not to be forgotten either was the grandeur of Pennsbury, the manor house of the Old Proprietor, inheritance of that worthy's grandson, Springett Penn, and recently residence of that youth's uncle, Mr. Thomas Penn. If the splendor of such an estate dared hardly be rivaled, it was to be admired all the more.

But Richard Peters was not to be a newcomer only to action and to signs of affluence. He was as aware of men as of things, and the press of circumstances did not hide from him the sturdy importance of outstanding Philadelphians. No individual aptitude that embraced a faculty for financial or political success was lost upon him. If he had felt awe in the presence of the Earl at Knowsley, at the least, there could be respect in his heart for the solid competence of the merchant-mayor William Allen giving his great dinner to citizens in the banqueting hall of the State House in precisely that September when Richard had acquired sanction, as it were, from good Bishop Gibson for rebuffing Mr. Cummings. The host was a Presbyterian, to be sure, he remembered, but already at thirty-two, Mr. Allen was a lawyer, merchant in a most thriving business, holder of tracts of land out in the counties, chief executive of the city, and, to boot, the son-in-law of Andrew Hamilton. All the strangers of note in the town had been added to the list of his friends at the banquet, and discerning judges of hospitality and decorum well might say, "That considering the delicacy of the viands and the excellence of the wines, the great number of guests, and yet the easiness and order with which the whole was conducted, it was the most grand and the most elegant entertainment that has been made in these parts of America."

Ben Franklin was a sly rogue, but the encomiums pronounced of William Allen's dinner in his *Pennsylvania Gazette* were not the only things to commend him as a printer for sermons defending Christian principles against a churlish rector. The fellow had got up from pennilessness. Although folk whispered that he had, no doubt, either bullied or wheedled his predecessors in the printshops of Philadelphia out of their businesses, and both Andrew Bradford and Samuel Keimer could testify to the shadiness of his transactions, he was more than a skillful agent to his own interest. If the former Governor, Sir William Keith, had dealt shabbily with him years ago in that old prank of the letters of credit, at least he had seen a means of discovering Franklin's affability to other folk of quality. Just thirty now, without education at Westminster or Oxford or the Temple, with only a craft mastered among the printeries of London during his sojourn in England, he was—so to speak—the man of the hour, associate of every man of learning in the city. His *Poor Richard's Almanack* was amusing

Aspirations of a Cleric

stuff, hardly of the quality of Addison's famous *Spectator* from which it quoted so generously, but Ben knew how to play with it, as well as with announcements and queries in his *Gazette,* to the entertainment of the town and the increase of his fortune. He was making a good thing for himself from his job of printing official publications for the Assemblies of Pennsylvania and New Jersey. Mr. Hamilton, Richard Peters never forgot, had helped Franklin to that emolument out of their own province. But the man's best stroke was his being the center and the life of his Junto. That body of cronies kept talk going, in their little coterie, of trade laws, mechanics, and science—perhaps too much, of government. It stood for ideas to a degree and for books. Out of it had come Franklin's scheme of a Library Association, and that venture for the spread of knowledge had won the favor even of James Logan, Philadelphia's chief aristocrat and Quaker, if Mr. Thomas Penn could be overlooked for a time. With the aid of gentlemen, the right volumes were being chosen and imported. Everything that Ben did prospered, and every one of his efforts kept the air of a benefit to the public. He was a man to vie with, despite the plainness of his origin, the frequent vulgarity of his associations, and the leather apron he bustled around in at his shop. Already Clerk to the Assembly, he was likely to be greater than that someday. He would hardly be chosen to the Council, Richard Peters found himself supposing, but Franklin would undoubtedly make his mark.

Then, always, there was the handsome, patrician-looking Andrew Hamilton to be reflected on. By no means inscrutable in manner, something obscure persisted about him—mystifying but provocative. Transparently Scottish in origin, he was not known to have told in Philadelphia what had been his parentage. His name, now that he had changed it—although from what was uncertain—was identical with that of a former New Jersey governor also of Scottish breed, whose bastard he may have been. But he chose not to go into his past with folk in any undiscriminating fashion. There might have been a bar sinister to cloud his birth. Some spirited violence in the eyes of Scotland's law might have made flight relevant, even imperative, from his home country. There was no doubt that he was now fully accustomed to having himself accepted as among the gently born. If he had begun life in America first as a classical scholar in Virginia, he had, on his marriage to the widow of his patron in that colony, become a gentleman of considerable property. Business interests had taken him from his acres in Accomac to new ones in Kent County, Maryland. Then, after a sojourn in England, he had returned from the study of the law at Gray's Inn, a barrister officially *per favor,* but in essence, a person of the most distinguished legal talent to pursue practice in Pennsylvania. In 1736, he enjoyed esteem as

Speaker of the Assembly, as a friend of the late William Penn, the Proprietor, as the master of Bush Hill—and, especially among the populace, as the defender, in a famous case at law in New York a year ago, of John Peter Zenger. In a fit of *noblesse oblige,* without fee or reward, he had gone to the capital of the province to the north and, by his eloquence and logic in a hostile court, won acquittal for a publisher from charges of sedition and—more satisfyingly to the mob, of course—sanction for freedom of the press in America even if a printer was pointing out corruption in officers of government. At Bush Hill, Richard Peters had been informed Andrew Hamilton treasured the little golden box in which the joyous citizenry of New York and the mayor there had given him the honor of the freedom of their city. For able men, the former Curate of Lathom Chapel knew, there was opportunity in Pennsylvania. Twenty-five years in the province had not been spent in vain by Mr. Hamilton. That sixty-year-old veteran deserved the recognition he had in Philadelphia and about the State House, whose beauty testified to his prowess as an architect almost as much as his acumen as an attorney at the bar.

Mr. Peters was not of Franklin's Library Association or the Junto. Also, he had reservations, as a cleric, toward the Masons, however much gentlemen of that fraternity associated with persons of Ben's set. But he was happy to realize that he was himself acceptable in Andrew Hamilton's circle. He liked, too, having James Logan's friendship. What a figure that eminent Quaker was, the most trusted man in Pennsylvania—and, now that Governor Patrick Gordon had died, in his capacity as President of the Council, the temporary chief executive for the colony! Logan's career was about forty years old in Philadelphia. Coming as the secretary of William Penn in 1699, he had served both that Founder and his children well during the long interval. Many a struggle had been his, many a responsibility, many an office. Quarrels with deputy governors, assemblymen, fellow councilors—all had been his portion. From many a charge and many a dispute in law, he had remained unscathed. His bearing was austere, direct, and harsh. He was even capable of splenetic wrath in words. If normally he took affirmation rather than oath, he was known to be capable of imprecations. Stories were told of how, Friend though he was from birth, he had fought doughtily against pirates who swarmed upon the *Canterbury,* as that ship was bringing him and his good master to America four decades ago. Penn, who had retreated below hatches lest he should break his Quaker principles against militancy, it was avouched, rebuked him when the vessel was cleared. He had energetically retorted that his patron had no right to reprimand him when he had not ordered him not to fight. Yet even in 1736, the most bookish and most

Aspirations of a Cleric

elegant aristocrat in the province on his Germantown estate he maintained the simple bearing and manner of a Quaker, ready to converse in quiet with either citizen or visiting Indian.

His "thee's" and "thou's" were strange to Richard Peters' ears, accompanying, as they did, so gracious a mentor, but Mr. Cummings' abused assistant could well overlook any differences in etiquette which did not mitigate his advantage. Indeed, there had been little notion in Richard's mind of withdrawal to Maryland after James Logan's letter from Stenton had reached him in June. The Councillor had written regretting the recipient's "cloudy thoughts" at that time, hoping the gloom of both his mind and his purpose might "be dispelled together." Mr. Peters rejoiced now at having taken at full value the consideration in Mr. Logan's sentence: "I want to have a great deal of close conversation with thee before thou engages ever for so long." He was fully willing to acknowledge then and now that the writer was one of his friends "not unfit to be advised with." Ben Franklin might have the Library Association, but Richard Peters was on the way to becoming an intimate of the man owning the greatest number of books in Pennsylvania, a scholar, a man of substance and spirit, though a Quaker. He cared not particularly that Mr. Logan was clinging obstinately to the garb and manner of an Irish father who had left the ministry, joined the Friends, and become the teacher of a modest school. There was talk in Philadelphia of the man's being of the ancient Scottish Logans of Restalrig, and certainly, the ring with which he sealed his letters bore the arms of the Logans of Oxfordshire; however frankly he might disclaim his right to them.

In fact, by the autumn of 1736, the troubled assistant of Archibald Cummings was employing his imagination admirably to the furtherance of his expert mundane gifts, and a year later, he could be happy that he had not only by his moderation saved Christ Church from a cleavage but also acquired for himself the esteem of men of affairs and could freely mingle with them. Moreover, his attitude was in no sense inconsistent with what he had written so affably to Mrs. Galloway. He had as high an opinion of religion as anyone had. He thought

> . . . a regard to God the noblest motive that can ever enter into the mind of man, and that all actions which proceed from this motive are best actions. Nay, whenever any one loses sight of his Maker so far as to be unconcerned to have His approbation of his conduct, he unmans himself and is but an elegant animal of the beastly kind. But there, where the intention is in the main good, cheerfulness and prudent enjoyment are by all means to be indulged.

IV

Inches of Earth

The capacity for work no less than the capacity for enjoyment was in Richard Peters, and after the rupture with Mr. Cummings at the church, he became a busy man at the Pennsylvania Land Office. From his predecessor, as his commission from the Penns required him, he secured the necessary official record books and papers and was soon deep in the multifarious and trying transactions of all those who took warrants and patents of the Proprietaries or who, by reason of incompetence, mischance, or calculation, forfeited back to them. Clusters of Irish folk or of Palatine Germans, whom he saw scrambling out of ships that brought them to the port or moving curiously from street to street, shop to courthouse, market to church, were all, he knew, prospective applicants for patents. His heart—though his head must protect his masters, quarrel, or repossess for them—was open to colonists, and he did not dislike immigrants the more for their being of upstanding stature or in decent habits. Day after day, he issued tickets to purchasers directing the Surveyor-General to have acres surveyed for the buyer, in this tract or that now being newly developed, or in that old tract where tenure had not been taken or possession improved according to the terms of an earlier warrant. Day after day, he made entries or scratched notations in his books. There were days, too, when he reflected on the unpopularity of surveyors laying out manors for the Proprietaries.

If he was too occupied in 1737 and 1738 to miss the color that had come into the city's midst with the visit of the chiefs of the Five Nations in 1736, he was not uninterested when James Logan reviewed Indian policies with him. He was quick to learn the wisdom of keeping the friendship alive with those proud wild people of the west and north, with red-skinned princes whose names only good Conrad Weiser, the interpreter, could pronounce on parley days—a friendship which meant not only maintaining the love of brothers between Onas, as always William Penn was designated in Indian councils, and the sachems and their tribes, but mediation between Catawbas to the south and west of Maryland and Virginia, and Tuscaroras and Senecas west of Pennsylvania, and Indian treaties for purchase of ever more land. He saw clearly enough the eighteenth-century way of uniting business with pleasure, did not marvel too much that James Logan should entertain redskins at his board in Stenton, did not refuse his smile when he knew that lengthy entertainment of the chiefs by white gentlemen could be discouraged by the unfortunate, but almost provident, presence of smallpox in Philadelphia. Always, the councilors were eager to protect the Oneidas or the Onondagoes from the sickness in the city to which their race was so much the prey always; the childlike guests were glad to be protected, granted they might be sent home with liberal provisions.

The interests of the province became, in brief, Richard Peters' interests. He followed with his customary candor all reports from the Assembly, all official exchanges between the Government of Pennsylvania and that of Maryland or Virginia, all preliminaries to treaties, all measures dealing with boundaries, all with counties, towns, and roads. He awaited with cheer instructions which it was known were to be forthcoming from the Court of King George relative to the amelioration of long-nurtured land disputes between the Penns and Lord Baltimore. He rejoiced in the closing days of August 1738, when, at last, propitious orders of His Majesty had been read and discussed in the Council of the province. He was conscious inwardly that, should the new Governor George Thomas and Mr. Penn think now to employ him on the commission which was bound to be created for surveying the line between Pennsylvania and Maryland, he would be glad to serve with that enterprise.

Once the boundaries were determined, land contests on the southern confines of Chester County would grow less acute, less friction would occur between claimants under grants from Lord Baltimore, and farmers possessed under grants by Thomas, John, and Richard Penn, there could be peace in the Land Office, and less vexation in the records. But more even than those considerations, Mr. Peters hoped. There was red blood in his veins; he would like to be stirring, seeing something more of land in the commonwealth to which he now belonged.

In fact, the Secretary of the Land Office experienced both a pioneering instinct and a genuine elation in April 1739. He could leave Philadelphia for an interval then to represent Pennsylvania with Mr. Lawrence Growden as his colleague on a committee of four members, including two gentlemen from Maryland, for the supervision of a staff of surveyors. As much as anybody's, it was now his obligation to determine the boundary between the two provinces.

That meant not only jealously guarding the rights of the heirs of William Penn, and carrying out the command of the King issued from his Court at Kensington, to survey a line westward from the Delaware to the Susquehanna "down so far South as fifteen miles and one quarter of a mile south of the latitude of the most southern part of the City of Philadelphia" and "on the west side of the said river Susquehanna down so far as fourteen miles and three-quarters south of the latitude of the most southern part of the City of Philadelphia." It meant a respite from tickets, warrants, and ledgers. It spelled novelty, journeying on horseback, and certainly no lack of future advantage to the secretary of a land office who admired men of affairs.

That he took his duties seriously, as well as with constancy and interest, his regular letters reporting back to Governor Thomas clearly showed. The script was always his, as were the minutes of each day's discussions with Commissioners Levin Gale and Samuel Chamberlaine of Maryland; however often, Mr. Growden affixed his signature, and the reports were meticulous. If once Mr. Peters' vocabulary had been that of the priest of religion or the barrister ambitious in his studies at the Temple in London; now it became fully of the surveyor. For a month, he learned to think in terms of meridian lines, pole stars above the Pole, vertical circles, chain carriers, circumferentors, and theodolites, and, when his mind was not exactly on fifteen miles and one-quarter mile south of the most south part of Philadelphia, it was on fourteen and three-quarter miles south. In another presumption, too, he was always fixed. Commissioners and surveyors were but men; it would be best to keep a close eye on every maneuver of his fellows. The instruments of Surveyor John Ladd for Maryland must be made to tally with those of Benjamin Eastburn of Pennsylvania; if they did not, correct allowances must be made. No surveillance by Richard Peters or his associate should be omitted.

On April 18, he took the opportunity, by Colonel Gale, who said he was going to Philadelphia to procure another surveyor, not only to inform the Governor of the troublesome behavior of the needle but to imply that the bearer of the communication wanted to be away in order to elicit in his absence from the rest of the commission some new secret instructions from authorities in Baltimore. It troubled him that attractions on the compass were not stronger in the spring than in the fall of the year, and he was none too satisfied to have the new lines keep crossing lines formerly surveyed and not always adding acres to the Proprietaries' lands. But it was encouraging to have Ben Eastburn predict, now that they had got something to the south of the old line run by John Taylor, they were bound to be gaining more and more.

Two days later, he admitted that the Colonel had gone to Philadelphia really for the purpose he had indicated and not for the one the writer had inferred. Yet the Maryland commissioner had been very uneasy before he left because of mistrust with regard to the needles in Mr. Eastburn's theodolite. Then, on comparison of the needles in the two theodolites, it was found the Pennsylvania surveyors had experienced no accident; the instruments were in harmony, after all, and Levin Gale's misgivings had begun to attach themselves to mistakes made by the former Jersey commissioners. On Monday, April 23, when that gentleman had returned to the survey, hours were filled with arguments between the two parties. The Maryland men, Mr. Peters reported, wanted the westerly line to be run for a distance of fifteen and one-quarter miles "upon the surface of the earth without any allowance for the unevenness thereof." The Pennsylvanians stood out for running it that distance in "an horizontal line, that is to say, that the altitude of the hills should be truly taken and a full and just allowance be made to them." On Tuesday, a compromise was effected, and Messrs. Growden and Peters accepted an allowance of twenty-five perches for the altitudes and the promise "that the rights of the several Proprietors to run and measure the fifteen and a quarter miles in any other manner should be saved to them." Superficially, it seemed no gain had been made for either side and opportunity afforded to the Penns and Baltimore only for continued procrastination. But Richard Peters could confide to Governor Thomas, when he wrote again, that Eastburn, who had been over the line last December and knew the altitudes of the intervening hills, was certain a twenty-five-perch allowance would in no way prejudice Pennsylvania's rights—and add the comforting assurance that the new line would continue generally to the south of the old line and save at least part of the good people of Nottingham Township to Chester County. Obviously enough, Mr. Thomas Penn's boundary agents were losing nothing for him and his brothers.

By slow stages, the group of commissioners and surveyors got their instruments, their horses, and themselves on from farm to farm, tavern to tavern—from Society Hill to Widow Parnell's to William Webb's—with lines running and minutes of agreement or disagreement being set down daily. On the 25th, there was mistrust again. At least Richard Peters, who rejoiced that day that an answer of approval had reached him from the Governor, was ready to write then that "although in his private capacity" Colonel Gale was a "fair and ingenious man," he and Mr. Growden were afraid the Marylander was acting under instructions "inconsistent with a disposition to run a fair line in conjunction with us." Indeed, the two suspected the Colonel was looking for some cause on which to break with them in order to have an excuse for his province to run a line *ex parte*. In detail, Mr. Peters pictured to his superior "the absurd character of a mere fool," which Levin Gale would attract to himself if he tried that sort of thing under the Great Seal of Maryland and the instructions of Governor Ogle. But presently, the Colonel grew tractable again, and the party got on westwards.

Before Sunday, April 29, however, there was further cause for umbrage and suspicion in the mind of Richard Peters. From Elisha Gatchall's, he wrote at length and reflectively to Governor Thomas.

Prefatorily, he remarked: "Men of skill can find a thousand objections against doing a thing that they have no mind to; this has been the case of our brother commissioners." Then he recounted his story. No sooner had the matter of running the line by a "superficial" rather than a horizontal method been settled than Colonel Gale began objecting to the use of Mr. Eastbum's half-chain. He argued his own "Gunter's chain made in London," a thing called a "whole chain" and four perches long, was a more accurate tool than Ben's, which had a length of but two perches, however strong that might be. Losing that argument because Eastburn's chain was discovered on examination not only to be exactly half of Gunter's product in length but much stouter and more serviceable, he next protested the half-inch added by the manufacturers to the two-perch length to allow for sticks and brush on the surface being surveyed. "It was," he said, "constantly giving the Penns an advantage." Shown then that his whole chain had two inches supplementing it for the same purpose, he yielded to the two surveyors, with whom he had carried on all his maneuvering in the absence of Messrs. Growden and Peters. But the next day, he was busy in the presence of the latter two men demanding twelve perches of advantage for Lord Baltimore against the inch excess in the measure of the half-chain being used.

Eastburn opposed the demand of Gale and Chamberlaine vigorously. He had never known any allowance to be made for such cause, the inch being added regularly to compensate for the "curves, bents, and baggings" of a chain. They refused to be satisfied by him. Growden and Peters had to inform them sharply their "niceties" were exposing them to a suspicion that they lacked the right "disposition for the execution of their commission" that the Pennsylvanians might as well break with them now as farther on. They were achieving nothing by their obstinacy.

Thereupon, the two Marylanders conceded and said they would require compensation only for half of the supplemental inch on Eastbum's chain. That allowance they would not give up. Peters replied that he and Mr. Growden would not yield their allowance at all for the stick. Rather for the authorities in Philadelphia and London, they would draw up minutes of the breach with the two and then themselves proceed to survey the Maryland-Pennsylvania line *ex parte*. Nor would they fail, "in their manner of drawing the minute up, *to mention the ten little sticks in such a light as will show how nicely observant you are of the most minute that may affect your Proprietary interest.*" Upon that threat, whether balked by the ardor of the Secretary of the Pennsylvania Land Office or by the more remote power of George II in Council at Kensington, the Marylanders again acquiesced, and the survey continued.

But Governor Thomas' correspondent had gained an idea. He set down many another detail, postulating minor gain or loss in territory for the Penns, informing officialdom of their progress on to Nottingham, telling of Colonel Gale's learning suddenly of the death of his only son and having to proceed into Cecil County to have further news of his wife and family. He wrote of a retesting of the theodolites to find the needle of those instruments still in harmony. Yet that was not all that his letter contained. It embraced two more items: One was Messrs. Peters' and Growden's reviewing with Mr. Chamberlaine the likelihood that Mr. Gale would not return and that in that event, the commission of the four men would cease, as legally it required two men from each colony, and they could proceed no farther under its terms lawfully. The second was—and the writer of it was most shrewd and expansive in explaining motives—a suggestion that Governor Thomas send on promptly a new commission to Messrs. Growden and Peters to continue the survey by themselves *ex parte* for Pennsylvania. Everything need not stop because of Colonel Gale's apparent defection—even though the man had insisted he would be back. His Honor, George Thomas, could take time by the forelock, was the implication, and authorize the Pennsylvania commissioners to achieve some real service to the future of the province. On the whole, there was nothing impolitic in the communication sent by Richard Peters.

That the Secretary's ruse worked was clear in his next letter, written on May 6 from Peach Bottom Ferry, on the east side of Susquehanna, for before that second Sunday for correspondence, the two Pennsylvania officials had received from the Governor their new commission and began planning to survey onwards tomorrow across the river toward the western limit of the King's Orders in Council of 1738. Mr. Peters could write now not only cheerfully of the nearly completed accomplishment of a solid duty, not only beg politely to disagree with the Governor about his wish to have had more of the trifling cavils of the Marylanders put into the minutes, he could write sympathetically of Colonel Gale. That good man had agreed to stay on and work with them last Monday on the west of the river but once more had had evil news of his family. One of his daughters had been taken ill with the measles. The other was expected hourly to be so. His wife had written she was quite comfortless. Regretfully, the Colonel had had to depart homewards to the relief of his family.

Ends about to be achieved to the advantage of the Proprietors, there was, in brief, no reason for not adding to business the tenderness of a gentleman. Presently, Richard Peters was back in Philadelphia with experience in travel and frontier communities added to his qualifications. He had proved some powers of diplomacy with representatives of another commonwealth. Also, the great seal of Pennsylvania had been affixed to an *ex parte* enterprise of a sort which he had some time earlier reflected could not, with dignity to it, be honored under the great seal of Maryland.

At any rate, he and Mr. Growden and Ben Eastburn had brought to George Thomas and the Council report of another week of surveying, duly authorized by them, and after the Marylanders had withdrawn. On the other side of Susquehanna, from the hickory tree designated by the King's Orders in Council marked with four notches for that purpose of continuation and beginning, they had extended their work toward the Potomac to the top of the most western of a range called the Kittochtinny Hills to a distance of eighty-eight miles, from their eastern starting point. They judged their line to be run far enough to settle the jurisdiction of the two provinces to fulfill the terms of their commission. They had ordered the surveyors to end there and to mark several trees with the initial letters of the names of their Honorable Proprietaries.

If Mr. Peters did not regard himself as a mercurial person, at least he took modest pride in his astuteness.

V

For the Good of Souls

Richard Peters' improvement of his secular gifts had other secular consequences. The cheerfulness of his letters back to England and the family awakened longings in his older brother, and by the time Richard had returned to Philadelphia from his exploits on the Maryland line as a surveyor and Proprietary agent, William had also begun flourishing in that budding metropolis. Yet Mr. Ralph Peters and his daughters in Liverpool were rather less pleased to have the elder son prospering in Pennsylvania than to have Richard recovering there from the misadventures of his past in London and Lancashire. For William had not only turned from tangled business affairs at home but left a family of four children and a wife behind him. More than that, he was ignoring the appeals of his sisters to come back and be reconciled with a mate of whom he had tired and leaving to his father the maintenance of both that lady and their offspring. It was a new sort of abandonment for a respectable barrister's household to contemplate. Mr. Ralph Peters was blunt. Through Peter Furnivall, trying to disentangle some of the defecting husband's obligations and credits in the English city, he sent curt word in July 1739 that he would not come to William's rescue except "you make friends and cohabit with your wife."

Miss Esther meditated much and lastingly. William's wife she regarded as a charming woman. She and her father loved the grandchildren. But she was neither as brusque nor as passive as her parent. Unanswered letters flowed from her across the Atlantic to William perseveringly. She reproved her brother's unkindness, described his children's persons and behavior, sympathized with her sister-in-law's struggle with poverty and illnesses, counseled the delinquent frankly upon his spiritual unhappiness, admonished him that that sort of unhappiness was worst of all in its separating men from the presence of God. But William Peters' consort might be charming or ill in health, his son Raphy might be doing well in school and behaving graciously to his aunts, especially on the approach of Christmas, his Willy might be a delicate child, his Nelly a pretty one, his Jemmy fat as a little pig—their husband and father had come to America to stay. There, he would court fortune, if necessary, even in his younger brother's shadow.

Conveniently enough to a man of William's conscience, respect for legal marriage and legitimate parenthood was not too imperative in Philadelphia. Ben Franklin, whose repute with women had returned from London with him none too savory, was living happily in a common-law union—and nobody was troubled. Mr. Hamilton's origin gave no one concern. William's brother's affair in Lancashire might have hurt him something at Christ Church. It had done no damage to Richard at the Land Office. Back in England, the tenth Earl of Derby had died, and the earldom had reverted to a distant branch of the family, not coming to Richard's friend Charles Stanley or that youth's sister, Richard's "wife." But no one in Lancashire had been particularly exercised as to how Charles and that lady were related to their late near kinsman. Certainly, they had had no claims to vacate Sir Edward Stanley, fifth Baronet, who had succeeded their relative as eleventh Earl. Thomas Penn, too, might be a bachelor, but here in the province as elsewhere, William Peters reflected, men had their ways. There were buxom enough charmers around Philadelphia and degrees of complacency. Well to take life as it offered itself.

So William Peters was rebuked rather than deeply contrite when Esther wrote again, in March 1741, of his "barbarity":

> Were you of the opinion of all considerate parents, you would think it an indispensable duty to take care of your children and see that they were brought up religiously . . . Can you reasonably expect them to love or reverence you as they ought? Would you think yourself obliged to your parents for bringing you into the world if they took no further care of you? Suppose we were brutes and had no soul nor were immortal. The consequence would be of less significance.

It half amused him that his sister could ply her style almost as well as Richard was managing his.

For William Peters knew, in much the same season as Esther's latest admonition reached him, that Richard was once more busy with his pen—and not merely in the affairs of the Land Office.

Death took Mr. Archibald Cummings in April 1741. Pious and proper grief followed in the parish. There was hushed talk of the need for a new shepherd for the flock. There were encomiums and conferences. There were thoughts of the need and of the essential qualifications of a successor to the late Rector. There was debate and, in due course of time, altercation.

Promptly on the 23rd, "The Humble Address of the Church Wardens and Vestry of Christ's Church in Philadelphia" was inscribed for the Right Reverend Edmund, Bishop of London. It pictured the mournful occasion. It recounted the interment of their minister on the day before with a "solemnity and regard becoming the universal good character and esteem which he bore among his acquaintance, of every religious denomination and society, for his learning, piety, moderation, and every other good quality that might adorn his sacred function." It spoke of Mr. Cummings properly as "His Lordship's Commissary," it commented on "the happy intercourse" which had always subsisted between him and the Bishop to the good of their congregation, it avowed the beliefs of its signatories that, in asking His Lordship to nominate a successor to his Commissary, they promoted the best interests of the parish and were the more assured of obtaining a person "every way fit and suited to the important trust." It reported that neighboring clergymen had offered to serve the church by turns until the next winter. It hoped, however, that before then, the Bishop would use his kind endeavors to send them a minister. It acknowledged His Lordship's benevolence in all his favors.

Among the signers of the address were Samuel Hasell and Thomas Lawrence, members of the Provincial Council. Among them were Peter Evans and Dr. John Kearsley, and in their number was Richard Peters. No one of the names of men who in 1736 had inquired curiously of Edmund Gibson, Bishop of London, whether the Province of Pennsylvania was annexed to his diocese, was in evidence. Certainly, in the document was no obtrusive questioning about His Lordship's function or his authority. Officially, indeed, the signature of the ex-assistant of Mr. Cummings and the present successful secretary of the Land Office was in the best of company.

But William Peters was not wrong in supposing that his brother was busy with paper and ink or that he was otherwise quiescent. Another storm, in fact, was about to brew in the clerical teapot of Philadelphia and the three lower counties on the Delaware. To a thriving secretary and a disappointed priest, death might spell opportunity as well as deference to an episcopal superior. Richard Peters was neither one to sleep nor one to be too oblivious if an ambition persisted in him. Nor was he unaware that by the same conveyance, there was going forward to the Bishop of London a second address—one resolved on by "the greatest part of the congregation" and signed by a long roster of names.

The clauses of this were several. First, it reminded His Lordship that "nine-tenths" of the church had made an application some years ago in the interest of the Reverend Mr. Richard Peters. Then, commending that gentleman's talents, it hoped that these might not be allowed to waste themselves in a "lay but honorable employment." It praised Mr. Peters' attachment to the constitution of the Established Church and his sincerity. It expanded upon his behavior at the time when, because of willful misrepresentation of himself, he and Mr. Cummings had been obliged to separate, telling of his noble refusal then to have a new church built for him by his friends and of his urging these to continue in attendance at services and to give their minister their usual support. It told of his valor on an occasion when the fanatic George Whitefield occupying their pulpit, he rose in open meeting and administered stern reproof both to that zealot's doctrine and his rant. It insisted on his moderation in the present juncture, when he had been told of the wish of the greater number of the vestry to have him immediately appointed to the charge of Christ Church and had determined never to resume "the ministerial function in these parts without first consulting your Lordship and having your advice and approbation." Conclusively, having extolled all the virtue of Mr. Peters and all the esteem of the parish for his character, it intimated to the Bishop what he might do to their advantage as a church and to Richard Peters' advantage as a saint rather than directly inviting him to do anything.

Eighty petitioners, in sum, choose to have their inclination rest on the knees of the gods rather than insinuate itself, as it were, upon the partiality of a prelate. More names appealed—however indirectly in Richard Peters' favor—than had appealed in 1736, and more goodly ones. If Stephen Vidal, Joseph Shippen, the two Ouches, and Evan Morgan signed again, there were also on the list William Till, Abraham Taylor, Thomas Hopkinson, Thomas Lawrence, Dr. Thomas Graeme, and many others.

Yet the roster was imposing rather than perfect, and some important names were lacking in it.

Indeed, more than vestry, wardens, and humbler laity, or prosperous merchants, or members of the Provincial Council had become interested in the problem of a successor to the learned but now lamented Mr. Archibald Cummings. That Commissary had belonged to the Church of England, and the clergy of that sacred institution had for two centuries not been without some authority in the appointment of their colleagues. The vestry of Christ Church had acted without consultation of the missionaries appointed by the Bishop of London to their flocks at Chester, at Newcastle, at Oxford in Pennsylvania, and divers other stations and the missionaries took it upon themselves to exercise their function. They, too, convened and despatched addresses to the Lord Bishop of London-although, unfortunately, not to recommend Richard Peters. Rather than that, they averred that any appointment of him would bring a deplorable disunity into the Philadelphia Church and a great detriment to religion. Documents from them began their voyage overseas to Bishop Gibson and the Secretary of the Venerable Society. The Secretary of the Land Office of Pennsylvania was not long in realizing that if he wished to return to his sacred calling as a minister and in a goodly congregation, he must do rather more than hope. Friends of his also realized that truth, and at the same time, when William Peters grew conscious that Richard had returned to his pen, others of the Philadelphia community were turning to theirs.

Four letters, in fact, were composed in Philadelphia on April 25, 1741, to be sent to Ferdinando John Paris, confidential agent for the Proprietaries in London and their solicitor before the Lords of Trade and other agencies of the Crown. All were framed upon a matter having nothing directly to do with government, although certainly they bore upon the functioning of the church and were designed to affect the action of a high-placed ecclesiastic.

Mr. Thomas Penn allowed himself a clause to dismiss provincial affairs and then, doing so without any delicate qualifications, informed Mr. Paris that his Secretary, Mr. Peters, had consented on the 24th to let the "majority of the vestry" use their interest with the Bishop of London to license him for the care of Christ Church. Sorry though he would be to lose that gentleman from his service, Mr. Penn considered it proper to inform the London agent that "he changes his station with my knowledge and approbation." He would especially have liked to leave his faithful servant in the Land Office now that he was himself planning a return to England, but he could not be surprised that a man of his talents was so much desired as a minister, and he requested Mr. Paris' interest in helping "the gentlemen of the vestry" with the Bishop. He added that Mr. Peters was writing to Mr. Paris "a full state of the affair."

Governor George Thomas wrote that a letter of Mr. Peters' was accompanying his and that, therefore, he need not himself add at length to what was being said by him to Mr. Paris. But the latter's application to Bishop Gibson would be very obliging to both Mr. Penn and his deputy, and Mr. Thomas intended himself to write to His Lordship at the next opportunity. Then he would inform that great ecclesiastic of the stand taken by Mr. Peters against Whitefield—a stand which had been of great service to the church and the government. He apprehended that Whitefieldian "partisans on one hand and some furious party zealots on the other" would endeavor to blacken Mr. Peters. Notwithstanding, he was convinced that "no man here or elsewhere" was so likely as that gentleman "to preserve unity in a church" or to reveal morals less to be reproached. Finally, he ventured the opinion—no doubt one relevant enough for the Philadelphia of 1741—that "If the Bishop himself were to reside here for twelve months, he would not escape scandal, nay, if an angel were to come down amongst them from Heaven, without a power to make the people better, he would not be able to please them."

The third and fourth letters of that same April day to Ferdinando John Paris were composed by Richard Peters himself. The writer, in his lay capacity, appreciated the importance of the London solicitor in affairs between the Penns and Lord Baltimore and knew how much he had to do with the preliminaries to the survey of the line between Pennsylvania and Maryland two years before. Now, in his conviction of prospective duty, he surmised that Mr. Paris might be as assiduous with a Bishop. Mr. Peters wrote, therefore, at length and with explicitness, if not with too unassuming a modesty. His first communication reviewed both the immediate past at Christ Church and the remoter past of five years ago, as well as past and present events in its author's thinking. It exposed the motive behind the invitation that had come to him from the vestry and abundance of other members of the church "to return to the exercise of his ministerial function": The year of his own assisting Mr. Cummings had "brought the church into a greater reputation than it ever had, either before or since." It explained that the leading spirits of the congregation knew that Mr. Peters' not being at present "in the exercise of his function was owing to his true regard to the peace and welfare of the church." They realized he was careful to make clear that he had withdrawn from the contest with Mr. Cummings in order to ensure the harmony of their parish. He recounted the happy opportunity, which had come after his rebuff and sacrifice, in Mr. Penn's offer to him of the secretaryship. He recalled his public firmness against Whitefield. He regretted, now that so many friends were importuning him to be considered for the vacancy in the church, there should be certain restless folk in the congregation already playing their old game against him. Some of these, in fact, were saying that in accepting the secretaryship, he had disqualified himself from ever returning to the exercise of his sacred function. Others remarked that the Bishop would be highly disobliged by any thought of having Richard Peters "resume the gown in these parts." Whitefieldian elements among them were maligning him as a "frequenter of taverns, coffee houses, balls, concerts, and assemblies," members of the parish, they declared, could not possibly, under the circumstance, think well of him. Such scandalmongering, in fact, had been a chief motive among others, he said, for his refusing to let the vestry consider him. Yet those gentlemen had insisted such malignant representations must not deter him. The Bishop of London would understand from what "hot men" the clamors sprang. Thereupon, he had assured them that he would not approve any action of theirs preceding His Lordship's approval. His oaths, when he took orders, he had said, obliged him "to consult and follow the directions of the Reverend the Bishops, and particularly of the Bishop of my diocese."

If, like the player queen in *Hamlet,* he protested too much, still he clung with a fine constancy to his ingenuousness as he set down his final sentences:

> As I am told, you are likely to be made use of by the people to act for them before the Bishop of London. I judge it proper to acquaint you with the part I take in the affair, which is no more than this: If His Lordship inclines to favor the application of such of the congregation as recommend me, I shall endeavor faithfully to discharge my duty both to the Church and to His Lordship. If it should be otherwise, I shall receive His Lordship's negative upon it as the result of his judgment on what appears before him and be thereby concluded, being inclinable to act the same dutiful part in this affair that I did in the former application, of which you are a good judge.

Everything in the letter implied that its writer would leave no stone unturned in the fulfillment of his destiny, whether in deference and obedience or service and duty. All that was exceptional about its contents was that they were addressed to a legal rather than to an ecclesiastical intercessor-that a lawyer of Thomas Penn rather than the clergy of Pennsylvania was to angle for an episcopal decision.

But April 25 was a stirring day, and, long as his first one had been, Mr. Peters felt obliged to address a second epistle to Mr. Paris. He had, in fact, got wind of what was being done by the owners of at least two names that had not been signed to the address of the congregation to His Lordship two days earlier. The later communication was designed, then, to supplement the first one as well as to substitute for occasional clauses. He mentioned the letters coming from Mr. Penn and Governor Thomas, but whereas Mr. Paris was to be free to show the first to the Bishop, the writer had no intention of having him afford His Lordship's view of the new one. That being true, he could present his version of things now transpiring. It seemed that Peter Evans and Dr. Kearsley had written to Dr. Thomas Moore, asking him "to wait on the Bishop of London in favor of some little paltry fellow that they may have the entire government of." So Richard Peters himself wished to prevent ill consequences "to this city and province by having a bad minister here" besides being willing "to oblige some old steady friends." Mr. Paris, he represented, could be very helpful, then, by waiting promptly upon the Bishop and showing him Governor Thomas' communication. "A first impression," he remarked, "is very material."

But quite obviously, his letter indicated that he desired more than Mr. Paris' promptitude to impress Bishop Gibson. Thomas Moore was a queer sort of man who knew how to secure the avenues to a great man. If Mr. Paris had any interest with the Bishop's "chancellor, or archdeacon, or chaplains, or his secretary," let him not fail to employ it in taking these off from Dr. Moore's influence.

Having ventured that prudent suggestion, he gossiped. In Philadelphia, his hearty friend, Mr. Lawrence, had "taken off" Robert Charles from concerning himself in the affair, a man on whom Mr. Peters' "opponents had great dependence." The other day, too, the writer had had the offer of "a joint certificate and recommendation of all the missionaries" but, doubting its security had rejected it. Now, he was expecting the people, since it was their affair, to procure "an ample certificate and recommendation for him from them." He must not omit his reason for refusing the dubious advance of the missionaries. The truth was, he had been told that one of them, Mr. Curry, had already been recommended to Dr. Moore by Peter Evans and his party. And, although their choice was one of the best of the ministers in the province, he was by no means fit for Christ Church.

Toward the end, Mr. Peters had to hurry to get his communication with the other letters on a ship for Liverpool, but he took time, amid final comments, graciously to suggest that if Mr. Paris could not succeed for him, but could name some other acceptable candidate to the Bishop, he would see that the man was handsomely supported by his friends in Philadelphia.

Yet, once Richard Peters' aspirations to renew his ministerial function had taken hold, he was not the man to forget obligations. He knew that he had the sanction of Mr. Thomas Penn in the province to give up his duties in the Land Office. He remembered, however, two points: he was a servant not to one only but to three Proprietaries; his commission had come to him actually from Thomas, John, and Richard. He must not, in negotiating with a bishop, neglect his secular patrons. So two days after the long letters to Mr. Paris, he got another shorter one off to the two brothers in London—of whom Richard, fortunately, had turned to membership in the Church of England; however, conventionally, Thomas might be exhibiting outward adherence to the Friends in 1741. In this epistle, he set down a brief narrative, proper compliments, open mention of the management being given to Mr. Paris, and regrets at the thought of discontinuing his secretaryship to them. One important point he did not omit: he would never have acquiesced to the appeal of the vestry and congregation had he thereby lost power to serve the Penns. In the state of the province, as it was then circumstanced, he assured them it would "not be unserviceable to their Family to have a good friend over the Church of Philadelphia." In any station, they could, too, depend upon the services of Richard Peters.

For an interval at the end of April, the pen of the Secretary of the Land Office, apart from work-a-day activities, was allowed to rest. But his mind remained active, and, keeping his wits provident, he continued alert to the tactics of his adversaries and meditated further upon his own. He did not hear the comments of those who insisted that John Kearsley, beloved builder of Christ Church, was right in refraining from giving his support to an agent of the Proprietaries. He was not present when scoffers told what they had known of the old altercation between himself and George Whitefield. He did not choose to recall too clearly the words of Mr. Whitefield's retort to him when last November he had risen in Christ Church at the end of that enthusiast's sermon and told the congregation there was no such term as "imputed righteousness" in Holy Scripture, although he could not quite crowd out of his memory the image of the man's producing a Bible and showing the very term there. But he could think of moderation and ways and means.

He knew of certainty in early May that the missionaries had met and actually signed a letter to the Bishop of London embracing a clause to "the effect that considering the present circumstances, it would break the unity and peace of the church to appoint Mr. Peters." He also knew that many of his friends were deploring the haste of their clergy, questioning the right of these to act for a congregation in America without reference to them or resenting the assumption of the clerical prerogative. He kept thinking. Then he found it opportune on May 7 to be in Newcastle, the seat of one of the three lower counties on Delaware, and on that date, two compositions acquired form.

One was an address of vestrymen of Christ Church to the missionaries of the Venerable Society in the province of the Penns. The other was a penning of his own to Ferdinando John Paris.

The address, a greatly extended document, began with the astonishment of the vestry at learning of "a very extraordinary letter" written by the clergy to the Bishop of London and concluded with a request not only for an acknowledgment in answer to the congregation but the transmission of a new letter of retraction to His Lordship. Its long middle ground reviewed the past and weighed the present. It told of Mr. Peters' disinterested declination to be considered for the charge without the Bishop's approval. It praised his fitness. Against a minority in the congregation, it vindicated his reputation and conduct. It admitted there had been "disadvantageous reports respecting his morals." It testified, however, that on examination, such charges were supported with no more truth "than that he had led a more gay life and had indulged himself beyond what perhaps became his character as a clergyman in several diversions and entertainments." It insisted that he had never in any of these "exceeded the bounds of honor, virtue, or modesty." It inferred that Mr. Peters' opponents were chiefly Whitefieldians, and, as it argued for having that gentleman returned to his function, and in the Philadelphia parish, it warned the opposition that "they could not serve two masters, the Church and Mr. Whitefield." More than all this, it indicated that the Reverend Mr. George Ross of Newcastle and their missionary group were now admitting that he had done injustice to Mr. Peters and acted rashly in the earlier "representing him to His Lordship of London" and that he was ready now to retract and set Mr. Peters' case "in a true light."

Richard Peters' letter of the same May 7th announced initially to Mr. Paris that his author was in Newcastle on a "very extraordinary occasion." He was, in fact, there to act as a "moderator between the missionaries and the vestry." Those gentlemen of the clergy, he recounted, "at the instance of two hot men," had signed a letter to the Bishop on April 23rd advising against having the unity of the church broken by the appointment of himself to its pulpit. The vestry, he said, were demanding that the missionaries retract their letter or be themselves exposed, but he had decided "to strike out a third way." He had, in brief, counseled the vestry to write kind letters privately to the clergymen requesting they do Mr. Peters justice and "undeceive the Bishop of London." This, then, he explained to Thomas Penn's London agent, was his errand there in the lower county, and Mr. Ross had promised to write immediately to His Lordship "acknowledging his rashness and precipitancy, giving me a good character and informing His Lordship of the truth that the people are so generally for me that unless I be appointed the peace of the church may be broken."

The visit of the "moderator" to Newcastle on the 7th bore fruit on the 8th and the 10th, when two retractions of the missionaries' April letter went forward to the Bishop, one from George Ross and the other from the Reverend Mr. Richard Backhouse of Chester. Both were full of apology and regret. One wisely defended the wronged clerical from charges of a too "gay" life. Each insisted upon his favor with the majority of the congregation. But Mr. Peters' labors for the vindication of his character and his priestly competence were not yet concluded. He was to be busy with correspondence—as also were others to be—for the remainder of May 1741. On the 11th, from Philadelphia, he wrote his first and only direct letter to Bishop Gibson. On the 14th, he was much occupied with one to Mr. Paris, which was to cover several enclosures. On the same day, Governor Thomas wrote again in his interest to His Lordship at Fulham. On the 23rd, the 25th, and the 30th, further lengthy communications to Thomas Penn's agent in London were composed. On the 14th and the 22nd, two churchwardens, William Pyewell and John Danby, remaining loyal to Richard Peters' cause, addressed themselves to the same recipient.

The letter to the Bishop was couched urbanely. It did not refer to any friction with the late Archibald Cummings. It recapitulated its writer's solicitude in 1737 to have continued to him, when he took secular office through material force of circumstance in that year, the "paternal regards" of His Lordship. It reasserted his disinterestedness with respect to filling the vacancy caused by Mr. Cummings' death. It told of a great part of the congregation who desired to see him again in the ministry and were recommending him to the Bishop for a license. It regretted the unaccountable conduct of the missionaries at the instance of Dr. Kearsley and Peter Evans. It informed His Lordship that two of the clergy, Messrs. Ross and Backhouse, had retracted their signing of the unfortunate letter. It inferred that other missionaries, more distantly located from each other than those two gentlemen at Newcastle and Chester, would also be retracting. It concluded soberly:

> If I am thought worthy of your Lordship's appointment, I shall pay all ready obedience to your Lordship's commands. I shall endeavor to deserve the affections of my brethren and promote in the best manner I can the good of souls and the interest of the established Church.

The Governor's letter of the 14th to Bishop Gibson told of intimate acquaintance with the late Mr. Cummings and sincere regard for him. It told of the importunity from many of the parish to Mr. Peters to take upon him the care of Christ Church. It admitted Mr. Peters had enemies, as an angel from Heaven would have if he ventured into Philadelphia. It praised Mr. Peters. It told of that young man's frequent lamenting the necessity of his having to live under another character than that of a clergyman, of his great desire to resume the gown on the first opportunity. It assured the Bishop that George Thomas had no other thought in making his recommendation than his affection for the Church, of which he had been a member from infancy. The letter to Mr. Paris, written by the two churchwardens, Messrs. Pyewell and Danby, on the same day, was rather more worldly than the Governor's. It resented with vehemence the "vile stab" given to Mr. Peters' character by the missionaries. It declared that because of "detestation for that underhand practice," many of the people were more determined than before to have Mr. Peters as their minister. It rejoiced that the two best of the missionaries, Mr. Ross and Mr. Backhouse, were retracting their precipitate earlier conduct in letters to His Lordship. It concluded with information to Mr. Paris that its two signers were taking care to "order a gentleman to make you a present for your trouble in this affair."

But compensation for the London solicitor's interest with the Bishop was not arranged only through the two churchwardens. Richard Peters' letter of May 14th to Mr. Paris went into great detail. It announced the three letters coming with it from Mr. Pyewell and Mr. Danby, from the two retracting missionaries and ten members of the vestry. It went into the malice of Dr. Kearsley and Peter Evans, it deplored their sense of "complete victory," it represented anew Mr. Peters' employment of pacific measures, it told how a letter from ten vestrymen had produced recantation from Mr. Ross and Mr. Backhouse, with a careful mathematical analysis it showed how, out of twenty vestrymen at the church, eleven votes for himself really constituted a majority of favor. It feared for the future of the congregation if he were not himself appointed to it. It expressed two other fears: Richard Peters was not certain the friendship of the best people in Philadelphia and of Mr. Penn would avail with the "noble person" whose favor he was seeking. There was an unpleasant apprehension in him that, his former application in 1736 not having had justice from His Lordship, he could not expect better usage from the Bishop in this. Finally—remembering that Mr. Paris, after all, was a lawyer and accustomed to fees—it announced: "I have desired Mr. Barclay to give you ten guineas for your expense and in part of the consideration for your trouble in this affair." The genial favorite of vestry and congregation but dubious petitioner to the Bishop of London did not indicate that out of a sum of guineas, a modicum might be employed to make His Lordship's chaplains less amenable to Dr. Thomas Moore's influence. It was enough for him to reason inwardly that if he were to oblige the Established Church by promoting "the good of souls" in Philadelphia, he would have to make terms with the evil times in which he lived.

But there were others besides vestrymen, Governor, and Proprietary, who revealed the proclivity to ink in May 1741. Mr. Ross was not to escape vilification any more than Mr. Peters during that unequal month. In charge of the congregation at Oxford, Philadelphia County was Alexander Howie, and Mr. Howie, not favorably impressed by the recantation of his two fellow missionaries, was willing to explain to Bishop Gibson the motives of at least one of them. He wrote frankly to His Lordship that Mr. Ross had not only signed the missionaries' letter but chiefly promoted it, and he deplored, therefore, the more his shameful retraction. That had come from no real change of conviction. It sprang rather from his wish to please Mr. Peters' staunch friend, Mr. Hamilton, through whom his son, young Mr. Ross, the lawyer, might have a future advantage. Then the father, suborned, as it were, by the legal fraternity, had corrupted Mr. Backhouse, despite the fact that both men knew with what "utmost freedom and deliberation" the April address of the ministers had been drawn up.

The Reverend Mr. George Ross, who got hold of an extract from Mr. Howie's communication, was incensed and fulminated to Richard Peters with both copy and the force of Latin. Calling Ovid to witness, he insisted: *Causa patrocinio non bona major erit,* and lamented his fellow missionaries' hardening themselves in crime. He regarded the "inconsiderable" Howie's presuming to acquaint the Bishop with the thoughts of the minister at Newcastle to be nothing less than blasphemy. He was grateful to Mr. Peters for having warned him against lying younger clerics. He asserted that Dr. Kearsley and Mr. Evans held those junior ministers "in a string like a pack of hounds," now they were being "let loose to hunt him down for morsels of bread." But he was willing to let his credit with the Bishop of London challenge their titles of respect.

Neither the terseness of Mr. Howie nor that of Mr. Ross was, however, to dissuade the Secretary of the Land Office from further deliberation on return to his ecclesiastic calling. Rather, both were influences to his making a further effort through Mr. Paris. Richard Peters found it important to inform that Londoner of the latest maneuvers of the missionaries against him and of his having obtained an extract of the substance of Howie's letter. He predicted the missionaries were ruining their credit with the Bishop. He explained that Howie "was a man of ill fame who by repeated misconduct had made Oxford too hot for him and was about to remove to Jamaica." He scorned Peter Evans for letting the renegade become a conduit pipe for himself to His Lordship. He admitted that Evans and Dr. Kearsley were not Whitefieldians, but he was certain that a new paper that those two were now fostering against him in the church was gathering to itself chiefly Whitefieldian signatures. He vindicated Mr. Ross and Mr. Backhouse. He theorized that if a stranger were sent to the church, it would make little alteration. The Whitefieldian group was bound in a quarter of a year to break it into two anyhow. He offered the opinion that having two churches and two ministers might be a good thing. The joint prudence of two leaders might help much.

In brief, he digressed very much in his letter of May 23, his emotions more transparently wrought than was usual with him. But he did not lose either full coherence or design. If resentment of Dr. Kearsley's influence carried him so far as to declare the Bishop would do him an injustice if he did not license him, he did not forget to remind Mr. Paris of his desire "for the good of souls and the service of the church." And he remembered two other Points. Mr. Paris was to peruse the letters he was forwarding before sealing them and committing them to His Lordship's hand. Moreover, he was to use "expedition in his attendance on the Bishop of London. The loss of a little time might be very prejudicial."

On May 25, Mr. Peters was still exercised, concerned in part with his own mode of overtures, in part for the temper His Lordship might be in, and in part for his rights as a priest and as a vestryman of Christ Church. His remarks about Kearsley and Evans, although "strictly true," might have been impolitic. His letter of the 20th to the Bishop, herewith enclosed for Mr. Paris' examination, might not please and was to be delivered only if Ferdinando John Paris thought wise. It might be best for His Lordship not to know that he knew of Mr. Howie's exchanges with Mr. Ross. For a time, he elaborated on the constitution of the Philadelphia church and the powers of the vestry to choose their minister. Then he contested an opinion that he said was being circulated in the province—that, in assuming lay duties in 1737, he had broken the 76th canon, which says: "No man being admitted a deacon or minister shall from thenceforth voluntarily relinquish the same, nor afterward use himself in the course of his life as a layman, upon pain of ex-communication." His defense was that he had not acted *voluntarily* in the time of Mr. Cummings—that an injurious act of the Bishop had then compelled his withdrawal. In fact, he was resolute now not to be deprived further from his chosen function, whether he should exercise it thereafter in Philadelphia or elsewhere. At length, he was writing, although he did not say so, as one might who had to provide an attorney with an argument. A canon, he realized, might frustrate his ambition far more surely than addresses and retractations.

At the end of the month, he was still concerned with the problem of his application, and on May 30, he wrote once more to Mr. Paris. Mr. Ross's letter of retraction had been detained by young John Ross, who "being no friend of mine," had taken care not to deliver it to him before Captain Buddie's ship, the

Adriatic, had sailed some days earlier for Cork. Now, he was forwarding it by another carrier and, unfortunately, unaccompanied by a letter that the sender had hoped for before then from Mr. Backhouse. He was diligent to explain that Buddie had brought with him duplicates of the letters sent in mid-month by Obadiah Bownes, embarking for Bristol on the *Concord.* He hoped all would arrive in due course. But he was most solicitous that Ferdinando John Paris should make political use of the several missives. He explained, therefore, that all had been left open for the agent's perusal before they should be offered to the Bishop's notice. Let him determine what to submit to His Lordship. He could adopt the belated epistle from Mr. Ross as the cue. When Mr. Paris should have read it, he instructed him: "You will please to seal it with a different seal from the rest." And cautiously, he added, "Indeed, every letter should be sealed with a different seal." In fact, as the ex-assistant of Mr. Cummings pursued his new candidacy, there seemed to be no reason for having the Bishop at Fulham Palace understand that the addresses to him from Philadelphia had not been sealed in that city, the offices of wax and signets, under the favor of a barrister in London, would be quite as satisfactory a means of closure. If the Reverend Mr. Peters was availing himself of a solicitor's services, the only correct thing was to have the solicitor party to the entire transaction.

Moreover, seals were always a matter of small concern. It was common enough for him to employ that of Governor Thomas when he wrote in his own name. That trinket was as useful as the pretty feminine head he sometimes stamped into the red wax on closing his letters. Was it of Venus or Minerva? He was not certain, but did the goddess' identity make any difference?

VI

Stone Wall at Fulham

In June, little doubt of his virtue troubled Richard Peters. He recalled with consolation that he was desired as a minister at Christ Church by many of the best people in the city. He remembered, to the relief of his conscience, that he had obeyed Bishop Gibson and not consorted with the Earl's kinswoman, of whom his sisters in England still spoke as his wife and with whom, as Esther wrote, they remained on cordial terms. He had been "gay" in Philadelphia but never in excess of the bounds of honor and modesty. Realizing that correspondence with agents and prelates in London was a slow process in view of the long voyages of sailing vessels between the two continents and tardy posts from seaports to the capital in England itself, he remained comfortable in his integrity and schooled himself to patience. Of reward and opportunity, he would hope for news in the late summer. Only occasionally did he look into his letter book to remind himself of points he had written.

Presently, in August, communications began reaching him from Ferdinando John Paris. The first one, written on June 27, brought some assurance. The late April and mid-May petitions and addresses had all reached Mr. Penn's agent, and the barrister had acted with intelligence after receiving them. In brief, he pre-read Richard Peters' letter to the Bishop, sealed it up, and by "a strange porter" sent it immediately to His Lordship. The other packets he chose sometime later to carry more openly himself to the prelate's lodgings in Whitehall. From there, the servants promised they should be taken immediately to Fulham. Then, on the morning of the day on which he was writing, Mr. Paris waited upon the ecclesiastic himself at his episcopal palace. He detailed meticulously the interview that had followed.

"I acquainted him," he said, "that at the desire of the churchwardens and vestry, and by the order of the Proprietor and the Governor, I waited upon His Lordship's license and approbation of you." The Bishop replied that he had received, but not yet fully considered, several letters he had received the night before. He had, too, had earlier communications telling him of Mr. Cummings' death and the wish of the clergy, writing formally, not to have Mr. Peters appointed to Christ Church.

Mr. Paris quickly apprehended that the ministers had been surprised into their request "with some art" by two uneasy persons. He ventured the opinion also that some of them would, in all probability, acknowledge a change of mind toward Richard Peters by the next conveyance. On the authority of the churchwardens and of the principal persons in the vestry, he assured His Lordship that they, who contributed to the support of the minister, had not been informed of the action of the missionaries and deplored any inclination of these to impose a minister upon them. Nor did they like the negative which had been put upon Richard Peters' character by the clergy. The reader in Philadelphia of Mr. Paris' words could appreciate the solicitor's prudence and courage in approaching his subject, to save a clergyman from imputations and protect the rights of a parish in the same juncture should have been calculated to appeal to an overseer of the Church. Surely, no prelate could relish precipitancy or prejudice in his subordinates. Certainly, none would wish to join in measures that might produce ill consequences in a congregation.

But Mr. Paris made it clear to his addressee in Philadelphia that Bishop Gibson also claimed rights in the matter. Whoever was the minister of Christ Church had also to be His Lordship's Commissary: His Lordship could not very well sanction appointing to the charge a man who had not only been opposed by the missionaries of the province but who, "in the teeth of one of the canons, had accepted and occupied a lay office." His Lordship admitted that his mind was not made up in the matter. He was thinking of sending some priest to Philadelphia to prevent difficulty through the appointment of someone there unacceptable to others. But he would consider the letters he had received for some time longer. On the sixth of July, when he should be back in town, he would be glad to see Mr. Paris.

But the sponsor for Thomas Penn, Governor Thomas, and the congregation was not lightly to be put off. He held out to the prelate on the evil of ignoring a "modest recommendation" from worthy folk, on the need to keep innocent clerics from imputation, on the importance of encouraging the worthy, of avoiding breaches and saving the church in those parts. For a time, he was satisfied he was bringing His Lordship to terms, that he was growing less determined. Then, disappointingly, Bishop Gibson recurred to the matter of his own authority. How could he approve for his Commissary, a man who had quitted his pastoral for a lay office? Mr. Paris came away chagrined.

But once he was come off, Mr. Paris acted naturally enough and thought of the things he might have said. Back in his Surry Street house, he had his doubts about the Bishop's right to have a commissary in Pennsylvania, in view of the frame of government in that province. He could entertain no cordial respect for an ancient canon which he was sure was "no jot of the law in England." So he was getting ready for another conference with Bishop Gibson, and Mr. Peters could depend upon his laying before His Lordship some clauses relating to preachers. Prudently, he sent word, too, that the vestry and churchwardens might fully expect his services in the cause of the people. That popular sovereignty might not agree with the operation of a church governed by a hierarchy, in brief, in no way dashed his zeal for a client.

Yet Mr. Paris, as his next letter—of July 7—indicated, was no person to work alone if he could have adjutants. Before a second visit to the Bishop, he had the suggestion from Mr. Barclay, who had transmitted ten guineas to him, that recourse to Philip Bearcroft of the Venerable Society might be helpful.

So he had turned to that gentleman, hoping to use him as a middleman, eager to pour all his views into the ears of the Secretary for Propagating the Gospel in Foreign Parts, alert for reactions from the designed intermediary. But Dr. Bearcroft had not proved clay. He conceded, as Mr. Paris said that he saw "no sort of necessity that the minister of Christ Church be the Bishop's Commissary." He intimated that if the Bishop did not hearken to the desires of the vestry, he "might be in danger" of losing that church which His Lordship "called his Metropolis in Pennsylvania." He was indefinite about the troublesome canon on quitting the ministry for a lay office. But he did not hurry away to the prelate's lodgings in Whitehall to further Mr. Peters' cause.

Mr. Paris had, in fact, gone without earlier heralds or outriders to his second meeting with Edmund, Bishop of London. Their conference was a lasting one, His Lordship assuming from the beginning of it a more militant attitude. He had considered deliberately all of the papers sent him. He had found all the clergy, six or seven in number, joined against Mr. Peters, and only two of them, he said, had retracted from their position toward him. He pulled out a little book and read what Ferdinando John Paris pronounced "a supposed canon," one which he said was Number 76. The fact stood fast that in exercising a lay office, the Secretary of the Pennsylvania Land Office had violated the canon. Moreover, the Bishop went so far as to remark that even the vestry, in their expostulary letter to the missionaries, had allowed that Mr. Peters "led a more gay life and had indulged himself beyond what became his character as a clergyman." In vain, Mr. Paris interposed, begging His Lordship to read the qualifying phrase from that epistle: "But not exceeding the points of honor, virtue, or modesty." For the Bishop remarked categorically: "He could not approve of Richard Peters. He wished the vestry would think of some clergyman who was already in Pennsylvania."

Mr. Paris answered all as best he could, then tried another tack. He proceeded to read letters in Mr. Peters' favor from both the Proprietors, Messrs. John and Thomas Penn, and from Governor Thomas. To disappoint both these excellent gentlemen and the vestry was unwarrantable. Furthermore, in disappointing the larger group in the church membership, Bishop Gibson would be making two mistakes. First, he would be refusing men who, only at Mr. Peters' request and out of his very great respect for the prelate, had forborne to name their minister on their initiative. Second, he would be negativing the clear natural right of the congregation to choose whom they wished for their rector. Quite in his manner of attorney, Mr. Paris argued two points in favor of the vestry and the congregation. By their voluntary maintenance of their minister, they were justified in having free choice. Furthermore, a clause in King Charles's Charter to William Penn accorded them the prerogative of selecting. Thereupon, he too produced a paper and read a clause showing sanction from the King for twenty persons or more to notify the Bishop of London of a preacher whom they wanted and then to have him. That privilege they could have secured to them "by any person deputed."

Indeed, waxing emphatic in his power as deputy, Mr. Paris next scored the missionaries for their busy intrusion upon the free choice of the vestry and warned His Lordship of sad consequences if he sided with the clergy. But his aggression only produced further emphasis from the Bishop. The prelate declared roundly and earnestly that he would approve of no one for their minister until the vestry of Christ Church gave up that right. Nothing of the solicitor's long persistence for another quarter hour of admonition against the ecclesiastic's hurting his own prestige in the colonies succeeded in modifying his attitude.

So Ferdinando John Paris closed his letter of July 7 from Surry Street rather lamely. He had taken recourse in a second visit with Dr. Bearcroft, who seemed to agree with him about all the errors the Bishop was committing and all the evils which would ensue from his errors. But the Secretary of the Venerable Society also confirmed his belief that His Lordship was "resolved." The London agent of Mr. Peters, in short, regretted that faithful and earnest though his endeavors had been, they had been attended with little success. Nor was his admission, by way of postscript, that he had received ten guineas by Mr. Barclay particular comfort to the correspondent in Philadelphia.

Yet Richard Peters continued hoping and looked up the clause in the charter on which his friend overseas was basing the force of argument. He could not quite see any phrase there which took from the Bishop of London right to approve or disapprove any Church of England priest in Pennsylvania.

Late in August, another letter reached him, with news of Mr. Paris' having received on the 13th of July a full quota of papers from his client and his friends in Philadelphia, of his having picked out pertinent ones of them, and posted with them to the Bishop, who had been too busy to receive him. He remarked, though, that he expected another audience with His Lordship and that he was glad for a new argument with which Mr. Peters' later letter had armed him. It was well to know that the Bishop had never really fully licensed Mr. Peters before, that he had only afforded him "a sort of extra-judicial and temporary permission." The prelate could not, therefore, be so dogmatic about Canon 76 that need not prohibit the Secretary from regaining his ministerial function.

But having encouraged his client to that effect, in other regards, he became profuse rather than inspiring. He did not now believe that he could procure for Mr. Peters any full license to preach in the Bishop's diocese. His Lordship would hardly consent to that permission if, at the moment that he did so, the vestry might choose Mr. Cummings' ex-assistant for their rector. Moreover, it would not be of advantage to talk of having two congregations in Philadelphia, as Mr. Peters in his letter of May 23 had hinted might be possible. The candidate himself had remarked earlier than that to the Bishop of London that he was not willing to press any application which would break the unity of the church. The writer, too, had to admit embarrassment with regard to the churchwardens and congregation, whose commission he had not to date been able to carry out.

Then, having fluttered in a hardly professional manner through a good many sentences, Mr. Paris tried to strengthen Richard Peters' expectations. For a time, he reasoned that the American plantations never were annexed to the Diocese of London. At the end of George I's reign, a very "spare" power had been granted to the Bishop to visit and superintend the clergy in America. Such a commission as Mr. Cummings' had come only from that limited authority. He suggested Mr. Peters find a printed copy of instructions to a commissary and assured him he suspected nothing in it would demonstrate the Bishop's privilege of annexing America to his diocese. But then once more, he fluctuated and counseled his correspondent that whatever he might urge in point of law might not be urged by expediency. In sum, Mr. Paris' letter of July 16, 1741, formulated no definite procedure. He exposed the learning of his profession rather than its effectuality and evaded every issue with a meandering discretion.

Then, as though he had accomplished something of weight, he postscripted again: "I have received from Mr. Barclay ten guineas, which he paid me by the order of Mr. John Turner."

Richard Peters read with increasing insight, but he let his dreams of being restored to his function linger on into September.

Two more communications from Mr. Paris presently arrived in Philadelphia. His sponsor had secured another admission to Bishop Gibson on July 20 and wrote on that day. His beginning could hardly be interpreted as auspicious. The new packets of letters had not varied the matter in His Lordship's eyes. The prelate declared he had determined not to appoint Mr. Peters. He reiterated his objection to Mr. Peters' having quitted his gown, departed from his function, occupied a lay office, and lived a gay life, not becoming a clergyman. Worse than all that, he added "that Mr. Cummings had been continually writing of the infinite trouble and uneasiness you gave him," and he foresaw "only mischief if you should get into that large cure of souls," which was, too, "a very valuable living." The Secretary of the Land Office of Pennsylvania found himself rebuffed, then, as he read, by a double reprimand. He had, according to the Bishop, sullied his position as a minister, and he, who had preached love, had reaped malice from a rector now dead and revered. Yet he must deplore rather than resent the indignities shown him if he would be true to his practice of moderation.

He followed Mr. Paris' defense to His Lordship, more with resolution than with pleasure. There was no surprise to him in the Londoner's rejoinder at Whitehall on Mr. Peters' always confining himself within the bounds of virtue and modesty. Second nature told him that Ferdinando John Paris was excusing himself quite as much for failure in his commission as he was supporting his client "in his unhappy dilemma." He was not too sure of his agent's authority when that gentleman informed His Lordship that "Mr. Cummings had always insisted that you had not had a full license under seal to exercise your function, but barely a permission to do so as long as Mr. Cummings thought it convenient." He was uncertain of the implications in Mr. Paris' next argument to the Bishop that, if Mr. Peters had exercised his function further with that bare permission, he would then have broken another canon. But he saw aptness in His Lordship's retort to that: "Then why did he not leave the place?" For he remembered well enough that he had continued to preach on alternate Sundays in Christ Church for many months after the difficulties had risen between himself and the late rector. He did not quite see the point of Mr. Paris' answer: "It did not suit Richard Peters' conveniency to be always passing and repassing between America and England."

Patiently the disappointed Secretary, however, perused the report of the rest of the conference: Mr. Paris' appeal for a license for him to preach at large in His Lordship's diocese without particular view to Christ Church, praise of his suffering for the "peace and service" of that congregation, his dutifulness in refusing appointment to the parish directly from the vestry, Edmund Gibson's refusal to license him under any circumstances, when the clergy had written so strongly against him, the solicitor's resentment of the clergy's "new invented contrivance to set themselves up as a body of people who would name, or exclude, any person they thought fit to succeed in any church in Pennsylvania." For Richard Peters knew that, whether or not Ferdinando John Paris had "pushed the matter to the utmost of his ability," he was to have neither license nor Christ Church. The last letter, of July 27, 1741, from the barrister on Surry Street, was not needed to confirm his knowledge that Edmund, Bishop of London, was "resolutely bent not even to license him to preach." From the dead cleric in his vault in Christ Church, Mr. Peters had drawn to himself the full effect of the "countercheck quarrelsome."

Yet Richard Peters was not one to remain inactive in mind, nor did he suffer from a dearth of ideas. He beheld the Reverend Mr. Aeneas Ross beginning, at the earnest request of the congregation, to supply the vacancy in Christ Church pulpit in September, talked on occasion with other vestrymen who accepted that arrangement until a regular minister should be sent them, attended worship with regularity, and was pleased to learn of the numerous baptisms the new Mr. Ross, in his zeal for the cure of souls, was recording.

But a number of his real thoughts he set down in a letter of October 24, 1741, to Mr. Thomas Penn, who had gone back to England. He recounted briefly the resolution of Bishop Gibson against him and admitted that the application for a minister, at least so far as it related to himself, was at an end. Mr. Paris' letters had, however, contained matter that might "prove of service to the church, and perhaps to the government." He understood plainly from them "that the Bishop of London is so far from having a right of appointing or presenting to any churches in Pennsylvania or even America, that he has not the right of licensing since America is not annexed to his diocese." If his reading of Mr. Paris was correct, would it not be worth Mr. Penn's while to consider this point: If the Province of Pennsylvania was not annexed to the Diocese of London, then his Governor might have the right of licensing and perhaps of presenting. Governor George Thomas might be instructed in the future to do so. Indeed, the thoughts he wrote to Mr. Penn took him further even than his surmise that the Proprietor of Pennsylvania, whether or not he was a member or clergyman in the Church of England, might direct his lieutenant in the province to license a priest to Christ Church. They took him on to an offer. "For my part," he wrote, "were it worth my while and I had your consent, I would immediately accept of the appointment of the vestry and procure the Governor's license, and should after that think myself as firmly and as legally possessed of this church as the Bishop is of his own bishopric."

That he might be suborning a rich Quaker, who had not withdrawn formally from the sect of his father William Penn, to supplant George II, the Defender of the Faith, and his archbishops and bishops in their ecclesiastical authority seems not to have occurred to Richard Peters in late 1741. But the practical sense of the man no more deserted him then than at any time. If he could not be a minister under Thomas Penn's sanction, at least he could continue as a Secretary of the Land Office. So he concluded his letter prudently: "However, it is not agreeable to me to enter into a sea of contention, and I shall, therefore, be exceedingly glad to continue in your service, wherein I will endeavor to give you satisfaction."

In brief, Mr. Peters was glad to get back to the parceling out of land. Mr. Aeneas Ross continued happily as supply in the Philadelphia parish. His congregation awaited a minister whom the Bishop of London should designate from his Palace at Fulham. The principle of church and state combined—at least of church subordinated to the state—did not come into effect in Pennsylvania. Erastianism was to have no undue advantage in religion in that province.

As for Ferdinando John Paris, that gentleman averred in January 1742, by letter to Mr. Peters, that he held to his convictions. "I am such a lover of liberty," he said, "and such an enemy to all undue usurpation of powers, either in civil or ecclesiastical affairs, that I am very much pleased your vestry are in a disposition not to admit any minister licensed by the Bishop to preach in their church. I think it a proper and a lawful assertion of what I take to be their undoubted right." One admission he made, however. For he added, "I am in doubt with myself, whether I should or should not acquaint the Bishop thereof." Then, having ventured that dubiety, he closed the matter with a simple directness: "I now send an account for my charges in that out-of-the-way and troublesome affair."

VII

Gossip and Politics

When, in March 1715, the Reverend Mr. Francis Phillips addressed himself to the Secretary of the Venerable Society on the subject of his troubles in Philadelphia, deploring modes of blackmail in the congregation of Christ Church and putting down Mr. Trent's threat to shoot him, he wrote of one further bitterness which he had to endure in his suffering. It seemed Mr. Robert Jenney had inferred that affliction was likely to be the mark of a "bastard" because it was so useful in recrimination. Moreover, that young priest had made the indiscreet assertion, Mr. Phillips wrote, "That I was predestinated to be damned because I was so severely pursued by calumny and reflection and for no other reason." Detraction was, apparently, the equivalent of guilt committed.

The assertion may not have been justified. Other causes than either malign destiny or boasting of the lightness of wives in his parish may have effected the trying expulsion of Francis Phillips from his charge in the bizarre era of Governor Gookin. But whether Providence or chance operated in his own clerical experience, Mr. Jenney found favor twenty-seven years later with the Bishop of London in 1742 and early in 1743, with the trust of that great ecclesiastic reposed in him, assumed charge of the Church of Philadelphia. In June, he wrote to his superior in England that he had received from Mr. Cummings' executors the printed copy of His Lordship's Commission from the King and that His Lordship might depend upon his best endeavors.

Richard Peters, receiving in much the same season reassurance from his patron Thomas Penn, agreed, on reading the latter's letter of February, that "a more unfit man might have been sent from England." The Proprietor regarded Mr. Jenney as of a good sort and heartily wished that he might "be a means to restore unity to your society." So his Secretary formed no notions of being a discomfort to the new rector, and indeed, the Reverend Robert Jenney could remain sanguine about everything in the first year of his charge. In June 1743, the congregation appeared "perfectly easy." In January 1744, he "thanked God" the church was in perfect peace "and the congregation very numerous." Seats for which people would pay, were they available, were much in demand. To add to his joys, the prospering rector married Jane Elizabeth Falconier Assheton, widow of Archibald Cummings, becoming that lady's third husband. If for the time his felicity was not complete, it lacked only because Mr. Aeneas Ross, beloved among the younger folk of Philadelphia, took occasional opportunities to marry his friends and baptize their children, which privileges of extending sacrament Mr. Jenney viewed as belonging decidedly to his cure.

On weekdays, Mr. Jenney's pewholder, Mr. Peters, devoted himself to non-clerical occupations. The Secretary of Pennsylvania's Land Office never languished for the need of things to be done. If he was not too pressed with warrants and patents, there was an abundance to write about to Thomas Penn in England. If he did not have to compose on matters of urgency affecting Mr. Penn's economic status or his political rights, there was always the opportunity to detail the misfortunes or the happy circumstances of the Proprietor's friends in the province. In the obituarial style, he excelled as in the exegetical, and he had a rare faculty for turning from grim sorrow to rapturous exaltation.

On an April day of 1742, he achieved that metamorphosis to perfection. Old William Penn's daughter, Margaret, wife of Thomas Freame, with her two children, Mr. Thomas and Miss Philadelphia Hannah, had just left the province for a sojourn in England, and he sat writing to that thirty-six-year-old matron and sister to the Proprietaries. If for a dependent on greatness, his air was rather intimate; his manner was meticulous and graphic as might be desired. "We are now mourning," he began of Mr. Penn's surveyor, "for the death of poor Mr. Steel . . . after one of the saddest distempers . . . a violent ulcer of so uncommon a malignity that scarce anyone could bear the offensiveness of it ... He was in continual pain except while under the force of an opiate from the first attack to near his decease."

Then, to strengthen himself—and presumably Margaret Freame—in the ethics of conduct, he digressed:

> Of what efficacy are care, temperance, moderation, a constant supply of good spirits and a strong constitution? All these were remarkably united in him, and yet they could not secure him from . . . more torment than what scarce at any time arises from a life of the most arrant dissoluteness. If propriety of conduct had not an irresistible force on a thinking mind, one would almost be tempted, from this and some other instances that I have seen, to disclaim care and prudence in the management of one's self.

Having, at the end of his digression, saved himself from moral heresy, the Secretary hoped for God's reward to James Steel, quoted the Savior's fine reasoning on "him that is faithful in that which is least," and enlarged by way of contrast on the decedent's debts, estate, and heirs, himself pleased that indebtedness was small compared with the fortune left to five daughters.

To add to a good measure of decay in humankind, the writer commented briefly on two other deaths, one without a will and another by consumption, and then, with an easily gliding sentence, shifted "to the land of the living."

Yet here, too, was a limitation. Apart from Mrs. Elliss and her family, especially Miss Nany, there were no ladies left in Philadelphia to compensate for the absence of Mrs. Freame or to keep Mr. Peters properly practiced in a gentleman's behavior in the company of ladies. With Miss Nany Elliss, he could "run over old times," but with the general scarcity of female conversation, there was "not so much as a little polite scandal to be picked up for the entertainment of a lady of curiosity."

The letter revealed nonetheless that one comfort had got both women and men through the long winter of 1741–42 in Philadelphia. "The pretty book of *Pamela*" had by some accident got into Mrs. William Allen's hands, and so into Mr. Allen's—and promptly "a most agreeable fund of discourse and reflections of the finest sort" gave life to conversations. Mr. Allen, the violence of whose views could generally be depended on, surprised the town by praising the book in the highest terms. More than that, he procured the privilege of reading Mrs. Allen's copy for George Thomas, and the Governor, were such a thing possible, was more pleased than Mr. Allen. From the favor of two such eminent gentlemen was "communicated such a fondness for the charming innocent that *Pamela* was in everybody's mouth and happy the person who could procure a reading." That Richard Peters himself also succumbed to the charm of the volume was evinced in his last words of it: "To be sure no book ever yet penned in my opinion comes up to Pamela, the model and envy of her sex."

If, however, he was quick to pass from death to life and from chat to literature, he could return as facilely to gossip. To the feminine ears of Mrs. Freame, he had other points to convey. Upon an old promise, he had married Miss Betsy Morris to Mr. Anthony White and, latterly, Mr. Andrew Hamilton to Miss Till. Then, from marriage, he passed on to another detail in family life, commenting that Mrs. Inglis had been brought to bed of a daughter and was as well as could be expected. After that, ceasing to give, he asked frankly. If Mrs. Freame did not think it too much trouble, he requested news of two ladies in England and "in what situation Mrs. Pearce's unfortunate affair now stands." And winding up his long commentary to the daughter of William Penn and Hannah Callowhill, he assured her that every minute would consist of ten minutes for him until he knew that she and Mr. Tomy and Miss Phil had safely arrived in London!

If, as time went on, his rapture diminished, at least his affability remained with him late in May of 1742, and as Mr. Penn's substitute, he waited upon the Reverend Mr. Bealer, pastor of the Moravians, who had just arrived in Philadelphia. To that ministerial figure, and through him to the Brethren, he tendered his own best services and those of the Proprietor and then, with proper ceremony, conducted him to Governor Thomas, who showed the representative of Count Nicolaus Zinzendorf the same official courtesy. Mr. Bealer, he remarked in his letter to his patron in England, had promised to wait upon him after a conference with the Count and that nobleman's fellow religionists. Yet despite urbanities in the interview with the pastor, misgivings remained in Richard Peters' mind. He promised he would get the best price he could for Mr. Penn's land. But he was dubious as to available good tracts since the most recent lottery adventures, and he feared he should not be able to bring the Moravians to anything like £50 per hundred acres.

October gave him the opportunity to expand upon matters other than dalliance among the ladies of Philadelphia or association with immigrant Moravians. The older Mr. Andrew Hamilton might have died in August 1741, when the Secretary was still dreaming of recovery of his ministerial function, and .that admired familiar might have passed away into half-atheist, half-Presbyterian shadows. Other pleasant comrades remained for Richard Peters and the election of assemblymen, burgesses, sheriffs, coroners, and assessors in 1742 bore fruit for him both in fellowship and politics. It was just the happening, he reasoned, to recount with a blending of duty and cheer. By way of induction, he confided in a long November letter that, after he had narrated what had transpired publicly, he would inform Thomas Penn of what had occurred before in private. Then, he staged his scenes effectively.

Some thirty to forty non-voting sailors, shipwrights, and journeymen from vessels in the harbor made their way at eight o'clock in the morning through Water Street and impinged upon Jersey Market, the place of the polls. Ubiquitous Israel Pemberton, concerned for any interruption to folk about to perform a serious function and certainly not loath to have the old Assembly reelected, happened along and inspired Mr. Allen and Mr. Lawrence to charge the seamen to disperse without offering any disturbance to the electorate. Those two eminent burghers warned that any interference might result in commitment to jail and severe punishment, their admonition assuming, more than either wished, the spirit of a taunt. But the sailors answered only that they were having a holiday and going out of the town to seek diversion in the countryside, and all would have been well had it not been for the persistent effrontery of Israel. That importunate Quaker, seeing one Captain Mitchell in the sailors' company supplied with a stick, demanded, "What business hast thou with that cudgel, friend?"

"It's none of your affair," rejoined the ship's officer, and by virtue of his answer, Israel Pemberton threatened the man with commitment if he had any evil design with his stick. Angered, Captain Mitchell attempted to strike his interlocutor and had perforce to be borne away by others. He departed "horrid mad," promising to find enough men to defend his person and to make the rascals who had offended him pay dearly for their insults.

For a time, there was a lull. At Jersey Market, where a thousand electors were gathering, strong for the old Assembly, and Mr. Allen, candidate for the Proprietary party, stood deserted with only some fifty men around him, inspectors were chosen quietly and took their place on the stairs to guard the election tickets being delivered by the voters. A band of sailors came again upon the scene, this time armed with clubs, but made no show of belligerence and started onward laughing in merry humor.

Then Captain Mitchell reappeared, an altercation began, and one exasperated elector tried hitting a sailor with a market rail and the iron hook attached to its end. That provocation was too much. Riot ensued. The offended shipwrights and journeymen "fell at a marvelous rate upon magistrates, constables, and gentlemen" without respect of persons or parties. Edward Shippen, friend to Richard Peters, tried diplomacy with the buccaneers, offering them drinks at Jonathan Robinson's if they would desist from their energy and be satisfied that no harm was intended to them by the voters. Good-naturedly, they accepted his invitation and followed him on an alleyway to Jonathan's. There, the innkeeper thought better of Mr. Shippen's proposal and, despite his generosity, declined to serve the sailors. The taverner's affront became the signal for emphatic redress.

Promptly, the ship's journeymen returned to Jersey Market and went on a rampage there. Five hundred Dutch were put to route, and bricks kept flying at innocent country people mounting the stairs to hand in their ballots. Presently, the sailors had made a clear stage for themselves and were dancing in glee outside the closed Courthouse doors. There was no going on with the rights of freemen for the interval. But the action of the protagonists was to have a counterstroke in the drama, and the mirth of the journeymen was short-lived. Provided with stout clubs, the outraged Dutch came back in droves, outnumbering the adversary, and, seeing themselves threatened with something more than Ned Shippen's ale, the intruders began making off.

Then came the final act. Richard Peters' pen moved briskly as he described it and provided a chorus in the same moment: "On this reverse of things, several magnanimous heroes made their appearance. Young Israel Pemberton, in particular, ventured out of the Courthouse chimney, and with him, Isaac Griffitts, Sam Norris, and other young men of that stamp came to the assistance of the Dutch and helped to drag the sailors to prison. To be sure, these deserved no pity, but to see those wretches, men of remarkable pusillanimity, lording it over the journeymen, who were pinioned and in the custody of constables who called their victims by the most vile names and beat them unmercifully, there was no man but what thought worse of Israel and his fellows than of the rioters."

Eventually, the scribe of all these matters, having pictured the tragedy of the unfortunates, was so complacent as to discover to Mr. Penn some of the strings that had operated the puppets of the play. In August, he wrote, it was expected the Dutch would be much divided in their voting and that there would be a warm and near contest. It was suggested then that four inspectors be chosen from each of the two contending parties, and that method of guarding the polls was agreed upon. But at the club at Postlewaite's, some gentlemen still felt apprehension, and to these, several ship captains offered what seemed timely counsel. They would suggest to a number of shipwrights and journeymen that they appear on election day, "thicken" the appearance for a choice of inspectors and be ready if they wanted to support the trial for the stairs. Nothing more than this had been ever mentioned to Governor Thomas, Mr. Allen, or Mr. Peters himself. "I assure you," he insisted to the Proprietor, "I am neither directly nor indirectly privy to these orders and to this conference with the captains. Nor do I know any more than that several of the Gentlemen at Postlewaite's and some of the captains declared they would not suffer any foul play in seizing of the stairs and changing men's tickets as they were bringing them to deliver. Of that practice, complaints had been deservedly made."

With that final assurance, he was content to let Thomas Penn behold for himself how the strings had worked—or failed to work—in an election that chiefly returned the old Assembly and chose Israel Pemberton as one of the two burgesses of Philadelphia. In truth, that such generally anticipated results should have ensued troubled the Secretary of the Land Office to no great degree. Nor was he perturbed that the account of the election and riot printed in the *Pennsylvania Gazette* did not corroborate his own in all particulars. If Ben Franklin did not give the hard-fisted Dutch special credit for the exploit but transferred it to the inhabitants generally, or if that newsman spoke less pityingly of fifty sailors "dragged one by one away from their ships and thrust into prison for their rioting," Richard Peters could only suffer Franklin to publish in Franklin's vem.

Late in 1742, the Secretary had other less colorful matters for his thoughts. He knew that Mr. Penn had journeyed into Northern England and, on his return to London, made a stop at Liverpool for a visit of some hours. Both he and William were pleased with the distinction shown to Mr. Ralph Peters. Richard was proud to learn that the Proprietor had passed the day with his father, enjoyed his hospitality, and was sending messages to him from older friends at home and greetings to the family of Andrew Hamilton. William was glad that Mr. Penn reported the visit had been agreeably spent and laughed at his good patron's admission that he had "a little too much drink," their sire, no doubt, had done the honors properly.

Weightier reflections sometimes kept Richard Peters' mind on Indian affairs. Always beyond tickets for surveys, records of transactions, warrants and patents, city lots, and manors was the romance of more land to be acquired, apportioned, surveyed, and sold or warranted. Treaties and purchases were constant subjects for consciousness. The Secretary realized that Mr. Penn's and his meditations flowed in the same channels, whether or not to the same advantage. He was aware, too, by this time that he must expect reprimands and compliments in letters from his master in England. So he half-wondered, half-guessed at what would be the Proprietor's response to counsel he had recently sent from Conrad Weiser. The interpreter had reported, and he had relayed word that the Six Nations were "immoveably determined not to treat with agents." "They wanted," they said, "to deal directly with one of the Proprietors from an imagination that the Proprietors never leave the keys of their money chest behind them—or, in other words, that their agents will not be so generous as the Proprietors themselves." Further Conrad had remarked, and been quoted, to the effect that "the lands at Juniata are favorite lands," and that he could not hope to persuade the Indians to part with Juniata. "The Six Nations did not even set such value on Wyoming or their other lands on Susquehanna."

The commentary might have almost any one of several issues. It might be an influence for bringing some members of the Proprietary family back to Pennsylvania; it might flatter more funds for expenses of treaties out of the Penns, and it might whet the desire for new purchases. Well to have it shaped to some useful end! Yet word from Thomas Penn that reached Richard Peters in December was not notably satisfying. The Proprietor admitted then that the guns bought for the Six Nations were what he had promised, but he questioned bluntly the expenses for entertainment of the Indians, "vastly higher than ever before," and amounting to £390.

The year 1743 in the province found Christians other than the laity of Christ Church at odds. In those stirring years when Whitefieldians kept breaking from presbytery or episcopacy, when dissenter quarreled with dissenter, and denomination with denomination, and the American colonies were everywhere harassed with disputes on doctrine, the Lutherans of Philadelphia debated matters of faith with the newly arrived Moravian followers of Zinzendorf. So one January day, Richard Peters, sensitive as he always was to disunity among the faithful, felt obliged to forget the secular affairs of Indians and Proprietors to do what he could to solve religious difficulties. At the instance of Count Zinzendorf and Mr. Bealer, he approached Pastor Behme, minded to "soften and accommodate the differences between the two parties," and supposing he had some influence with the Lutheran. But his conjecture, it seemed, was wrong. For the moment he broached the problem, the eyes of the disciple of Martin Luther "struck fire."

"I would as soon," shouted Pastor Behme with passion, "agree with the Devil as with Zinzendorf."

Mr. Peters tried mollification for a time. Indeed, he expatiated on "the Christianity of the Lutheran's temper." Yet it was all in vain. He had perforce to withdraw, disappointed. In fact, he left the pastor with an "abundance of contempt" in his heart, sad that the German should be so "hot and indiscreet" a person. Israel Pemberton himself could have done no more with the man. The Secretary hoped that at Christ Church, the new rector would have happier experiences with his flock than could be possible among the followers of Bealer and Behme.

By the spring of 1743, circumstances for Thomas Penn's Philadelphia agent were growing more easy and clear. The old regret for the obstinacy of the Bishop of London was wearing off. If he could not reconcile pastors and missionaries, at least Richard Peters was having favor from mundane authorities. In mid-February, on the resignation of Patrick Baird, George Thomas proposed him for Secretary and Clerk of the Provincial Council. He was unanimously accepted, admitted to the presence of that dignified body, given custody of the seals of state from the Governor, and instructed to prepare the necessary bonds. Within a few days, his friends, Mr. Till and Mr. Strettel, two of the Councillors, had superintended delivery of the Council Books and papers to the new appointee, and he and Mr. Baird had interchangeably signed for possession of those precious documents of state. The addition of a new function disturbed Mr. Peters no whit. If his responsibilities increased, there were amenities to compensate.

In April, Thomas Penn's responses to the late letters of 1742 came, and if he must follow their several points with mingled feelings, he could yet find satisfaction among them. He prided himself that he could take approval and rebuke with equal grace. If Mr. Penn endorsed any view that he offered, whether it came from Conrad Weiser, James Logan, or himself—and indeed, he did not always distinguish between ideas that emanated from those two men from ideas that rose in his mind—he took pleasure from the endorsement.

The Proprietor's letter of February 26 interested him much. Thomas Penn announced that he had been much concerned at the news of the election disturbance, found the riot unwarrantable, and wished the magistrates had taken more pains to suppress it. But, although he ventured "you should have discouraged the proposal," he did not task his Secretary on that point, for he knew "the heats with which such contests have been carried on," and he suggested only that "in the future, all belonging to us will remain neutral." He wrote commendation, too, of the seemly behavior of William Allen on the day of excitement. On Indian affairs, however, he was something more austere. He began that he was pleased in everything relating to the last treaty, then qualified "to except the paying of half the charge of the entertainment of the Indians." For, as Mr. Peters realized, the Penns were accustomed to having the expenses of such projects provided out of public rather than Proprietary funds. Regularly, they insisted that treaties, which guaranteed the greater safety of the people, should be paid for by them through grants and levies voted by the Assembly. Furthermore, the Secretary knew that the Proprietors would not admit to the validity of their having to share in appropriations for the common defense. Lands granted by the Crown in England for signal services to the monarch were free of real taxes levied on other sorts of estate. The charter to William Penn was but a Crown grant *in Excelsis,* carrying with it all such exemptions as had been merited by the achievements of Admiral Penn for the Stuarts and warranted to his son, the Founder of Pennsylvania, in the royal gift. Richard Peters had been trained in the law. It was not his fashion to condemn any gentleman's wholly legal rights. The Penns granted privileges to settlers and let the folk of the province protect their privileges through the lawmakers whom they chose to elect into their Assembly. Thomas Penn might well enough dislike a frugality on the part of the legislators. In the summer of 1742, the great chieftain Canassatego of the Six Nations and James Logan and the Council had agreed that the Delawares must vacate lands at the forks of the Delaware, which earlier that tribe had sold to the Proprietaries. The arrangement had been effected quite as much for the convenience of settlers as for the promotion of Penn interests.

So, Secretary Peters could sympathize without particular reservations. If Thomas Penn regarded it a trick of the Assembly to claim a shortage in the public funds and persuade the Council to contribute from the Proprietary coffers, his subordinate in the province could accord with his superior's interpretation. In fact, what Mr. Peters liked among Mr. Penn's remarks on Indian affairs was his responsiveness to a proposal of his own. In Conrad Weiser's name, he had hinted at a better purchase than "at Juniata." He read with pleasurable anticipations Mr. Penn's comment: "Your proposal to sound the Indians about another purchase was well judged. I should be glad to purchase Wyoming with the lands below on Susquehanna first and am really indifferent as to Juniata. If Wyoming were bought, I should let most of it lie for the use of the Family." Richard Peters knew that the beloved hunting grounds of the Delawares on the east branch of Susquehanna, whatever their sacredness to the Indians, were rich as whole English counties. He knew, too, that what letting land "lie for the Family" meant to Thomas Penn was the laying out of manors luxuriantly fenile. It was his duty to foster rather than discourage "Family" dreams.

He did not repine, then, as he observed the Proprietor's chidings. "I think," wrote his patron bluntly, "the charges for your expenses into the Jerseys are great, and I desire you will be as frugal on such occasions as decency will admit of. Ten pounds is charged as part of the expense of your journey, which is a considerable sum." Further, he accepted as but a pan of the day's work in the Land Office Mr. Penn's rebuff to him for having issued to Thomas Howard, at the rent of a shilling, a warrant and patent for ten additional feet to a city lot against the Proprietor's instructions. Indeed, he intended to retrieve the warrant instantly, as Mr. Penn demanded to be done, by Mr. Howard's punctual reconveyance of the ten feet of ground back to their owner. Also, he promised himself to obey what the Proprietor underscored: *"and never let me see another instance of your taking such a liberty."*

Resolute rather than abashed, he read other more gently couched phrases: Mr. Penn offered words on the Reverend Mr. Robert Jenney, on the death of that excellent man Ralph Peters of Liverpool, of which his son had learned earlier, on three poems out of Dr. Edward Young's *Night Thoughts,* published during the last year, which he was sending to his friend. The generous donor of these commented that human conduct was very justly depicted in their sentiments upon "Life, Death, and Immortality." Mr. Peters noted with due restraint of feeling that they had afforded the giver "an entertainment agreeably melancholy."

Yet it is just possible that a letter from Thomas Penn, which reached him a month later in May, touched the now secularly minded Richard Peters more deeply. Chief Justice Jeremiah Langhorne, once sponsor for the assistant of Mr. Archibald Cummings to the Bishop of London, had recently died, and to the vacancy left by that gentleman's death, Governor Thomas had elevated John Kinsey. The Proprietor, however, was so gracious as to remark that Judge Langhorne's office was one that he had wished Mr. Peters to have "as the person we thought best qualified to discharge it." It was a comfort to the Secretary of the Land Office, the Pennsylvania Secretary of John, Thomas, and Richard Penn, and the Secretary to the Provincial Council to be appreciated with that high confidence. So complimented was he, on the whole, that he could concur with his great friend in England in his conviction that Colonel Thomas was a good governor who had not accepted "pecuniary recommendations" before designating Mr. Kinsey as chief jurist in the province.

Moreover, there was no particular reason for a clergyman now prospering in two lay functions to wish to sit on the Bench.

VIII

Chagrin and Some Business

The mirthful William Peters might correspond with Thomas Penn on the subject of a marine painter whose works hung on the walls of the Peters family in Liverpool, desiring Mr. Penn to find for him a copy of the man's "Borromean Islands," he might desire a violin to be sent for him out of England by the Proprietor, or that some player of the harpsichord be encouraged to embark for the colonies. His brother's meditations in the late autumn of 1743 were upon subjects more serious than art or music. The flush of increased importance that came with the assumption of responsibility for the great seal and charge of the ponderous volumes recording the deliberations of the Provincial Council had begun wearing off. There was more of Mr. Penn's mingling of compliment with reproof. Richard Peters liked better the Proprietor's declaring "his appointment to the new Secretaryship was his due." He thought the good man was most kind when he continued, "What I hinted before was as a caution to a proper frugality, but I would by no means have you want what is handsome and like other of the best people in Jersey." He quite saw Mr. Penn's point of William's being able to help him in the Land Office and to relieve him at times for his obligations in his second service. He understood the Proprietor's caution "as to the more mechanical part, neatness and exactness in keeping the Council Books." He would carry out instructions and employ only the most careful of clerks for the copying of entries. He liked being the transmitter of Mr. Penn's greetings and those of Mrs. Thomas Freame, his sister, to Mr. Lynford Lardner and Mr. Penn's young friends in Philadelphia, Nanny and Dick Hockley. But Richard Peters had misgivings in November 1743 upon social conditions in Pennsylvania, and he was really more fond of reproving others than of being himself reproved. He wrote apologetically to the Proprietor, thanked him for suppressing a letter of his to the Board of Trade, and appreciated his just observation "on my bungling manner of making up my letters, which I will endeavor to amend for the future." But at the 'same time, he addressed what he regarded as a sympathetic ear, and gravity came into his tone in the personal part of a letter to Thomas Penn:

> I assure you Philadelphia is not the least altered from what it was when you were here and that the merest trifle in the world will be made a town talk. Everything proper or improper, of a public or a private nature, is constantly bandied about in the two coffee houses. One set of politicians is sure to espouse one side, and for that very reason, without any regard to right or wrong, the other set will take the opposite side. And there is nothing in which they can agree.
>
> Such is the natural and constant consequence of republican principles, and it is to be found in this province to a higher degree than I have ever known anywhere else. I know nothing so pleasing and so recommendable as an openness and freedom in conversation, but I protest there is such an imprudent use made of almost everything that is said in public that, contrary to my natural genius and temperament, I am grown silent in company. Towards the fall of an evening, I often choose to take a nap that I may have no part in the conversation.
>
> I give you these accounts that you may form your notions of things. Amidst so much fire, I don't know, but a little of the flames will stick to me. Were I not in a public station, I should probably know much more. But I hope a regard to my character and to your interest will preserve me from doing anything to the prejudice of either.

It was distinctly more pleasurable for Mr. Peters to write of plans for a garden. He had now established himself in Francis Knowles' house and had a tolerable space of ground. He informed Mr. Penn, which he was already preparing against next spring. Modestly then, he suggested wishes to the Proprietary: "As I know you are a good judge of what flowers and flowering shrubs will do for this country, so as to have them in agreeable succession, I would be highly obliged to you—if a ship comes out early in the spring—to send me a quantity of roots and seeds." Further, he hoped Mr. Penn would excuse the freedom of his suggestion, as none of his other acquaintances in London could judge how to choose for climate and soil in Philadelphia.

But in the winter of 1743–44, it was not to Richard Peters that "a little of the flames" was sticking. Town talk was, in fact, rather more free in that season about his elder brother than about himself. For, although the lawyer William was now making a successful way in the Philadelphia courts, he had continued to disincline from the admonitions of his sister Esther. That good woman, indeed, had written him in vain about the unhappy scorbutic palsy that had seized on her poor sister-in-law in Cheshire and of his son Raphy's visit with her to his mother at Christmas. Later, she let Raphy himself write about his little brother Willy's death and the death of William Peters' father. The youngster indulged an eighteenth-century boyish sentiment on Willy, "taken out of the world so soon, but in all probability happy, for it is certain, we must all launch forth on the brink of eternity sooner or later so we ought not to murmur which of us it pleases God to call first." He was sorry to be the messenger of his breaking of his leg on the way to school. He was curious as to what might be his father's plan of education for him. He was sorry to acquaint his father with the melancholy accident: "I mean Grandpapa's death, which is certainly the greatest misfortune which could have fallen out, particularly to me, for it grieves me to think of it, and much more to say that he was the only friend I had in the world." He wrote of his being "with Mama, who is but in a very indifferent state of health. She has been ill above half a year of a palsy, which I believe was occasioned by fretting for your misfortune." But neither admonishments from Esther Peters, melancholy news from Raphy, the boy's interpretation of his mother's word "misfortune," nor catastrophes in three generations of a family circle in England were availing with William Peters during a gossipy winter in Pennsylvania.

Philadelphians did not know these matters of correspondence in detail, but there were folk who knew that Richard Peters was enduring "no small uneasiness for his brother." And in March 1744, interested ones of them were aware that another death had occurred in the Peters family connection in England. For in that month, young Richard Hockley was writing to Thomas Penn that William Peters is now "married to a girl that he kept in the country and had two children by her." Having lost his first wife, the English Elizabeth Bayley, the widower was prompt to contract with a second one, American Mary Brientnall.

Yet if his brother could not resist the buxom charms of a rural female, Mr. Richard Peters, in the raw province of Pennsylvania, could not hold out too long or too sternly against the humors of the city. For the well-to-do, he realized, it was an indulgent world. The Earl of Derby could hardly have felt contempt for William, or the late Mr. Hamilton, or the living Ben Franklin. Men, it seemed, were men. And now to the light-of-love William had come lawful wedlock in Trinity Church, Oxford, if not through Mr. Jenney at Christ's. On the day of the second marriage, happily, the two children of the contracting couple were both baptized and thereafter, William's provincial flame could bear her children under the benefit of the clergy. The good-natured Richard Peters could look more tolerantly now on his two-year-old American nephew William, and the uncle's affections turned warm to the three-month-old Richard, Jr., legitimatized by the ceremony of January 30, 1744, and, at his christening of the same day, named for his father's brother. In fact, the Secretary could, in due course, reflect with cheer on having helped infant Dicky's parent to an envied appointment and seeing him become Register of the Admiralty within King George II's Province of Pennsylvania. William's interest in ships and marine pictures could be turned into practicable channels.

The summer of 1744 brought on the necessity and the rigors of making a new Indian treaty. In March, the French King declared war upon George II. Before the end of that month, the English monarch had responded with a declaration of his own and given to his subjects, as far as depended on them, to distress and annoy the French in their settlements, trade, and commerce. Orders went out to England's ships of war and her privateers. They were followed by the action of His Majesty in Council instructing the governments of the colonies in America. It behooved Pennsylvania, Maryland, and Virginia to think about their relations to the Indians upon their western boundaries and on the relations of these to Frenchmen in their western lands. Moreover, Virginia had been at odds for some time with the Six Nations on the question of whose was the right to the land beyond the mountains. Clear terms with the Indians were important. Governor George Thomas and Conrad Weiser knew, as also did the better minds of Maryland and Virginia, that steps that would prevent any French alienation of Indian regards for their provinces would be eminently wise. The southern colonies must have an eye on the Catawbas and the Cherokees, Pennsylvania and New York to the Six Nations. So there followed much of correspondence amid governors, of necessary directions to intermediaries, of the sending of interpreters and invitations to the Six Nations. In the late spring, Mr. Peters was in frequent conferences with the Governor for the Penns and in constant communication with officers of state in the other provinces. Toward the close of June, he accompanied several members of Council and George Thomas to Lancaster to a conclave gathering there, and for two weeks, he was absorbed in business among commissioners from Maryland and Virginia, councilors for Pennsylvania, and sachems from the Six Nations—tribes, in the absence of the Mohawks, represented by the Onondagoes, Senecas, Cayugas, Oneidas, and Tuscaroras, and known also in their multiple strength as the Iroquois. The aging James Logan had not been able to come on from Philadelphia, and his pupil in Indian affairs, Mr. Peters, realized that he and the Governor must avail themselves all the more of the indispensable services of Conrad Weiser, experienced interpreter for the province.

Colorful but occupied days ensued in the frontier town. On the 22nd, Governor Thomas was welcoming to Pennsylvania the Honorable Thomas Lee and Colonel William Beverly from Virginia, the Honorable Edmund Jennings and Philip Thomas, Esquire, of Maryland, and, even prouder in bearing than these southern aristocrats, the two chieftains from the forests, Tachanoontia, the Black Prince, and the venerable Canassatego. The ceremony in the Courthouse began with a serving of wine, punch, pipes, and tobacco to all. Then, the day being Friday, the Governor offered the opinion that the Indians must be tired after so long a journey and that it would be well for them first to have a rest of three days and begin conference on Monday when he would address all the gathering.

But from the beginning, it became clear that the stately Canassatego intended firm dealing with the Virginians. Onas was not there in person (having in the character of William Penn died some twenty-six years earlier). Lord Baltimore was there only in his figmented personality as Tocarryhogan. Still, it was hard for Richard Peters to realize that Assaraquoa, as the Indians by custom named the Governor of Virginia, was also not in the midst of his commissioners. For the Six Nations king's meager words in rejoinder to George Thomas' courtesy were most emphatically addressed to the ears of the missing executive. After first acknowledgment of the Pennsylvanian's kindness, leaving it to that gentleman to appoint hours for a conference as he chose, and indulging the hypothetical Governor of Maryland to a similar privilege, Canassatego changed manner:

> As to our Brother Assaraquoa, we have at the present time nothing to say to him, not but we have a great deal to say to Assaraquoa, which must be said to him at one time or another. But, not being satisfied whether He or We should begin first, we shall leave it wholly to Our Brother Onas to adjust this between Us and to say which shall begin first.

Just so abruptly did proud and regal words initiate consultation, and in the days that followed, a contest, although carried on with all outward civilities, grew tenser between Commissioner Thomas Lee and the Indian chief. The Virginian claimed for his province, without the need for further subsidy to the Six Nations, the great valley region beyond the mountains. Canassatego claimed all that territory for the Iroquois by the right of conquest over the Catawbas and Cherokees. Each had evidence, one in deeds he quoted, the other in tribal memories often confirmed by treaties in the past, for his position. Through formal addresses, rich in the beauty of phrases borrowed by earlier agents from the Indians, through the ceremonial presentation of belts of wampum, received with equally ceremonial shouts of approbation from the deputies of the Six Nations, through fumes of wine and tobacco, through Indian examination of gifts: pounds of vermilion for painting faces and chests, flints for arrows, jewsharps, hundredweights of bar lead, pounds of shot, half-barrels of gunpowder, strouds, shirts, duffle blankets, and guns—Richard Peters remained ever conscious of the two forces really pitted against each other, whoever served as mediators or victims in their protracting debate. Well enough for Governor Thomas to say all have come to enlarge the fire which had almost burned out between Maryland and Virginia on the one hand and the Iroquois on the other, well enough to wish to brighten the chain which had contracted some rust, to attempt renewing the friendship which Marylanders, Virginians, and Six Nations hoped would last as long as sun, moon, and stars should give light—Virginia and the great warriors from Onondaga, induced to come to the conference by Conrad Weiser, were transparently at odds. So the Secretary of the Pennsylvania Council kept his eye on Colonel Thomas Lee and his thoughts interested for Thomas Penn.

At the end of two weeks, the shade of Assaraquoa, as it were, had been vigorously dealt with, and the militant pride of Canassatego had been properly appeased. Terms were drawn among the commissioners from the three provinces and the Six Nations. Feastings came to an end, values of thrifty but placating amounts in goods, money, and promises were given to the Indians, and the frontiers of three provinces, at least for an interval, were delivered from the menace of French and Indian compoundings. Moreover, when Richard Peters could have copies of the treaty, reports of the councils, of the preliminary correspondence, of the spirit of three colonies, and accounts of the costs all in order for posting to England, he would also be able to narrate privately by letter to Thomas Penn the course of the great consultation in Lancaster. He had not watched Thomas Lee and the Virginians and Marylanders in vain. Conrad Weiser, called Tarachawagon by the Indians, might, as the complimentary name implied, "rule the Heavens," Governor Thomas might gather to himself the glory of the great achievement in the frontier courthouse, but Richard Peters did not let himself be forgotten.

His subsequent letter to the Proprietor told a full story. It began with the excuse of an extreme business which kept Mr. Penn's Provincial Secretary from sending by this conveyance copies of his Warrant and Patent Books and then moved briskly to the subject of Conrad Weiser. Dr. Graeme, fortunately, had been able to send the interpreter a prescription which had relieved the good German of another illness, and Conrad had managed to get on to John Chambers' Mill, meet the Six Nations chiefs, and escort them to Lancaster. All that was as it should have been, but, unluckily to Mr. Peters' view, there had been other hitches. The commissioners from the two southern colonies had met in Annapolis previously meditated having New York in the conference—a detail which did not eventuate, but, most significantly of all, agreed there "that Conrad Weiser could not be depended on." Virginia had provided no goods for the Indians; Maryland's plan to have goods on hand had been miscarried by the sudden death of Colonel Levin Gale, earlier deputized to purchase them. Amid such circumstances, it was easy for the Provincial Secretary of Pennsylvania to anticipate what would be the behavior of the Southerners. The Pennsylvanians had provided their proper assortment from vermilion to duffle blankets, and Governor Thomas was a man of mark. Jealousy and arrogance from the others could be apprehended toward the representatives of Penn's interests.

The Virginians, indeed, began with a high hand. They would admit no claims of the Indians upon their westward lands: they made it clear that they would not pay sauce to the Governor of Pennsylvania for lands already their own and that they were not going, if the treaty proved successful, to let Colonel Thomas have the credit for the engagement. At Philadelphia, even before they got to Lancaster, they had sung the praises of their own former Governor Spotswood. But George Thomas was a match for them, in a strain between raillery and earnest playing off their hero in his ambassadorial exploits earlier at Albany and questioning their claims. In fact, he produced letters from Governor William Gooch showing them terms that the executive had agreed on for the Indian lands and requests from him for the offices of the governments of Pennsylvania and Maryland. Moreover, in pursuance of Colonel Gooch's letters, he had sent Mr. Weiser to the Indians at Onondaga to tell the chiefs in council that the Virginians would satisfy them for their lands.

The haughty Thomas Lee softened somewhat at being told such matters pointedly, and there was talk of his sending an express to Virginia for orders for him to buy goods to compensate the Indians. On promises, then, from the two other provinces, Governor George Thomas resumed preparation of his great speech to the Six Nations. But the other commissioners kept hoping in vain for a new interpreter from New York. Word had come into the Virginians' possession, originating from the Commissioners on Indian Affairs at Albany, to the effect that their interpreter had instructed that the Indians when questioned as to whether they had demands for land on Virginia, should answer that they had none. So it remained important for Mr. Peters to keep a tab on Colonels Lee and Beverly; he knew the two southerners would not hesitate to take any *carte blanche* extended them.

It turned out as he and George Thomas expected. When Colonel Beverly brought back from Thomas Lee the letters of Governor Gooch, entrusted to the Virginia commissioner for his perusal by the Governor of Pennsylvania, one letter was missing.

There was an inquiry. Colonel Beverly told Richard Peters he had handed him all the letters of Gooch sent by Lee; Colonel Lee told Mr. Peters he had sent by Beverly all the letters received from Colonel Thomas. The Secretary and the Governor of Pennsylvania were themselves "very well persuaded that Colonel Lee had fraudulently kept back" a letter. It was the one from Governor Gooch that admitted the just claims of the Six Nations on the western lands of Virginia, which had disappeared.

But the game of cat's-paw against cat's-paw continued, and the treaty went on. Responsibility for the expenses of the several pairs of commissioners came under dispute, and payments were adjusted, Pennsylvania meeting one half the costs and the visiting colonels the other. To clear themselves of suspicions of any two provinces conniving against a third, the three sets of envoys elected to take quarters in three different public houses, and the Virginians were indulged to the first choice of hostelry.

On the 22nd, the first brief, formal conference occurred. Canassatego, responding to Governor Thomas, spoke briefly first to the Pennsylvania commissioners, second to those of Maryland. Then, manner changed abruptly; he turned to the Virginians, and Conrad Weiser, sensitive to the alteration of tone, "stopped a little for expression" as he interpreted the old sachem's words.

The proud Colonel Lee stiffened: "If the Indians had nothing to say to Virginia, Mr. Weiser could tell Canassatego, 'Virginia had nothing to say to them.'"

Fire came into the eyes of the Virginia planter and the Iroquois. The interpreter felt an embarrassment coming on him from the all too similar words of the two men. Both repeated. Then the Colonel, with the New York letter from the Albany commissioners in his pocket all the time, chose to be at once histrionic and designing. With emphasis, he insisted: "Mr. Weiser has given Canassatego's words a false turn," and he produced the document he had on his person while the good Conrad pondered on the behavior of the southerner and, being wise, kept his own peace.

Chagrin and Some Business

During the three days of wait for the Indians to rest from their journey, of course, there was talk despite the fact of separated residences in three public houses. Thomas Lee argued that Canassatego had admitted in his brief speech that the Indians had no claims on the western lands, and the Pennsylvania interpreter had falsified his words. He kept the Albany commissioners' letter much in evidence. Yet he promised that he would no more speak of it to the Indians, lest he put into their heads the notions of making a demand on Virginia. He was militant and conciliatory, hot and cold, but did not abandon his mistrust of Weiser—best card now for his own obstinate position.

So the guests of the three public houses found it well to confer in one of them. Governor Thomas repeated the substance of Governor Gooch's letters; he mentioned with firmness the copy, originally made by Mr. Peters, to be sent with Conrad Weiser on his mission to Onondaga, the copy of the most material one of all of them. Moreover, he informed Colonel Lee that that letter had been entered into the Council Books of the Province at Philadelphia. All that he did *not* say was that he and Mr. Peters were both convinced privately that the Virginia envoy had purloined and suppressed the original text from Gooch.

His general forthrightness seemed to avail. The Maryland commissioners concurred with Governor Thomas' position and boldly pronounced Colonel Lee to be wrong. Neither Edmund Jennings nor Philip Thomas spared the Virginian. Yet the arrogant impugner of Conrad Weiser's integrity and Canassatego's rights did not lose immediately. For, in fact, the writer of the long account to Thomas Penn reported that, before Governor Thomas' speech should be made on Monday, the 25th, the group of commissioners agreed that, although the Indians' claims on Virginia for lands were true claims, they should not be mentioned in the Pennsylvanian's address when he opened the council. It seemed best to all to be diplomatic, avoid dispute, and enter only into the minutes the truth of them. That would keep the Pennsylvania records accurate and in harmony. What it might or might not imply with regard to the Six Nations for the interval was unimportant.

The appeasement of Thomas Lee, however, did not solve all difficulties. Conrad Weiser's feelings also had to be considered. The worthy interpreter, annoyed by the Southerner's suspicions for a time, was resolute, for his own honor's sake, not to sit further in council with the Indians. Richard Peters had either to mollify him or suffer the treaty to disintegrate. The Indians became uneasy at the thought of another possible intermediary between themselves and the provinces. They appealed for a conference involving themselves, Conrad, and Mr. Peters. The Secretary of Pennsylvania, to save the right-hand man of the whole ceremonial series, had to submit to divided councils. Indeed, he consented to let thirty of the Indians meet with Mr. Weiser and himself in his own quarters at the public house in which he had been established apart from Virginians and Marylanders. For to have an ambassador's reception all to himself in no sense irked Richard Peters.

At the gathering in his room, Canassatego became the central figure. The Indian complained that the Virginia stranger had ill-used the Six Nations. He deplored the man's indiscretion in telling them they had come to be paid for land they had no right to. He doubted, then, that the Iroquois could agree with Virginia or Maryland. He asked whether they might, on the continuance of the treaty, have the liberty of consulting from time to time with Mr. Peters. Canassatego did not wish to disagree with anything through having misunderstood the Pennsylvania commissioner. Through Conrad Weiser, he begged the Secretary to inform the other commissioners of the proper methods for dealing with Indians at a treaty. For his fellow tribesmen, he promised Mr. Peters that they would so manage, if they quarreled with the Marylanders and Virginians, that they would not prejudice Pennsylvania. Brother Onas could be sure they had a grateful sense of his friendship and honorable dealing with them. They would never fall out with him but would take his country into their care and prevent any harm coming to it. All this liberty they took unto themselves with the Secretary because they were sure that the Proprietors would employ no man as an agent but one who had a hearty zeal for the service of the Indians.

In brief, the letter of October 13, written some months after the events of June and July 1744, made it apparent that without Richard Peters, the process of the Lancaster Treaty would have been more rough. Mr. Penn's agent had reconciled Conrad Weiser to his duty, kept Canassatego faithful, and joined sturdily with Governor Thomas in effectuating to the good of the provinces in America the wishes of George II in his Court at St. James. Mr. Peters could well afford compliments, then, to others as well as himself. He remarked on the strict and ample justice of Onas, intending that Thomas Penn should refer that appellation to himself no less than to his father. First, having written that the Indians feared they were observing a new behavior in Conrad Weiser toward themselves, he spoke of the great attachment of the Six Nations to the interpreter, whom they claimed as half their own. They wanted, he said, to have Conrad come always to their councils and advise them on treaties. To confirm their goodwill to Tarachawagon, they gave him a bundle of skins, and in the presence of Mr. Peters, he promised to act toward them as he used to do.

Yet Peters was careful not to omit the fact that the interpreter had got 30 pistoles besides some former presents from Virginia as payment and £100 from

Chagrin and Some Business 75

Maryland. He gossiped of how thirty pistoles had come to Conrad from Colonel Lee for bearing out with the Indians the right of Virginia to precedence in the talks because she was the oldest of the three colonies. He was also concerned in his last paragraphs about informing the Proprietor in England how worthless the secretaries had been brought on from Maryland and the other southern provinces. Only his own minutes had been accurately taken.

Lancaster had been an achievement for Richard Peters in the summer of 1744. The glow of his experiences there endured for the long interval of supervising the entry of records into the Council Books, catching up with the duties of the Land Office and despatching full copies of all matters to Thomas Penn. But it did not preserve him altogether from concern or prevent him from offering the Proprietor frequent news of Governor Thomas. That executive came back from the frontier town with what seemed a slight but what proved to be an obstinate cold. By late autumn, the Secretary, who had been sounding the great deputy's powers of discretion and oratory, was also lamenting his infirmity. On five different vessels, he was sending ominous letters to England for the consideration of the Proprietor. It was his opinion that the Governor would turn from the skill of Philadelphia doctors to that of physicians in England by the next spring. He was suffering from a fixed pain in his breast. Dr. Thomas Graeme, for ten days together, had tried to raise a spitting, but the invalid had not responded to the treatment attempted. Although now downstairs again, the vegetable diet prescribed for him was lowering his spirits without in any way reducing the pain. Mr. Peters was frankly alarmed. If Providence had been pleased to continue the health of George Thomas, all would have been managed to the greatest advantage both for the province and the Proprietaries. Now he knew into what parties Philadelphians were already split. It would be far worse if "what I fear should come to pass." It seemed, indeed, that the Penns had better be ready to choose a new governor. The troubled Secretary warned them how bad things might be if Colonel Thomas died and the province had to have the aged Mr. Logan, or weak Captain Palmer, after him ranking senior in the Council, acting during an interim. Pennsylvania's problems were calling for "consummate skill and prudence" in difficult months. An absolute necessity might any day be facing the Proprietaries.

In short, if Richard Peters were not touched with too much sorrow for the Governor's illness, he would have the Penns know he was acutely concerned for the business of the Commonwealth. In his own way, he enjoyed throwing off hints to his masters.

IX

More Business and Some Beatitude

After the Treaty of Lancaster, Richard Peters could say, as once Virgil's hero Aeneas remarked of his share in the Trojan War, *magna pars fui.* Certainly, he had deported himself in the council with the Indians as a leading figure, and whatever Governor William Gooch achieved there through his chief Virginian sponsor, Thomas Lee, was managed only with Mr. Peters' sanction. It was but natural, in consequence of his *coup d'état* in the frontier community, that the thriving Secretary should regard himself as a versatile and gifted executive. He acted for the Land Office, he acted for the Council, and he regarded himself as envoy plenipotentiary, always as though *in extremis,* for the Penns.

But during the next few years after 1744, he was really more of a clerk to the province, recording minutes or entering land transactions, than an agent on his initiative. What he achieved by his direct means in the political or social life of the commonwealth was slight.

Moreover, Governor George Thomas neither succumbed to his illness in the autumn of 1744 nor repaired to England in the spring of 1745. Instead, that capable leader, no longer the salaryless victim of the Quaker Assembly whose bills he would not sign, enjoyed both respect for the success of the Lancaster Treaty and a new period of favor and continued in his office as pilot of Pennsylvania for two more years. He, rather than the Secretary, bore honor for command of affairs.

Yet Mr. Peters needed not to suffer for lack of occupation, repine at his superior's eminence, or envy the success of his brother William, now established in the Vice-Admiralty Courts of the province, and exercising successful domain over the record of "Acts, Causes, and Businesses," as his commission instructed him to do. Tickets and patents at the Land Office drew plentifully upon Richard's time. Records of errands taken at Governor Thomas' behest by Conrad Weiser provided him with abundant copy for his Council Books. So he was satisfied with an occasional exploit, did not forget that he had been an active agent in 1744, and remained interested in all Indian matters, whether between the Cherokees and the North Carolinians, the Catawbas and the Virginians, the Six Nations and the Delawares and Pennsylvania. Land and diplomacy continued habitual factors in his consciousness, even though not to the displacement of cheer and piety. He was not at the helm, but he was enough in the stir of things, with England at war with both France and Spain, not to find life hemming in too close on the imagination. Where he did not experience it immediately, he could at least mentally revivify. News in American ports was always absorbing. This French man-of-war or that Spanish privateer was reported to be threatening English transport at sea or American shipping at Atlantic coast inlets from Virginia to New York. The air was full of menace. Every measure to forestall catastrophe in Pennsylvania held Mr. Peters' attention. He hoped there might be no more reverses for the colonies, like the ill-fated expedition to Cartagena in the Spanish War in 1741. He was alert to anything which might be done to the French on the St. Lawrence far to the north. He was awake, especially to the vaunts and maneuvers of Peter Chartier, a trader in the Alleghenies who had just gone over to the French and was suspected of efforts to alienate the Shawnees to the interests of the King of France.

The spring and summer of 1745, in fact, provided Governor Thomas and his Council with an abundance of concern. Virginia wanted a new conference with the Indians, hoping to improve relations between the Catawbas and the Six Nations as well as to secure her frontiers, and desired Pennsylvania's mediation at Onondaga. Philadelphia wanted no new perils in the west by reason of Chartier's defection. Massachusetts was arming an expedition under Governor William Shirley against the French at Louisburg and desired supplements of men, provisions, and powder from the province of the Penns. The Duke of Newcastle, writing from Whitehall, signified the pleasure of His Majesty George II that if Commodore Warren found it necessary to employ his strength of ships against the French in defense of Annapolis Royal, Pennsylvania, like other colonies in America, should supply the Commodore with assistance, whether of men, provisions, or shipping. Delaware Indians, sent by their King Olompias first to Shamokin and then to Philadelphia, brought twenty pounds' worth of skins with them, assurance of their friendship for Onas, and required a present in response. So Richard Peters was kept busy reading and recording documents of state, affixing at intervals the authority of the great seal to Governor Thomas' instructions or impatiently waiting for action from other instrumentalities of government.

Through the invaluable Conrad Weiser on the one hand and proper executive diplomacy on the other with the Assembly, problems had to be ironed out as best they could. The cunning of Governor Shirley in capturing Louisburg helped with the Assembly. Although inhabitants of the Province of Pennsylvania were not apt to praise the achievements of men from another colony, they could be pleased that demands for militia did not have further to be pressed on them. Once the victory in Cape Breton was *fait accompli*, Governor Thomas was able to place an embargo on powder, enjoin William Hill, keeper of the powder house of Philadelphia, from letting any more of the precious stock flow into private hands, and ensure refurbishing, when necessary, of the exhausted magazines of the New England colony. The Assembly, no longer obliged to offend its Quaker members by considering appeals for raising and paying a regiment of Pennsylvanians, was gracious enough to vote four thousand pounds for the King's use in the purchase of bread, beef, pork, and flour as the Governor should think most fit, so much by the grace of William Shirley of Massachusetts. Even King Olompias profited from the new tractable mood of the Assembly, having a present of fifty pounds in return for the Delawares' twenty pounds' worth of skins.

Mr. Weiser was hardly less helpful than the New England general. His early June visit to the Six Nations also worked out conveniently for the government in Philadelphia. The Indians at Onondaga received Conrad with heartiness. Welcome too were his companions: Shikellamy, the beloved Oneida chieftain, always the leading figure at Shamokin, one of Shikellamy's sons, and the affable half-breed Andrew Montour, the courier of the forests and already a veteran diplomat.

There was first private conversation between Canassatego and his white brother and guest, Tarachawagon. The instructions from Governor Thomas to his legate were read and interpreted, and Canassatego's "good offices" were promised to assist Conrad.

On the next day, the 9th, chiefs of the Oneidas, the Tuscaroras, and the Cayugas, and one chief of the Senecas were at hand to hear, on behalf of their brethren, what the interpreter and representative from Onas would have to say. Mr. Weiser announced his purpose in coming. The Governor of Pennsylvania had sent him with a message that concerned the Iroquois' brother Assaraquoa of Virginia. At their council fire, he laid down a string of wampum and then reminded them of their agreements with Tocarryhogan, Assaraquoa, and Onas last summer in Lancaster. Then he addressed them on Governor Gooch's wishes that they hold a congress with the Catawbas on the subject of peace, shrewdly suggesting on his initiative, rather than on that of Assaraquoa himself, that they meet with their old foes in Williamsburg. He knew that the Six Nations would regard with suspicion any hint that they assemble in towns or country of the more southerly Indians. So he assured them they would be kindly entertained at the Virginia capital. Moreover, they could depend if the Catawbas, after the overtures, sent no deputies to Williamsburg on having the Catawbas turned over to them for punishment according to their deserts. Besides, ample reward would be given to all Six Nations deputies who went to Virginia. The laying down at that point of a second string of wampum produced "Jo-hahs" of joy from the younger sachems. Tachanoontia, however, having first maintained a few minutes of grave silence, repeated the whole of Conrad's speech so that all hearers might completely understand it.

Then, the emissary in another address made clear the wishes of Pennsylvania. He told of the rebel Chartier, of depredations of the Shawnees inspired by him upon Ohio traders, of King George's demands that he be punished and that the Shawnees make restitution of goods and prisoners they had seized under his evil influence. He laid down a third belt of wampum, was glad to hear responsive "Jo-hahs" accompanied by clamors against the Shawnees, listened respectfully to the Black Prince's repeating of his second speech, and perceived that all his words were being received cordially.

In due course, full answer was made him, and all the information Governor Thomas had ordered him to elicit was secured. It was not agreed that the Six Nations would send deputies as far as distant Williamsburg, or that they should disgrace themselves by going to their foes' country on errands of peace, or that they should travel by roads not properly cut for them. But it was agreed that either the French or the Shawnees should compensate for Peter Chartier's evil-doing among them and that the Iroquois would not war on the Catawbas. Tachanoontia spoke gracious regret for Chartier's conduct, regarding that as an open breach of the peace against the Six Nations by the French. Conrad Weiser could bring all that news back to the province, Governor Thomas, and Mr. Peters. He could also bear word, on the fact of which he had not challenged directly in an open conference, that the Iroquois were in communication with the French in Canada. He could tell, however, that not too many of them were treating with the Governor at Montreal or too eagerly. He could report, too, the hospitality extended in Tachanoontia's house: a plentiful dinner of hominy, dried venison, and fish, and after the repast, a dram all around. His friend, Shikellamy, and his son, Andrew Montour, and himself could start back from Onondaga for Shamokin, Tulpehocken, and, ultimately, the capital of Pennsylvania.

But before Richard Peters was to enter record of the exploits of Massachusetts' mailed fist on Cape Breton and the narrative of Conrad Weiser's use of the velvet glove at Onondaga into the Council Books of the Province, another event was to impress itself on his mind.

In June 1745, he was, in fact, more the chief functionary of the Land Office than the Secretary of the Commonwealth. There was no meeting during that month of Governor Thomas' aides and advisors, and Mr. Peters had the opportunity of service to the Penns in another fashion. As though he might be proceeding to a feat in surveying such as he had participated in six years earlier on the Maryland-Pennsylvania line, he rode off from Philadelphia to supervise the laying out of a new project beyond Susquehanna. The Marsh Creek lands were more vigorously to be converted into the Manor of Mask.

The Land Secretary knew something of old Mr. Penn's charter from Charles II; he knew well enough Thomas Penn's liking for having the best plots in any survey reserved to the advantage of "the Family," he knew that "the Family" believed it had better control of any development of countryside which was made manorially. The antiquated medieval terminology of the charter, in fact, in no way disturbed him. It was proper enough for the Penns to have freehold from the King; he saw no legal necessity for their granting freehold to occupants who might esteem land in a manor less than property which could become wholly their own. In brief, he was going off to his business beyond Lancaster soberly.

The Penns had the privilege under their charter of erecting into manors any parcels of land in the province which they chose. Settlers taking privileges there were entitled to have their own courts baron to exercise immediate jurisdiction over and for them. They had their function of frankpledge—whether they called it duty or right—to maintain discipline and peace among themselves or their stewards. They had the right of the consideration and interest of the Lord of the Manor for and in themselves. On good soil, they had the opportunity of raising full crops and the duty only of paying a moderate rent. So long as they chose to keep any tenure within their own or their heirs' possession, they could hold almost as in fee simple. They had but to remember that they could not sell any such tenure or any part of it out of their own or their heirs' possession and that, on any such design of alienation out of their family privileges, both their tenure and land reverted to the Lord of the Manor.

It was not a bad system, as Richard Peters saw it. Prospectively, tenants could make a good thing of it. Poor immigrants were hardly folk to own much land in their names. Freehold contributed rather surely to the evils of republicanism; the acres of Pennsylvania might be prosperously cultivated under a scheme that tended to keep gentlemen in control of property and Government.

It was not, however, until Mr. Peters had got to Marsh Creek that he could behold, with full power of insight if he chose, the spirit of back inhabitants and settlers in Pennsylvania. So it was with cheer that he proceeded to the scene of the Manor of Mask, the cherished land project of the Proprietors.

Accompanying him were the sheriff, a group of surveyors, two chain carriers, and the Surveyor-General of Pennsylvania, William Parsons. The latter added to his professional expertness an ability to speak "High Dutch," and for that reason, had been "judged proper to go along in order to pacify the frightened people."

Yet "Dutch" did not avail as a linguistic medium for addressing determined Scotch-Irish settlers, and, despite an earlier miscalculated attempt to erect a manor at Marsh Creek, Secretary Peters met with some surprise. Mr. Parsons' power of quieting unrest proved less than his reputation, and his function, as Surveyor-General, of executing the land warrant was scarcely more impressive. A previous hint to Mr. Peters that the chief dignitary would do better than his subordinate, Mr. Cookson, had been obviously misleading.

For, as soon as the first tree was marked for the beginning of the line of the survey, and the chain began to be stretched, two groups of back inhabitants flew at the carrier, wrenched his instrument from his hand, and broke it. At the same moment, all fell a-shouting: "There would be no manor laid out there. They had settled their land as other folk had settled other land. They were ready to pay for it on common, not on manorial terms." The justices in Richard Peters' entourage ordered the obstructors of Mr. Parsons' men to disperse, or "they would proceed against them as rioters." They said they did not wish to have innocent men involved with guilty ones. They invited those who were peaceably inclined to the project of Mr. Penn's manor to ally themselves with the officers of the peace and assist in the suppression of the offenders—not going so far, however, as to suggest eventual obligations of "frankpledge."

But to the observation of the Secretary of the Land Office, few of the farmers responded to either command or appeal of the magistrates or divided perceptibly from their fellows. Indeed, the Surveyor-General's setting of his compass a second time and the carrier's obvious intention to renew the use of his now-repaired chain were signals for a new phenomenon. A body of some seventy joined circlewise around Mr. Parsons' instrument and began narrowing in upon it, the front ones on foot, the rear ones on horseback. Then Thomas Hooswick, declaring he spoke for himself and the settlers on Marsh Creek, informed Mr. Peters and the Surveyor-General with no uncertain emphasis that "no lines for a manor would be run on that tract." Further, with his friends ringed stoutly behind him, he proceeded to take Mr. Parsons' compass out of his hands while other settlers possessed themselves of the chain.

The consequence was that there was no more effort on that day expended upon the Manor of Mask. The wish to accomplish that project might persist longer in the dreams of Thomas Penn. Yet that is not quite what Secretary Peters said when he reported the episode to the Proprietor. His account was meticulous in respect of rather divergent points. He told, in fact, more of what the forces of law in Pennsylvania debated and intended than of what they performed. He did not say that the surveying party thought it better to retire from Marsh Creek, spare further harm to their instruments, and not risk instant indignity to their persons. What he did say was that he had been for "committing" the fellow Hooswick, and Justice Smout had agreed with him but that the other magistrates had ruled against such procedure on the immediate occasion. If Hooswick were seized, they could expect that champion to be rescued by his comrades and the minority of sheriff's men to be roughly treated. "No one knew to what length matters might have been carried." It would be far better to withhold commitment, be sure to list the names of the rioters, make indictments, and press prosecutions later. They could subsequently have warrants for arrest issued from the Chief Justice of Pennsylvania, have the perpetrators of the violence removed from local jurisdiction to Philadelphia, have them jailed in the capital and tried before the Supreme Court, where the authority of the Government could be "undoubtedly and sufficiently vindicated."

Then, having predicted to Thomas Penn the eventual panacea in the law for the disorders beyond the Susquehanna, Mr. Peters conveyed three other items of knowledge to the Proprietaries. He had warned the people at Marsh Creek to keep off certain boundaries of land, which he indicated to them particularly. Within those boundaries must be forty thousand acres in all, twenty thousand of which were worth certainly £40 a hundred acres or £8,000. Examination in the books of the Land Office did not reveal more than a dozen earlier licenses or warrants, or for more than two thousand five hundred acres, for minor tracts in the Marsh Creek region. Just so did he advise Mr. Penn of profits which he might have one day from his dream Manor of Mask and quiet his conscience with respect to any lands previously granted, without manorial obligations, in the fertile and contested neighborhood. Just so did he find, like John Falstaff, that discretion is the better part of valor. Just so, too, did he fail to note that in the spirit of the settlers of Marsh Creek was not zeal for disorderly riot but an individualism that would one day portend broad revolution.

There were, however, other details, more personal than the present failure of the majesty of the law, which Mr. Peters could set down in letters of the late spring of 1745 for the reading of his friend and master in London. Thomas Penn's one-time linen-merchant partner, Richard Hockley of Hull, had died ten years before, and his widow Mary, remarried to John Shewbart, an innkeeper of Philadelphia, was now established with her three children, Richard, Ann, and Samuel Hockley, in the Pennsylvania city. Mr. Penn's letters to young Richard always bore an affectionate *in loco parentis* tone, and Mr. Peters knew how favorite with the Proprietor were at least two of Mary Shewbart's young people. Long paragraphs on Nanny slipped into his letters, then, between accounts of Callowhill Market lots or of Indian affairs, when that fragile maiden began a decline.

His eloquence modulated to its tenderest vein. The Secretary pictured to the old guardian of the young woman's family each stage of her illness, every symptom of her fever and coughing, every treatment tried by her physicians, the twenty balsam drops which she took three times a day on the recommendation of her brother Richard. He told of the marvelous beauty of her dying. Just before the last struggle, she had formed a short and expressive prayer and sung a hymn of her own, composing with a clear and exact tune, which so surprised her brothers and her mother that they could not stay in the room for tears. So much good sense, unaffected tranquillity, and substantial solid piety had appeared in her behavior throughout her long sickness that an enduring impression was left on all her friends, who would, he thought, be the better for it. Indeed, had Richard Peters been favored to witness the death and glorification of a saint, he could hardly have felt greater beatitude than when he described Nanny Hockley's last hours.

Answering word on the subject of the young woman came in subsequent months from the Proprietor. Mr. Penn had had no hope of Nanny's recovery from the time of his first account of her illness. But he wrote most responsively on her value as a person and her behavior before and at death. He was confident that her presence of mind in the last hours "proceeded from a certain assurance of her approaching happiness." Such faith was "no doubt, the greatest blessing in this life, and more to be desired than the highest honors." He was aware that the affection shown by Mr. Peters during Nanny's long illness, "though due to her own merit, was not the less for the relation she stood in to me," and Thomas Penn would "always consider it as such."

The Secretary of the Land Office and to the Province could, in fact, experience an inward pleasure at having the Proprietary so grateful to him for his kindness to Mary Shewbart's daughter. He knew of Mr. Penn's consideration for the Hockleys and their mother when transplanted from England. Lots had been specially held for their domicile and John Shewbart's business in spirits and bricks in Philadelphia. Nothing, Mr. Peters felt, commended his master more than his guardianship of an old friend's progeny. And Nanny Hockley had fully merited the affection of her father's former partner. In life, she had shown herself the very exemplar of virtue. Often in later years, the Philadelphian correspondent would read pensively the epitaph on the tomb of the dead girl in its honored place in the aisle of Christ Church and the eloquent words that closed it: "which removed her at the Age of 24 Years singing in the most devout Strains and making Melody unto the Lord in the very last Moments."

Yet Richard Peters remained himself at least intermittently mundane, and the creature of earth, and that he was not entirely translated into a spiritual being, was evidenced in contemporary hints he threw off to Thomas Penn on the subject of William Evans. He had not forgotten that that young man's father, Peter Evans, had wickedly conspired some years before with Bishop Gibson of London to keep him from the cure of souls at Christ Church. Shrewdly, then, he regretted that Mr. Penn had yielded to a promise extorted from him by the late Clement Plumsted and that he had appointed a young man, who had just inherited £10,000, to his deceased father's lucrative office. The commission was, as Mr. Peters reminded his master, "in the name of the Proprietors and during the pleasure of them and their Lieutenant Governor for the time being." Yet delicately, he left the matter to the good judgment of his superior—a fastness of discretion to which he might confidently commit all things. He must not press the fate of his old enemy's son too diligently.

And having refrained to that wise limit, he proceeded comfortably instead with his duties as Secretary, neither pushing prosecution of the "frightened country people" at Marsh Creek too hard nor becoming too apprehensive that Governor Thomas, in spite of the pain in his breast, held on in his office. Month after month, he recorded the responses of what the Council wanted to do in furtherance of the Colonial cause so ably supported by New England victories on Cape Breton, or the veritable attitude of the Assembly, or the missions of the interpreter, Conrad Weiser.

Like other Philadelphians, he became more prey in 1745 and 1746 to rumors of shoals of French and Spanish privateers sailing off the Virginia capes, threatening inroads into the Chesapeake or up the Delaware as far as the city. Excitement, then as ever, was not a thing to be rejected by his mind if exhilaration could be drawn from it and no present damage. Yet if he was always ready for a narrative of evil or good or for labor in the ledgers of the province, he also kept an ear open for phrases of piety. A letter brought to him at the end of February 1747 by the son of plain Conrad Weiser and referring to Romans 8 gave him great pleasure. Not only did it extend the interpreter's regard for the Secretary, it revealed "a strong and lively sense of religion in Conrad's mind." Indeed, as Mr. Peters thought, the passage to which the good man of Tulpehocken referred "put all humane philosophy to the blush." The Secretary might have put off the cloth of the clergy for the garb of a lay office. That was no reason for his abandoning the work of spiritual instruction. He was glad to write at length to a disciple willing like himself to confide in the superiority of Christian belief to the most admired passages in ancient philosophy. "How flat, after all, was the observation of Socrates as he took the hemlock: 'Whether or no God will approve of my actions I know not, yet this I am sure of, that I have at all times made it my endeavor to please him, and I have a good hope that this my endeavor will be accepted by him.'" How satisfying in comparison, argued Richard Peters, was "that noble plerophory of confidence, that full assurance of faith with which the apostle expressed himself: 'We know that all things work together for Good to them that love God. He that spared not his own Son, but delivered him up for us all, how shall he not with him freely give up all things. For who shall separate us from the love of Christ?'"

X

Little Less Than Treason

Mr. Thomas Penn was of comfortable mind in the spring of 1746. To him, as to other folk in London, good news had come out of the north, and he was gratified to have the rebellion in Scotland at an end. He could write with cheer of the English victory over the clansmen in Inverness some four weeks earlier. He could rejoice, too, that presently, he might have, in the company of Mr. Hamilton of Philadelphia, pleasures of conversation worth far more to a gentleman of honor and sense than attendance at plays being performed by Monticelli or Garrick. On the 14th of May, he sat amiably, if somewhat soberly, setting his thoughts down for both Governor George Thomas and James Hamilton of Bush Hill, son of the late Andrew Hamilton and a gentleman now minded for a voyage to England and a sojourn in town.

Especially gracious was Mr. Penn to the prospective guest from Philadelphia, writing as he did half as a man recognizing an equal in social privileges and intellectual powers, half as an elderly person who would encourage his junior.

Frankly, he did not think thirty-five was an age too great for action. Mr. Hamilton's demurrer to his advancing years had only grown from his "inclination to an easy life." In fact, after the middle thirties, one could have "as good a relish for all that is agreeable as at any time before." Thomas Penn would only be elated when the visitor got on to London to substitute the society of a sensible friend for the thin food that the theatre affords to the human mind.

Fortunately, he did not have to retain his animadversions on what had happened to Prince Charles Edward, or the Camerons, or Mackintoshes, or Frasers, in and after their defeat at Drummossie Moor until the voyager from America should present himself at his lodgings. Inert to old rumors of the onetime Jacobitish tendencies of his father, beneficiary from the Stuart kings, William Penn's son could write from the normal point of view of a burgher subject of Hanoverian George II—of anxiety now past and relief now ensuing. "We have been for some time in a disagreeable situation here, with many people fearful of the worst consequences. But, for my part, I was very easy on every other account than that the rebels were very troublesome to the people among whom they were and put the Nation to a very great expense to oppose them." What he had confided in was that England would never accept a change of government. Now, all the affair was happily ended, and the Duke of Cumberland had given the followers of James Stuart's son considerable reason to repent their folly. Most of their best clans were destroyed. They would not be able to do any more mischief "in our time." The loyal subjects of the King were safe. Charitably enough, Mr. Penn wished that folk in Pennsylvania might be as well provided.

To George Thomas he wrote in much the same spirit on the same day, although somewhat more explicitly, of the battle that had occurred on April 16. The duke's army, he recounted, had not above eight thousand men but was so properly drawn up that, had there been many more of the rebels, it would have been in no danger from them. The carnage had been dreadful, and "some people called it cruel." But the writer thought it very necessary, for the Highlanders "were only to be kept quiet by fear, they had no relish for the fruits of peace and industry." And, whether he was writing to the Governor or Mr. Hamilton, Thomas Penn was no man to concern himself uniquely for a wild and unfrugal people. The tragedy of the Gaels, fighting for an old cause against the Sassenach and by mistake identifying that cause with the last ambitions of scapegrace remnants of the Scottish royal house of Stuart, was not his tragedy. He could not countenance treason to the King and Parliament in England, and his own affair was more properly Pennsylvania.

That is to say, it was as if Pennsylvania in 1746 was really the affair of anybody in particular.

Just a week before the Gael lost at Drummossie Moor, the ultimate battle in his centuries-old struggle against Anglo-Saxondom, copies of a letter from the Duke of Newcastle, composed at the command of His Majesty, had gone from Whitehall to America. Despatched by express from Boston, presently, one example of the document went on to Governor Thomas in Philadelphia, and in the first week of June, the Council of Pennsylvania and the Governor were regarding the Assembly as responsible for action. The King, it seemed, was sending five battalions of his troops under the command of Lieutenant General St. Clair to go from England as soon as possible, with a sufficient convoy of men of war to Louisburg, whence, with several regiments being sent from Gibraltar and other troops to be enlisted in the colonies, they would proceed to the reduction of Canada. His Majesty was planning to remove the menace of the French to the provinces by consummating against that race the victories General Shirley won on Cape Breton during the previous year. So Governor Thomas had to initiate matters, and the Assembly had to be called upon. The King's message had spoken for four companies of one hundred men each to be raised in Pennsylvania, with arms, clothing, and provision for these. It had explained that the quotas raised would be sent to Albany, to be there under the command of Lieutenant Governor Gooch of Virginia, had called for persons acquainted with the navigation of the St. Lawrence River, had hinted that colonial troops should share in any booty taken from the enemy, had hazarded the information that General St. Clair, acting for His Majesty's Government, would make reasonable allowance for defraying the expense of the projected campaign. Formally, George II and his ministers had resolved on the defense of America, and they were expecting the provinces to be interested in their own protection.

Yet although the initiation of efforts to put the King's wish into effect in Pennsylvania was prompt, effectuation of them proceeded desultorily on both sides of the Atlantic. It was easier in London and Whitehall in 1746 for ministers to rejoice at the Duke of Cumberland's signal victory over the Highlanders and easier for functionaries in Philadelphia to proclaim the blessed deliverance that came out of that event to His Majesty's subjects than for anyone to find an immediate means of discomforting Canada. On July 14, the Provincial Council approved a draught offered them by Governor Thomas in a proclamation of a day of rest "from all servile labor" and of prayers and sermons to be observed ten days later. Drunkenness and all other forms of licentiousness were to be eschewed, as all might discover on reading the words posted at the Courthouse or printed in the *Gazette*. In the battle of Culloden, God, it seemed, had first visited Pennsylvanians like other English folk with punishment for their sins and then sought through the triumph of His Royal Highness, the Duke of Cumberland, to awaken all to a "juster sense of His peculiar and distinguishing blessings to the British Nation above all the Nations on Earth." Moreover, in His goodness, He had gloriously rescued His children from "a bloody rebellion carried on by the son of a popish pretender, encouraged and supported by our ancient and inveterate enemies the French and Spaniards, and by that monster of iniquity the court of Rome." In addition, several weeks after celebration of the day of thanksgiving, the Council subscribed to "a humble address to the King's most Excellent Majesty," and words were set on their way praying there might never be "wanting one of your royal blood to sway the British scepter, or command the British armies, in valor and conduct equal to the glorious instrument of the late signal victory."

Days of religious observance and official assurances of loyalty, however, required far less time than raising an army or equipping an expedition to vie with the achievements of the English victors over the clans at Drummossie Moor. Recruiting companies for Governor Gooch was simple enough. Four were assembled and sent off to Albany. The Assembly voted for funds for clothing and provisions. The Governor, out of his private purse, advanced money for arms, which he expected to have repaid subsequently by allowances from either a repentant Assembly or a materializing Lieutenant General St. Clair. But the Quaker majority in the House could not compromise with their principles enough to grant sums for weapons or powder, allowances from other governments did not compensate for the fact that funds were not punctual in arriving from the royal treasury in England, the four companies stayed on at Albany for a twelvemonth or more without having either promptness of pay or orders to march, the regiments of St. Clair did not make appearance at Louisburg, and everybody's business seemed to be nobody's.

George Thomas regretted his generous advances. The Council appealed in vain to the Assembly for renewal of subsidies for the companies of Captains John Deimer, William Trent, John Shannon, and Samuel Perry. Those gentlemen, their lieutenants, their ensigns, and their men waited impatiently for new clothes, installments of pay, and adequate provender. The Assembly argued it had been willing to supply funds for a campaign in the summer of 1746 but not for anything like a standing army kept idle at Albany. Officialdom and commonalty alike awaited further communication from the Duke of Newcastle. In the autumn of 1747, it was finally known to the Council that "His Majesty had laid aside for the present the late intended Expedition against Canada" and that steps were to be taken to meet what charges for the army from Pennsylvania were not to be defrayed by their Government, and that General William Shirley and Sir William Pepperell would continue to be key figures with Commodore Knowles, acting for the defense of Nova Scotia and Louisburg.

But before late autumn of 1747, a great many other things had been coming under the cognizance of Richard Peters.

He had promised himself during the last month of 1746 that he would try to be more circumspect in his talks than he had been when earlier he wrote to Mr. Penn of the demise of Governor Lewis Morris of New Jersey. Mr. Penn did not esteem what he had said of Morris' going out of the world so "unlike a man of good sense" or of his showing "a ridiculous fear of death." Mr. Penn thought "a serious deportment very proper" at the time of dissolution. He did not like the unbecoming mirth of Richard Peters' comment on the end of the executive of the neighboring province. So, the Secretary to the Proprietor intended to be sober in 1747 and to reveal the good sense of a modest man. For a time, he held to his purpose, as his February letter to Conrad Weiser by its straightforward piety demonstrated. Yet he did not cease to be quite himself as the months lapsed.

In their course, he had both his satisfaction and his astonishments. The Assembly eventually stretched its grants for the companies at Albany from an initial £5000 to something over £6000, it remunerated Governor Thomas for his private outlay to something above £200, and it permitted the shrunken coffers of the province to be drawn on to the sum of £550 to repay certain innholders for dieting the soldiers of Pennsylvania. It was something to add a report of such considerations to the minutes of the Council, factors slightly more tangible than the spiritual inherencies, for divine rebuke or heavenly charity, in Drummossie Moor.

Moreover, although he did not enjoy the prospect of having Captain Anthony Palmer, as the senior member of the Council, become the lieutenant executive of the province in an interval between two deputy governors for the Penns, Mr. Peters did not too much dislike the thought of having an ailing governor withdrawn. Knowing always that Pennsylvania needed a strong and able guardian, he had notions of the relevance both of George Thomas' taking farewell of the Council and Assembly for a visit with physicians in England and of James Hamilton's departure to that same country in the pursuit of pleasure and knowledge. Furthermore, he conducted himself with gravity when news arrived in Philadelphia in early May of the death of Mr. John Penn, eldest but invalid and least active of the three Proprietaries. With interest, he guarded his clerks' entering the items of business into the books of the Council, but he was hardly unaware of points either omitted or inserted by implication between the lines recording correspondence of Governor and Assembly on the retirement of George Thomas or loss in the family of the Penns.

In a message of May 5 to the Assembly, the Governor condoled with that body, his words citing the "humanity, good nature, and affability" of the deceased Proprietor and instancing John Penn's regard for their liberties and the public good. He complimented them on having "two worthy branches of the same family" left to further their comfort. On the 8th of the month, by formal acknowledgment, the Assembly condoled with him on the loss that the province had sustained in the death of one of its Proprietors. But the House chose to remark nothing more of John Penn while they enlarged rather pointedly on "the benevolence, generosity, and public spirit of our late worthy Proprietary, his father," still fresh to their view. From William Penn's descendants, the Assemblymen did nothing more than hint that "they would hope for the continuance of a like beneficence."

On the point of Governor Thomas' retiring for his voyage to England, ceremonies were at similar cross purposes. The Executive indicated by solemn address his wish to collaborate with them in any last service to the public which they might desire to perform, then offered some defense of his administration in "difficult and tempestuous times." His intentions had always been good. He would leave it to others to judge "whether any degree of prudence or skill had appeared in his conduct." The reply, which was presented to him three days later, was studiedly courteous. It referred to Governor Thomas' want of health, wished him a prosperous voyage and restoration of strength, admitted his abilities and skill, besides his integrity, but, conceding nothing out of its authority or wisdom, observed that "a variety of sentiments" between legislature and administrator must be expected in tempestuous and difficult times, and knew of no further public service in which to participate with him.

Richard Peters, of course, understood everything and took all in his stride. If Thomas had to go, there was no point to repining at President Palmer's acting *ad interim* in the gubernatorial function. Old goutified Mr. James Logan had insisted he had not been a member of the Council since Colonel Thomas' accession and now urged his own absolute resignation and the removal of his name from the roster of the body. So the Secretary knew he must not grieve at having a lesser figure temporarily ensconced in the saddle of state. There was always Mr. Penn to be written to about what an executive was attempting, be he Lieutenant Governor or President of Council, and in Philadelphia itself was Mr. Lynford Lardner, Richard Penn's brother-in-law, with whom the Secretary could converse in quiet surmises about what were the intentions of the Proprietors with regard to George Thomas, illness or no illness.

To satisfy him also in the summer of 1747 were other matters of moment, discretion, or charity. Anthony Palmer and his Councillors had many things to decide on, were often in session and acted—as Mr. Peters thought sometimes—firmly. They furthered the work of the courts, seeing to it that the horse thief, Hugh Bruslam, despite his petition of inability to pay, should not be discharged from the Philadelphia jail until his fine of ten pounds had been met. They compelled the counterfeiters, John Thomas Jones and Stephen Barnes, despite their petition of embarrassment, not only to have their stamps for milling pieces of eight destroyed, but to stand themselves in the pillory in partial evidence of their disgrace. They refused to save the burglars Patrick and

Michael Burne, two Philadelphia laborers, from the hanging to which Judge William Till in a late court of Oyer and Terminer had sentenced them. They directed and won of the Assembly the charity of clothing and food for Spanish prisoners about to be exchanged. More than supporting the institutions of justice and the opportunities of kindness to the unfortunate, they maintained through Mr. Peters and Mr. Weiser a wise intercourse with the Indians, and they acted with discrimination with regard to sickly ships coming from the Barbados and healthy ships filled with Palatinates coming from Europe. Drs. Graeme and Bond were kept busy testifying whether or not vessels should enter the port of Philadelphia, fevers from the south were warded off, and immigrants from the east were admitted.

In addition, the Council showed wise attention to marine matters. They were not scornful, as were the Assemblymen, of the implications of a bold exploit that occurred in Delaware Bay, somewhat downstream from Newcastle. Instead, they began a serious, prompt investigation of the affray and put their statesmen heads together on the matter of pilots. What had happened made excellent substance for depositions, and, preliminary to recommendations of the state, the Council Books filled up with that form of legal testimony, phrased often in vivid narrative.

Recorded versions showed that two householders of Apoquinimink Hundred, four miles north of Bombay Hook, Edmund Liston and James Hart, were plundered of furniture, bedding, apparel, and a parcel of slaves by the daring stroke of a bevy of Spaniards. For a time, a pilot boat rested at anchor out on the bay. Then, early in the afternoon of July 12, a smaller boat took off from it for the shore, and the Quaker Liston's daughter was suddenly interrupted as she and her slave were gathering crabs to behold the young Negress seized by a crew of Spaniards, tied and thrown into the craft from which the marauders had issued. Brushing on by the astonished white maiden, the men came inland to Friend Liston's establishment armed with guns, pistols, and cutlasses, declared they belonged to a Spanish privateer, demanded the farmer's Negroes, money, and keys, presented their pistols to his breast, made up bundles of his goods to carry to their boat, and forced him to lead them to James Hart's house. There, after a siege of the more militant neighbor's residence, they repeated their outlawry, accumulated about seventy pounds' worth of the second owner's movables, and added to their previous loot two slave women, one the mother of a suckling and their two children. Their raid achieved, the Spaniards—there were nineteen of them, according to the depositions—slipped back to their boat, away to their pilot ship, and disappeared with both vessels.

But that did not end the story of them. Bernard Martin, commander of the ship *Mary of London*, also had a tale to depose to and was corroborated by another deponent, his mate, John Cowan of Philadelphia. Both asseverated "on the holy Evangelists of Almighty God." Returning from a passage to Antigua, their vessel had sailed up Delaware Bay to within sight of Cape Henlopen when, at seven on the morning of July 14, a privateer sloop of ten guns appeared menacingly. Captain Martin made a firm show of resistance and prepared for an engagement, and the interloping ship made off. But an hour later, a familiar-looking pilot boat took a position as if coming to guide the *Mary*, and, unsuspecting, her master stood to for it to come alongside.

Then occurred the second surprise on the water approaches to Philadelphia. The pilot and two other men seen aboard the steering craft turned magically into thirty-five Frenchmen and Spaniards, who swarmed out of their hatches and up over the rail of Bernard Martin's vessel, used their muskets with promptitude, one ball grazing the captain's cheek, and possessed themselves of the *Mary*. After that, they tacked, careful not to crowd the sail, and stood out to sea. Moreover, they conversed freely within the hearing of the overmanned captain, mate, and crew. "Now that they had provisions, they were ready to rejoin the privateer to which they belonged; soon, they would be cruising, as of old, about the capes of Virginia and Cape Fear." The next morning, they were rather less talkative but quite as capable of action. With a forthright gesture, they put Captain Martin and seven of his crew aboard the pilot boat, told him the ship was his to command, and themselves sailed away on the *Mary of London*.

The audacity of the Frenchmen and Spaniards was, then, something for Philadelphia and the province to take note of, and, except for the Assembly, the topic of privateers did not lose interest as August, September, and October succeeded. More and more, it was argued, from the increased molestation of Philadelphian and colonial shipping off the coasts of Virginia and North Carolina and the ever-growing impudence of the French and Spaniards, that raids were due to be made on the Port of Philadelphia itself. Further depositions offered evidence to the Provincial Council both of the rapacity of the foreign sloops and the double-dealing of American pilots and pilot boats. To be owner of a pilot boat was to be suspected of giving comfort to the enemy and receiving material advantage in return. With talk of perfidy and violence ever in the air, merchants, laborers, and gentlemen meditated much in defense of their goods, their houses, and their persons. Certainly, numerous citizens would have said Thomas Penn's hopes had not been granted and that they and their fortunes were not as well provided for as the beneficiaries of the victory at Culloden. The

Council, under Anthony Palmer, generally offered a friendly ear to appeals and representations. But it was not so with the Assembly. The Speaker of that House, John Kinsey, and his Quaker colleagues regarded as suspect all the evidence of the depositions. They saw no need for new regulations of their own on the licensing and control of pilots; their religious principles made it impossible for them to sanction the creation of a militia and the purchase of arms. Moreover, they did not forget the four unused companies of Pennsylvanians maintained to no purpose for the past year at Albany. They were not to be wheedled into new subsidies by pretexts or the advocacy of military procedures. Mr. Peters, in brief, beheld the Honorable Anthony Palmer's administration kept as ineffectual in handling the Assembly as from time to time were the Proprietary lieutenant governors. Indeed, it was easy enough for the Secretary to the Provincial Council to be sober in the summer and autumn of 1747.

Yet his experience was not altogether monotonous. If September brought to him an ephemeral chagrin at having been reprimanded with Lynford Lardner by Thomas Penn for having unseasonably announced to Governor Thomas that his commission was made subject to supersedure by the death of Mr. John Penn and the change in the Proprietaries by reason of that demise, at least the same month brought from Thomas Penn criticism also of that Governor's withdrawal in May whereas he had promised to continue in office until June. And the early autumn brought another personal satisfaction to Richard Peters. A letter written during the summer by the Proprietor fretted considerably about Mr. William Allen, but it was full of esteem for James Hamilton. That latter gentleman, come on to London after a two-month stay in Ireland, was proving everything "in honor and gentleman-like spirit" which Richard Peters had described him to be, and Mr. Penn was frankly delighting in his society. If there were no present words of praise for the Secretary's conduct of the Land Office or the orderliness of his Council Books, it was nevertheless gratifying to know that one's friends had become friends. In fact, Mr. Peters was entertaining a hope with regard to Andrew Hamilton's handsome, knowing, and affable son. He meditated that the companionability of the Philadelphian might be a sort of compensation to Thomas Penn for the recent loss of his beloved brother, but he thought farther than that for the Province of Pennsylvania.

When he was not too absorbed in his reflections, however, the Secretary had other facts of experience to contemplate. Cordial relations with the Indians remained a prime concern, and the Philadelphians, who in the autumn of 1747 were neither agreeing with the sentiments of the Assembly nor hanging diligently upon the problematic authority of the Council, were a subject for new interest.

Mr. Peters, in fact, kept laying before the Board letters and reports from Mr. Weiser. Proper attention had been given in early July to the grief which Shikellamy, Taghneckadorrus, and other Oneidas and Cayugas at Shamokin were bound to feel at the death of a Proprietary. Conrad had eulogized their brother John Penn in a gathering with them at Paxton and, knowing the genuineness of their sorrow had bestowed on them twelve silk handkerchiefs to wipe away their tears for their friend. Information, too, was conveyed to Philadelphia from Shikellamy that fine English clothes distributed to Indian women and children at Oswego were keeping the Six Nations firm in the English interest. Later, the news was less pleasing. In October, Mr. Weiser found Shikellamy and most of his family at Shamokin suffering from a fever and had to ply every medicine and every skill in the use of it in which Dr. Graeme had instructed him to recover the Oneida and his progeny. Olompias of the Delawares had died, and his successor—important as a possible friend or foe to the province—had not been chosen. Such was the fear of sachems that the one of them elevated to the new rank of king would soon be bewitched by some envious Indian. So both Mr. Weiser and Mr. Peters were concerned, and only half of the difficulty was solved when a present of clothing from the province was forwarded to the cured Shikellamy to replace the apparel he had foolishly given to Indian doctors to heal him, and the corn which his horses had foraged on while he was sick. Yet there was comfort in the fact that information came to Mr. Weiser in November that the Twightwees beyond the mountains in the Ohio country were dissuading tribes neighboring them from the use of the French hatchet. To the Secretary, ravages on the English and Irish back inhabitants of the province during the coming winter seemed less likely.

At least it was true in the autumn months of 1747 that Richard Peters was less aware of the Six Nations and their allies than he was of his neighbors. A much-circulated anonymous pamphlet called *Plain Truth* had won great response in the city, as so often it seemed did items which issued from the press of Ben Franklin, and Philadelphia was astir. Everywhere were talk, arguments, witticisms, sly smilings. Some readers were scornful, some impressed with the weight of the pamphlet's thesis, some entertained with the elegance of its Latin exordium, shrewdly quoted from Sallust. Occasional ones thought the style rather too learned to be the composition of a tradesman, as the title page of its first edition pronounced it to be. Others averred that Ben Franklin's translation of the prefatory Latin for the benefit of those who did not know that classical tongue, when added to the second edition, showed openly enough who the real author had been. Some remarked pointedly that the benedictional prayer which closed the piece ought to move even a Quaker. Richard Peters saw considerable force in the initial Sallustian phrase, *Capta urbe, nihil fit reliqui victis.* He realized that, should a swarm of French and Spanish privateers take Philadelphia, little would be left for the conquered and not too much for the Penns. So, although he was Secretary, he offered no noisy objections to a work that postulated the origin of government in a people rather than in a prince or a proprietary.

He was more concerned to note the results of the pamphlet. *Plain Truth* challenged Pennsylvanians—English ones, who derived from their ancestors' "zeal for the public good, military prowess, and undaunted spirit," Irish ones whose sires had opposed James II at Londonderry, and in their heroic resistance during the siege, won glory for themselves and imparted lasting valor to their sons, German ones, brave and steady, whose forebears had always maintained the character which Caesar had given them for courage. It called for protection-as might an oration of Cicero-of wives, parents, and children, of homes and shrines. It pictured imminent bankruptcy in trade with persuasion hardly less cogent. It argued eloquently: *Libertas et anima nostra in dubio est.* It drew sad parallels of peril from Scripture. It preached forthrightly that Heaven helps those who help themselves. With philippic force, it warned that timorous prayers and womanish supplications are not so likely to bring Providence to one's side as they are to provoke God to wrath and indignation against one. If Ben Franklin had penned the document, Mr. Peters admitted to himself, Ben had written effectually if not too wisely. And, on the whole, Franklin's saying, "The way to secure peace is to be prepared for war," was not very different from old James Logan's argument, offered even to Friends, that there was no sin in defending oneself, however wrong it was to offer offense and violence of one's initiative.

But whether *Plain Truth* had been the cause, whether dire danger in Delaware Bay and as far up as Bombay Hook—for the pamphlet had not failed to depict in a footnote the spoliation there of Edmund Liston's household—was responsible, or whether some collective lust in the blood was asserting itself willfully—the last months of 1747 saw something new in Pennsylvania history. On every tongue were the novel words "Association" and "Associator."

Assemblymen frowned. Councilors put their heads together and pondered. Representatives of them waited upon officers of government. An instrument for an Association was drawn, a great public meeting was called, and printed copies were distributed, winning instant approval. According to Ben Franklin, before the gathering disbanded, one thousand two hundred signatures had been secured, a scheme of companies was effected, and, promptly after the assemblage, committees of ladies were at work upon silken colors and mottoes for the divisions of Associators envisaged. Anyone who loved devices could delight in a lion erect, one forepaw brandishing a naked scimitar, the other holding the escutcheon of Pennsylvania, and signalized as *Patria,* or an eagle, emblem of victory, disporting an *A Deo Victoria,* or an armed man with falchion in his hand, and symbolizing Heaven's aid to the valiant, *Deus adjuvat Fortes,* or a city walled round, with the glowing conviction: *Salus Patriae Summa Lex.*

So, not to his surprise, Secretary Peters found himself taking note of an important meeting of the Council on November 27 and receiving directions. A letter, in fact, was drawn to the Proprietaries to be forwarded the next morning on the London ship then leaving port. The phrases of the official document were carefully shaped. They reviewed the course of events, unfortunately not changed for the better, declared the "naked and defenseless" condition of the province so fully known to the French, regretted the faithlessness of the pilots on Delaware Bay, apprehended an attempt on the city in the next spring at the latest, pictured prospective plunder by a cruel enemy and inhabitants prospectively left to the exercise of the brutal passions of a set of banditti, recorded that many Philadelphians intended to send their families away for safety.

From its introduction, the letter that Anthony Palmer and eight of his fellow Councillors sanctioned went directly into the matter of an association for defense. It told of many hundreds who had resolved to learn military discipline, form themselves into bodies, and assemble such arms for themselves as they could. It said a scheme was being entertained for erecting a battery on the river below the city and predicted that applications were likely to be made to the Proprietaries for some cannon for the battery. It announced the Council's approval of the Association and the motive behind it. It surmised that the Assembly would not concur and not gratify any applications for aid coming from the Associators. It confided that if the Penns approved the measures for the public safety that the Council was supporting and did not neglect its hint for a subsidy of cannon, the city would "owe its preservation, under God, to the same Family from which it had its birth and foundation." It indicated that the merchants of Philadelphia were petitioning the Lords of the Admiralty for a man-of-war to protect sea lanes for them to New York and to make periodic visits to Delaware Bay.

To Mr. Peters fell the duty, once the letter had been inscribed, of rounding up the nine signatures of the Councillors. But privately, he had another obligation to perform, and he knew his best tact would be required. On the next day, writing of other affairs to Thomas Penn, he allowed himself a moment of gossip, remarking, "Mr. Edward Shippen is likely to come into an abundance of trouble by marrying Mrs. Newland, her husband being alive and well in the Barbados and it is said intends him a visit." But on November 29, as once more he sat pen in hand, he adhered without any asides of scandal to his purpose of informing the Proprietor what he knew of the Association.

He did not, however, write without diplomacy or adroitness, nor did he omit the forethought of keeping his position as noncommittal as possible. He opened with a notion "which people said the French had got" to quit their cruises in the West Indies next spring, descend in shoals on the Atlantic coast and, using American pilots, make an attempt on Philadelphia itself unless men-of-war at New York or Virginia would intervene. So, at least, numerous tradesmen were saying. Moreover, the Quakers had been making the situation even worse. They had been conducting an inquisition upon members of their own persuasion to find who of them had contributed to the recent "manning out of the *Warren,* privateer on our coast, in order to drive away the French and Spanish privateers that infested the Bay last summer." The odium of their inquisitorial methods had exasperated not only supporters of their congregation but also those of all the other Pennsylvania flocks. That state of affairs made Ben Franklin really apprehensive of a visit from the French and taking advantage of the people's fears. Ben had first conversed in the matter with Messrs. Francis, Coleman, and Hopkinson, then taken the character of a tradesman and, in a paper, fallen afoul of both the Quakers and their strongest opposers. This had been designed, on the one hand, to animate all the middling persons to undertake their own defense and, on the other, to tempt Mr. Allen and his friends, the gentlemen, to publish a vindication of their own past conduct and follow it with overtures to identify themselves and their interest with all who would promote the public good. Franklin was quick with offers to publish gratis all papers to that end in the *Gazette* or, if there was no space there, in separate pamphlets to be sent with his newspaper to every one of its subscribers.

The scheme bore fruit. Verses promptly appeared praising Robert Barclay ("taken, Mr. Peters supposed, out of one of the magazines"). A quotation from that writer's *Apology* on the subject of defense was given notice with the addition of "some sly but strong observations which any pious and well-inclined Quakers might make." Then, when these first efforts were dividing moderate men from bigots and causing outcries against the inquisition of the Quakers, "a strong and pathetic appeal to the people, mostly of Franklin's own doing," came out to win marked success for the ruse.

On November 17, tradesmen to the number of one hundred and fifty met in Chancellor's sail loft and were addressed by Franklin. Ben shrewdly addressed them first as the movers of everything useful in Philadelphia, instancing their establishment of the Library Company and the Fire Companies. Then suddenly, he drew a paper out of his pocket and read them a draught of an intended Association. The tradesmen were all at once for signing it. But "No," says Ben, "let us not sign yet; let us offer it, at least, to the gentlemen, and if they come into it, well and good! We shall be the better able to carry it into execution."

That artifice also had prospered. For "all the better sort of the people met on Monday at the Coffee House, where Franklin produced his draught, and it was unanimously agreed that several copies should be printed and signed at the New Buildings the next night." The signing had been effected, and Ben had just told Mr. Peters there would be a thousand hands to the document by evening.

Such was the "relation" that Mr. Peters composed for Thomas Penn to supplement what, of course, the Proprietor would read from the official letter of the Council.

But it was not in the Secretary's genius to stop with bleak facts, and he subjoined commentary. Now that he had written down everything that had come to his knowledge, he observed that he had "no hand in it, neither privately nor publicly." Moreover, there were points he must make in justice to Mr. Allen. When that gentleman had communicated the affair to Richard Peters, "which was before it was reduced to any settled form or plan," he told him, Franklin and all the others concerned wished the Secretary to be acquainted with every step. They had nothing in view but the security of their lives. They thought they were at the same time doing the Proprietaries' true service in defending the country by an Association, which the legislature had refused to do. They were, therefore, expecting the countenance and assistance of the Proprietaries, and they wished to depend on Mr. Peters to make their regards known to the Proprietors' Family. They desired the Proprietors to believe the Associators were heartily in their interest, as vast numbers would accede to the Associators, it would be mightily to the advantage of the Proprietors to encourage their organization by a generous supply of cannon and small arms.

> In short [Mr. Peters concluded] the scheme took its rise from the just fears and apprehensions which all sorts of people were under for their lives and properties, and, tho there may be at the bottom of it a personal antipathy to Quakers, who brought the Country into this dilemma, yet they really desire to recommend themselves to the Proprietaries. I have

had no time to consider the paper called "The Association Paper," of that I will give you my opinion by the *Beulah*.

Mr. Peters' conscience was clear. His behavior had been described to his superiors in England, for the next month, he could perform the function of his office as the Council commanded.

On December 7, nearly six hundred Associators drew up under arms before the Courthouse, and to them, the Secretary delivered a message from the Councillors. "I am commanded," he said, "to acquaint you that your proceedings are not disapproved by the Government, and that, if you go on and choose your officers according to your articles, commissions will be granted them."

Two days later, he was busy with a proclamation of a fast to be observed, on command of the Government, in January by all the religious societies. Intervening days filled up with correspondence with governors of other colonies.

Then, on December 29, Mr. Peters laid before the board a number of blank military commissions, saw these signed by President Palmer and the four eldest members present at the meeting, and was ready for the next step.

On New Year's Day, there was a great ceremony at the State House. The Associators again appeared under arms. They chose their officers, and their officers had their names entered by Richard Peters into their commissions in the Council Chamber and departed, each with his own credentials. The captains and ensigns, all of whose names the Secretary wrote down with either "Esqr." or "Gent." appended, elected their superior commanders and asked for commissions on the next meeting of Council for Abraham Taylor as their colonel, Thomas Lawrence as lieutenant colonel, and Samuel McCall as major. Two of the latter, Mr. Peters realized, could hardly sign such papers, for they were themselves well-known members of the Provincial Council, but he knew their colleagues could act for them in that delicate issue.

Just so was the Secretary occupied in the presence of the people of Philadelphia on January 1, 1748, a passive instrument of their will—and Mr. Thomas Penn three thousand miles away across the Atlantic. But, as he saw marching men outside the windows of the State House and beheld silk pennons fluttering to touches of breeze their mottoes of *Semper Paratus, Pro Aris et Focis, In Nomine Domini,* and *The Lord our Banner,* he kept wondering what the great Proprietor really would think.

Correspondence across the Atlantic, whether private or official, was a matter of many months. During the interval between January and March, while word was on its way to Mr. Penn, his Secretary in the province was keenly aware of the growth in popularity of the Association. In February, commissions had to be filled out for goodly numbers of gentlemen associators as officers for Philadelphia, Bucks, and Newcastle Counties. In March, there were lists of them even longer for Chester and Lancaster, the names so numerous that space was not available (or not used) for "Esqr." and "Gent." to be appended for the back inhabitants. In April and May, when the Council no longer had to act on the problems of military but unofficial defense through the Association, the minutes of Mr. Peters filled up with further intercolonial commentary on privateers and Indian affairs.

In June, the reflections of the Proprietor arrived. But Mr. Thomas Penn's mind could hardly be described as having been comfortable in March when he wrote. Richard Peters' friend, Lieutenant Lynford Lardner of the City Associators and brother-in-law to Mr. Richard Penn, found it easy enough to infer rebuke to himself in a letter from the older of the two remaining Proprietaries and, as a connection of the Family, read the missive with attention.

> The paper called "Plain Truth" [wrote the rich man from London,] I am afraid has done much mischief, as such a spirit raised in a people cannot be of any service, but under proper and legal regulations. I am sure the people of America are too often ready to act in defiance of government they live in without associating themselves for that purpose. "The Association," as printed, I have seen, and I admire that any man used to thinking seriously could imagine such a military establishment legal and proper, but I shall send the President and Council the Attorney or Solicitor General's opinion upon it.

The letter to the Council, being official, was more temperate. Mr. Penn had observed with great concern the apprehension of the Board. If their information that the French would be sending a considerable force in the spring was to be depended on, they had great reason to be disturbed. It was clearly the business of Council to do everything in its power for defense and to endeavor to raise in the people such a sense of danger as would induce them cheerfully to obey orders and discipline. "Unfortunately," the writer remarked, "the copy of 'The Association' which the Council had sent was lost, but it was probably the same as the printed one he had seen." If so, he could now observe, "Though on the one hand, we shall on all occasions desire to join in every fit proposal that may contribute to your safety, we must on the other with great caution object to any proposal that is liable to great objections. We have great doubts whether this is not liable to such objections." In fact, he was dubious that the Association might render unsafe the persons who had joined in it. He was uncertain whether it was warranted by necessity. He would, however, have Mr. Paris obtain and send to Council the thoughts of the Attorney and the Solicitor General upon the matter. The Councillors could wait for present advices. With that mild injunction, the Proprietor ended, and he set down in his letter no promise of cannon or even small guns.

A brief communication, addressed to Richard Peters on March 29, notified that gentleman that Mr. James Hamilton had been appointed Governor for Pennsylvania and would probably reach Philadelphia late in the summer, and was news highly satisfying. Something indeed might be hoped for in government, the recipient thought, with the son of his old friend Andrew Hamilton in office. He must not repine too much, therefore, at Mr. Penn's saying it was very uncertain, on account of the condition of his affairs in England, when he could visit the province again.

Nor need he to repine personally at what Thomas Penn elaborated to him in a long letter of March 30. For the moment, no harm done; he could incline with a sympathetic ear to the views of the distant Proprietor. The honored gentleman began punctually with his "concern." He regretted frankly that their apprehensions of danger had hurried the people of Philadelphia into such an "Association" as he had been told of. If they had had no governor and no constitution, their conduct might have been very proper. "But to establish a military commonwealth in your government," he warned gravely, "is, I am afraid, acting a part little less than treason." Instead of so radical an action, the people should have first requested the President and Council to appoint an officer to train them and then put themselves under the direction of the Council's appointee. They should not, on their own initiative, have presumed to establish a military council and then have held themselves accountable to it. In brief, Mr. Peters could see they had, on their own authority, erected a government within a government, and Thomas Penn was certainly of the opinion that "no set of people could do that without rebelling against the King's authority." During the rebellion two years before in the north and Scotland, all "associations" had been regarded as illegal. And even then, men did not pretend to erect a constitution but only raised men to be put under the command of such as King George should appoint.

So the Proprietor hoped sincerely that the President and Council had, in the commissions they granted, made it clear that the holders of them were responsible immediately to the Council itself. Mr. Peters could understand they would be called to strict account if they had let their power out of their hands.

Vigorously, Mr. Penn protested: "It is strange people cannot walk in a plain path. When men set up for refined politicians, everything which plain common sense dictates becomes beneath their notice." Moreover, if the procuring of arms was a good thing, the legal government only ought to have formed a body of men and accorded commissions. As matters had been described in the letters from Philadelphia, the people were acting only by will of their own. Such license they could never safely be allowed. It was directly contrary to the rules established by all nations in such affairs.

More vehemently still, he insisted:

> This Association is founded on a contempt to Government and cannot end in anything but anarchy and confusion. The people, in general, are so fond of what they call liberty as to fall into licentiousness, and when they know they may act, at least they are told so, by orders of their own substitutes in a body and a military manner, and independent of *this Government,* why should they not act against it.

Then, modulating his concern, he told his Provincial Secretary more gently that he was going to have Mr. Paris procure the opinions of the Attorney General and the Solicitor General and forward them to the Council. He would procure them himself, but he was setting out for Bath, it happened, on the day after tomorrow.

But he did not close softly, for in his last paragraph, he wondered how Mr. Logan could acquiesce in the Association. He scoffed at Mr. Peters' assurance that the Associators justified what they did on the plea of necessity. He demanded whether there were any more necessity than to apply to the President and Council, and he answered the supposititious question with an emphatic "Not the least!"

The Secretary meditated, not philosophically on either republicanism or on folk dressed in a little brief authority, but rather on what would be the relevant answer. On June 13, 1748, he, who had neither inspired the Association nor in any individual way fostered its development last year, now wrote suavely of Ben Franklin's scheme. Diplomatically, he omitted the name of the progenitor, as the understanding Proprietor also had done. Wisely, he refrained from opposing any of Mr. Penn's arguments. He may have fairly surprised himself in offering some defense of the project. But he made no mistake in keeping his slate clear of intrusion, and naturally, he began that he was "truly concerned" by what Mr. Penn had said. He was in hopes, however, that the Proprietor's notions having derived, as he supposed, from his having perused only the Association paper, the matter would be seen in another light when Mr. Penn realized that the Associators had "never acted but by orders of the Board." The Council's "leaving them to choose their own officers was looked upon by the Council only in the nature of recommendation." Such, too, was the tenor of the commissions that the holders of them received their orders from the Governor for the time being according to the "Rules of War." The Councillors had it in their power to revoke the commissions at any time. Although the rules agreed to by the Associators were oddly expressed and in rather too general terms, they were only intended to make learning military art easier and the management of musters more commodious. The Associators respected discipline, not action. They never had any thought of acting independently of the government. They were surprised to have their intentions misconstrued. If they "should have missed it in the form," they had always had recourse to the Council, behaved "with remarkable dutifulness, order, sobriety, and quietness," never overlooked "their submission to the King and his representative here." Besides, they were all hearty friends to the Proprietors and fully expected the Proprietors to countenance their behavior. It was true also that they had set the minds of the citizens at ease. The dangerous schemes which, Mr. Peters had been informed, were brewing at Havana against Philadelphia were more likely of frustration. The Secretary could not extend his approval lightly. But "Justice extorts from me," he concluded, "what I have said and indeed it would induce me to say everything I could for them."

Richard Peters may not have understood revolution as intuitively as Thomas Penn. The Proprietor may or may not have been given legitimate cause for concern. But the history of the next nine months brought neither anarchy nor sacking. Instead, it brought Mr. James Hamilton as Lieutenant Governor to the province, the end of King George's War, with the restoration of Cape Breton to France, and greater security to England at home by an unhappy barter of gains which offended New England, the removal of apprehensions of any further visiting of Spanish privateers in Delaware Bay, and chances of revival of trade.

Late in November 1748, the Secretary could recite his joy and that of the people and gentlemen at the arrival of the new Governor. He regretted cursorily when he wrote that, as the guns of the Battery below Wiccacoa were not loaded, no public salvos were possible. But he complimented Thomas Penn on phrasings of letters brought from him by Mr. Hamilton to the Council, which made all faces flush with pleasure.

Moreover, in the following spring, aware of the continuing happy fortune of the province, he could write with enthusiasm of Mr. Hamilton's pleasing manners. The master of Bush Hill had been amazingly altered during his visit to England. Now, "a most judicious affability sat gracefully upon him." His old stiffness had disappeared amid gentlemen of distinction in his mother country. Mr. Peters' only fear was that the low mercantile conversation of Philadelphia might undo the perfections of James Hamilton's carriage and air. Deportment in that city seemed "to go insensibly into the indifference of men of business and tattle."

XI

Cabins and Academy

As early as 1732, the name of Thomas Cresap had become malodorous to the servants and wards of the Proprietors of Pennsylvania. His appellation, one to be spewed rather than conjured with, was much on the tongues of magistrates, Councillors, and Deputy Governor. Persons who believed it their duty to protect the long-suffering Indians held him in contempt. Officials who regarded narrowly the pretensions of Lord Baltimore on the southern, unestablished boundaries of the province suspected justly enough that Cresap had the countenance of Maryland and anticipated trouble from him. The Conestogoes, just west of the Susquehanna, had no sooner had the protection of Governor Patrick Gordon and Pennsylvania and been rid of the interloper Edward Parnel and occupied that departed figure's illegally raised cabins than the man "and some other people of loose morals and turbulent spirits" had appeared, disturbed the peaceful allies of the Penns, burned their homes, and destroyed their goods. Justices of Hempfield, John Wright and Samuel Blunston, had dutifully rendered full account of Thomas Cresap's misbehavior to the authorities of Philadelphia. But his act did not offend the nostrils of Lord Baltimore, and five years later, his reputation was still fair in the Colony of Maryland; however black and foul it had become within more northerly degrees of latitude.

The borders of the two provinces were not yet determined. The code of the two Proprietors admitted tacitly the wisdom of keeping settlers at cautious distances away from either temporary or supposititious lines; the practice of settlers was often less prudent. Moreover, it could not be demonstrated with overwhelming proof that either government did not connive at any form of settlement, which might eventually bring advantage to its own domain.

Indeed, before Richard Peters came into the Land Office of Pennsylvania, the way was wide open for Thomas Cresap, dignified with the title of Captain by Maryland, to become a celebrity. In the late autumn of 1736, he had attained that distinction. His name was in general circulation, blasted in Philadelphia and honored in Baltimore. By the spring of 1737, it was known even to George II at Hampton Court, and the occasion there for an act of state sternly enjoining Pennsylvania and Maryland to keep the peace until His Majesty should have further instructions for his subjects and territories beyond the seas. One gave credence to Thomas Cresap's story, in accord with one's politics or one's domicile. If one were of Pennsylvania, one believed that a number of Germans who had occupied lands beyond Susquehanna, supposing them to be in Maryland, had, on discovering themselves settled on forbidden acres in Pennsylvania, promptly transferred their allegiance to the province of the Penns, accepted its jurisdiction, and vacated their fields. Also, one accepted the tale that Cresap himself, ensconced in 1736 among these ex-supposed-dependents of Lord Baltimore, was quick to encourage a new immigration of lawless folk from the southern province to fill up the abandoned cabins of the new dutiful Pennsylvanians. In the difficulties that followed, magistrates from Lancaster County attempted to evict Captain Cresap before he should be surrounded by other spirits as truculent as himself.

A lively narrative was soon corroborated by deponents from Lancaster. Pursuant to several warrants issued against Thomas Cresap for the murder of Knowles Daunt, the sheriff of that county called to his assistance twenty-four men, crossed to the west side of Susquehanna on November 22, and planned to surprise the interloper the next morning at his house. But the Marylander was not surprised and had instead to be besieged for a day. With six men in his cabin, he let the constables read the warrant, declined to surrender to Pennsylvania law, and declared he and his companions would resist to the death. Beleaguerment of his position began, and hour after hour, he held out obstinately. One person in his coterie, less violent than the others, managed to outwit his control by escaping through Cresap's cabin chimney. The rest of his followers had to be smoked out. Indeed, at sunset, the Sheriff of Lancaster and his aides succeeded in setting fire to the establishment. They shouted they would quench the flames before floors and roof fell if only Cresap would surrender. But his response was that of a desperado. He would neither come out himself nor let his wife or children issue. Rather than that, he forced these latter into the positions most exposed to the rifle shots of the besiegers and, for some time longer, held the fort with his comrades firing at the justices and their posse from points more protected. In the end, so the Pennsylvania story went, Thomas Cresap's house crashed in flames, and the persons of the culprit and three companions were seized. It appeared openly that he intended to have his wife and children burned in his house, and he was carried off to Lancaster and Philadelphia to meet the further process of the law. In total effect, the disorder led to one death in the *melee,* one of the interloping Marylander's gang shooting another by mistake, and to one wounded shoulder among the Pennsylvanians, one deputy having received a shot through that member.

South of the undetermined line, the account was recited differently, and in Baltimore County ran a simpler tale. The warrant calling for the seizure of Thomas Cresap as the murderer of Knowles Daunt, all Maryland knew, was unjustified. The death of the unfortunate Daunt had come about entirely as a matter of self-defense on Captain Cresap's part. Moreover, the absconding Dutchmen had defected to Pennsylvania in spite of the pleas of their lawful governors; the substitutes designed for their emptied settlements had made proper petitions for occupying them to the Governor of Maryland. It was, in fact, the servants of the Penns who had become truculent while the great suit-at-law between the Proprietors of their province and those of Maryland pended in the King's High Court of Chancery in Great Britain. So violent had the Sheriff of Lancaster County been that with a group of turbulent companions, he had crossed the Susquehanna, set fire to a house in which were innocent Thomas Cresap and his family and six friends, shot at that persecuted householder and his children and companions even as they were escaping from the flames, and then, to add ignominy and insult to riot and rapacity, carried several of his harmless victims off to Pennsylvania gaols. In short, Maryland did not believe that Thomas Cresap had called Sheriff Samuel Smith of Lancaster County and his assistants "damned Scotch-Irish sons of bitches," or "the Proprietor and people of Pennsylvania damned Quaking dogs and rogues." Rather, the southern province accepted the ill-starred and evicted householder as a gallant and intrepid hero of the border, protested that, ever since 17 p, the denizens of the northern neighbor kept conspiring against him, and repined that he should lie in a Philadelphia prison.

Be the truth what it was, Thomas Cresap came to no hanging in Pennsylvania. The two provinces accepted the will of the Crown in 1738, boundary wars simmered down to the surveyors' disputes in 1739 between Colonel Levin Gale and Mr. Secretary Peters of Pennsylvania's Land Office, and Maryland prisoners, on order of His Majesty George II, were released from Philadelphia gaol buildings. Only a technique for ouster and unapproved, warrantless settlers had been perfected, and a few rancors had been stored away in human hearts.

By 1743, the notorious name of Thomas Cresap had been substituted for that of George Whitefield. Zeal for religion rather than the passion for defending the border and Proprietary rights was then consuming the mercurial elements of Philadelphia. Pious clergymen of the Church of England trembled alike for their pulpits and their flocks. Orthodox Quakers and Presbyterians were disturbed about their meeting places and followers. Mr. Richard Peters, lately a reluctant applicant for "the cure of souls" at Christ Church, deplored the vogue of the evangelist whose enthusiasm so fascinated the people of Pennsylvania and kept all sects in unsettled confusion. It troubled him that even the partial sanction of a man like Ben Franklin should be accorded the enthusiast. He did not esteem Mr. Whitefield. He was not interested in that zealot's thoughts of a charity school. He saw no reason for Ben Franklin's wish to convert an institution for orphan boys tainted with Whitefieldianism into an academy. So he listened with dull ears to certain proposals made to himself by the excellent leader of the Junto, founder of the Fire Companies, and inspirer of the Library Association. He preferred, he told Mr. Franklin plainly in 1743, to adhere to his employment with the Proprietors to make no compromise whatsoever with Whitefieldianism. Mr. Franklin might have his jest of wishing to entertain George Whitefield at his house "not for Christ's sake, but for his own," he was not himself convinced that Mr. Whitefield did anything at all really for Christ's sake. Interested though Mr. Peters was in the education of youth (he once had been tutor and guide to some young kinsmen of the tenth Earl of Derby), he did not consider Mr. Franklin's idea timely. He did not himself care to become the head of an academy, which should, in its physical contours, be reconstructed out of a Whitefieldian environment. He preferred better auspices for the founding of a college. With an emphatic "no" in 1743, he declined to enter into the scheme of the printer and tradesman, a brilliant child of nature but no trained academician. Instead, during that year, he entered into his new duties as Secretary to the Council of the Province.

But matters were different in 1749. By then, Mr. Peters had become a figure in Pennsylvania. He had the confidence of the Proprietors. He was the intimate of the Board, the well-known friend of Governor Hamilton and Mr. William Allen, and latterly, on the recommendation of Mr. Thomas Penn, not only Clerk to it but also a full-fledged member of the Provincial Council. A made man, he could solicit rather than accept patronage, and he could solicit patronage from those most properly in position to accord it. The close of King George's War with Spain and France had made Franklin's Associators folk of less moment, the silence of guns in the Battery at Wiccacoa less shameful, and the taint of treason in *Plain Truth* less palpable. Richard Peters was willing to risk in 1749 an approval, which he had not thought it wise to lend in 1743.

The year following the cessation of war was indeed one for the advancement of enterprise, culture, and piety. It was one to seize on for good works. Conrad

Weiser and George Croghan had penetrated to the Ohio in 1748, set the Union Flag of King George waving at Logstown, drunk the health of His Majesty with many an Indian chieftain assembling there, and Senecas, Shawnees, Wyandots, Mohawks, Mohicans, Onondagoes, Cayugas, Oneidas, and Delawares all had pledged peace with the English. The frontiers promised to be quiet. Movements of traders in the western unpurchased lands were secure. There was no fly in the ointment save the tactics of the ambitious Virginia Company of Thomas Lee. Settlements, towns, schools, and churches in the purchased areas all might be fostered under the initiative, the wisdom, and the benevolence of the Proprietors. It was Richard Peters' honest wish to further every one of the gracious acts of these, to acclaim their unfailing interest, and, where advisable, to suggest their possible conduct.

He desired their consideration, when he wrote to the Penns, of a proper person to educate to succeed Conrad Weiser as Interpreter to the Indians, although he could not approve of Conrad's recommendation of Andrew Montour—for, though the half-breed had a good character among the Indians, he was an extravagant and untractable fellow who kept low company of which he was more than likely to be the dupe. He desired the Proprietaries' favor of a charter to Christ Church, which seemed the only possible means to infuse a spirit into the people of that congregation, which had not one farthing in bank, although their edifice was too little by one half to hold the members attending services there and really needed division into a second flock with a "chapel of ease" to be set up for it, and, despite the frequency of its worshipers, was without steeple, gates, wall, and bells. (He was tired of being kept "begging all round the town for contributions" for it, he declared in July.) He was pleased to write of the Assembly's passing an act for the erection of York County, prompt to request orders for patents of the grounds in which the public buildings of the county seat, York Town, should be built, confident that Mr. Penn would sanction the gifts of pieces of ground already made there by Governor Hamilton to every one of the religious persuasions on which to build their meetinghouses and churches.

Furthermore, he had thought of another sort of public donation which the Proprietors might advisedly make. If the giving of land for places of worship had the effect of encouraging people to come and live in a new town, there was another thing that would exercise the same happy influence. Nothing, he wrote in October 1749, "would be more serviceable than to give a lot for a school house, to build a school house yourselves, and allow a small stipend to a schoolmaster." Anything of that sort would "set such a useful, nay absolutely necessary, a matter in some sort of forwardness."

Yet, in truth, Richard Peters was employing prospective common school education in York as only a preface. With brisk *a propos,* his letter veered into its more definite purpose. "Now I am on this head," he continued, including in the sweep of his idea Messrs. Thomas and Richard Penn both, "I am desired to send you each a pamphlet entitled 'Proposals Relating to the Education of Youth in Pennsylvania,' and to support it with the warmest recommendations in my power." Endorsement from him, he admitted modestly, was unnecessary, in view of what Governor Hamilton was saying "in every proper place of Mr. Thomas Penn's zealous intentions to promote such a design." Yet he would venture "to tell you that most of the people of substance in Philadelphia are exceedingly well inclined, if one may believe their professions."

Those, of course, would soon be tried by the call for subscriptions. But there were genuine sponsors of the *Proposals.* Although Mr. Peters had not heard the Governor mention what he would give, he understood that Mr. Allen intended to give £100 per annum for seven years. Other good news was that Messrs. Franklin, Hopkinson, Coleman, and Francis, who had drawn up the scheme, were being generally applauded. (Although Mr. Hopkinson was in a deep consumption and not likely to live long to enjoy his esteem or to add to his already numerous services to the Penns.) Besides, the initiators had already in mind both a headmaster for their school and a site for it. Mr. Penn remembered, no doubt, Mr. David Martin, the Sheriff of Hunterdon County in New Jersey. He was "a perfect good scholar, and a man of good temper" and has been "prevailed upon to quit his Sheriff's office" for the distinction of being Rector of the Academy. As for their schoolhouse, Mr. Franklin, who was "an active genius" in the whole matter, had a solution to offer. Once Mr. Martin had accepted, the leading spirit in the pamphlet proposed quite the proper edifice. Now, the trustees of the great building which the Whitefieldians erected and where Gilbert Tennant was preaching had consented to spare two-thirds, or at least more than half of the structure, for the uses of the new school. The plan was to run off a section by a cross wall, divide that space into four apartments, and make ready for four different masters to sit in their classrooms. Indeed, all was going so well that one might fully expect "the zeal, ability, and diligence of the gentlemen proposed to be Trustees of the Academy will carry it much farther in a little time."

Then, having prefaced with a conjectural schoolhouse in York, Richard Peters waxed ultimately into peroration on measures which he did not choose to declare too manifestly had sprung from Ben Franklin:

> Whoever reads the proposals will, I imagine, see in the authors such a reach of understanding, such a clearness of head, such a wisdom and penetration, such an accuracy of expression, and such a copiousness of matter as will put it beyond all fear of want of success. If the administration of the Academy be committed to them, which it will be, though perhaps in conjunction with the Governor and Mr. Allen to give it the greater weight, I understand there will be a formal application to the Proprietaries that they would please to be at the Head of the Trustees and to patronize and encourage the design.

Only one reservation clung to Richard Peters' mind as he framed his long letter. He had not been in Philadelphia when all the proposals were brewing, so he could not have as perfect acquaintance with them as the Governor would have. Mr. Penn could expect a better account from Mr. Hamilton.

But there was no undue delicacy in the epistle which he wrote four months later. He had long known the elegance and the munificence of Mr. James Logan's library. He had seen the Greek Classics, all in folios of the best editions ranging the shelves of that excellent gentleman, with all the Greek, Latin, and French mathematicians, all the Byzantine historians, all the collections of Grevius and Gronovius, every curious Latin and Greek text in historical literature way down to the invention of printing. He had envied and admired all those noble evidences, in tooled bindings, of individual culture and humane achievement, of the flowering life of the ancients and the scholars of the European Renaissance. He had for a decade listened to Mr. Logan's fluctuant efforts to decide on the mode of endowing Philadelphia with those precious volumes, amassed at a cost of more than a thousand pounds. He knew of Mr. Logan's wish to erect a library facing the State House and to make by some wise reservation of ground rents and other rents a permanent gift for the encouragement of learning in the city and province. He had known regularly of the benefactor's overtures to the Proprietors for aiding the folk of Pennsylvania. Now, in February 1750, he chose to use both the philanthropist's benefactions and his ambitions prefatorily. He began, therefore, with full fervor:

> Mr. Logan's heart beat high all the while I was mentioning to him how handsomely you spoke of him and his charter, and he desired me to tell you that he was very much obliged to you. As fire covered with ashes, though seemingly extinguished, if the air gets at it, blazes out afresh, so his esteem and affection, being loosened by your kind expressions, broke

out into a glow of friendship, and he will by the next conveyance come to some resolution about the mode of his donation, and let you know it by me.

So warm, in fact, was the Secretary's phrasing that one might have supposed Thomas Penn, an even greater benefactor than the aged donor of his volumes.

But Mr. Peters' real subject in February was, as it had been in October, the Academy, and once his figure of speech had been consummated, he was glad of a chance for a more sober narrative on more secondary benefactions:

> Our Academy cuts a figure in print. I really thought the formers of the scheme had engaged people to carry into execution some feasible part of the plan, to make a beginning with, but I do not find that they have. So far they have done no more than print a collection of every thing of the kind that they could get together, and they call it a constitution. Yet with this they have done a great deal: they have bought the new building and lot, they have raised an annual subscription for five years which will amount to upwards of £800 a year, and they are now altering the south half of the building into four rooms for four masters. What is to be done next, I cannot tell. Mr. Martin, it is said, was engaged some time ago to be the headmaster. But he has been in town, and, though we are good friends and, at the importunity of Mr. Allen, I have become a Trustee, yet he has never opened his mouth to me about it. I asked Mr. Franklin, who is the soul of the whole, whether they would not find it difficult to collect masters. He replied with an air of firmness, "Money would buy learning of all sorts," he was under no apprehensions about masters. But for all Mr. Franklin's sanguine expectations, it is my opinion that they have undertaken what is too high for them and will not be able to carry it on. Not but that I heartily wish they may. I shall do all in my power to spirit them up, but I find the matter is not wholly understood among them.

Thomas Penn, however, failed to be unduly moved by either the confidence of Mr. Peters' first letter or the hesitant dubiety of the second. He wrote Governor Hamilton, who the Secretary had said was vouching for the Proprietor's generous intentions, that the proposal in the pamphlet for the education of youth was much more than he ever himself had "designed." He thought it aimed at far more than was necessary in the province, where "the best of our people must be people of business." For such activity, he did not regard public schools or universities as fitting youth. He could see no real advantage for Pennsylvania in the proposal. He doubted the need to establish an academy to draw young gentlemen from the islands thither for education. Moreover, he found people in England thought the Americans were going too fast in such matters, giving too many fools among the King's subjects at home an opportunity to spread their fears "that the colonies will set up for themselves." He would write Mr. Hamilton further on another occasion. Yet his deputy could say to the gentlemen of Philadelphia that no charter should be granted to their enterprise. Mr. Penn had every intention to promote the real service of the province. He had no intention "to make it a great nursery of learning or to put it in the power of anyone hereafter to do it." Few children, he was sure, required more than a common school education. The proponents for the Academy were setting "out too great at first."

A letter of the same February of 1750 to Richard Peters carried the same attitude, with perhaps somewhat less detail. Mr. Penn had read the proposals, but the scheme suggested was so different from what he had contemplated that he would leave it to the gentlemen of Philadelphia to go on independently of the Proprietors as they should themselves deem proper. He had not mentioned it to his brother, Richard Penn had a family to provide for. He was soliciting the opinion of a learned friend, whose view he would presently send on with his own to Governor Hamilton. At the time of writing, he believed it "imprudent to establish so extensive a plan on annual subscriptions." Mr. Allen's proposals were very handsome, but some estate of the same value would be of greater use. The plan, or rather the "essay towards a plan," was prettily drawn. Mr. Penn knew Mr. Martin but was "no judge of his qualifications." There would, in his own opinion, be few children for many years in the province to whom "an academical education would be useful." For traders and farmers, that sort of training was wholly unfit. Indeed, it might prevent their application to business. On the whole, he never wished "to see a large number of children educated in that way."

Yet the Secretary did not become too reflective on receiving Mr. Thomas Penn's letter. He may have smiled wisely to himself at the Proprietor's appended pleasure on having the County of York established by Act of Assembly. He may have been forbearing when he observed that his superior in England had offered no penny for school building and no penny for a stipend of schoolmaster at York Town. What he did do with certitude in 1750 was carry out the Penns' behest in another matter of business.

The withdrawal of James Logan from active affairs had left Mr. Peters the most important man, after Conrad Weiser, on Indian problems in Pennsylvania, and Indian problems were, in his and Thomas Penn's view, urgent in 1750 as always. So, the Academy out of his mind, the Secretary set forth in mid-May on an important mission to the back parts of the province. With Mr. Weiser, he went to the new County of Cumberland, resolute to support the magistrates there in their duties against trespassers on Indian lands. First, they had rendezvous with George Croghan and presently were attended there by five Indians. Two of these were sons of the late Oneida chieftain, Shikellamy, who came from Shamokin and were capable of transacting business for the Six Nations; two others had just arrived from Allegheny, a Mohawk named Aaron and Andrew Montour, the interpreter at Ohio. Speaking for his companions and having a message to the Government of Pennsylvania from the Ohio Indians and the Twightwees, Montour desired a conference, and it was forthwith arranged for to be held in the presence of four justices of the county. On the 18th, the five Indians expressed themselves through the well-known half-breed. They said they had thought a great deal of what Mr. Peters and Mr. Weiser had imparted to them: that the two representatives of the province "were come to turn off the people who are settled over the Hills." They were pleased to see them on that occasion. Indeed, the Council at Onondaga had this affair exceedingly at heart. It had been particularly recommended to them by the deputies of the Six Nations last summer. They desired to accompany Mr. Peters and Tarachawagon. Yet they were afraid, "notwithstanding the care of the Government," this new attempt might prove like former attempts. The people would be put off now and next year come again. If that happened, the Six Nations would no longer bear it but might do themselves justice. So they recommended, once Mr. Peters had turned off the trespassers, that the Governor should place two or three faithful persons west of the mountains who would be agreeable both to him and themselves, with commissions empowering them to remove everyone who should presume to settle on the unpurchased lands of the Six Nations. To enforce their words, they gave a string of wampum and received one in return from the magistrates, assuring them they would perform their duty.

All indeed worked out at George Croghan's post as the most conscientious agent of the Penns could wish. Armed with the sanction of the Iroquois, fortified with his lawful resolve that no new Indian wars should ensue through illegal settlements in prohibited territories, Mr. Peters could press his purpose of preserving order and peace among the back inhabitants assiduously. He intended to stand for no such maraudings in Cumberland County as had infested Marsh Creek and the Manor of Mask.

Presently, a triumphant progress was taking place.

On Tuesday, May 22, Matthew Dill, George Croghan, Benjamin Chambers, Thomas Wilson, John Finley, and James Galbreath, all esquires and all justices, were assembled around Mr. Peters to uphold the law at a favorite hunting ground of the Indians, twenty-five miles from the mouth of the Big Juniata and ten miles north of the Blue Hills. There, they proceeded from cabin to cabin, summoning forth possessors to the number of five. Of one after another, they demanded of William White, George Cahoon, and David Hiddleston by what right or authority they had possessed themselves of the land at Big Juniata and erected their log houses thereon. White, Cahoon, and Hiddleston admitted frankly they had no right or authority for their behavior—that the land belonged to the Proprietors of Pennsylvania and surrendered themselves into custody. George and William Galloway, however, resisted, and those two, having got to a distance, shouted back, "You may take our land and houses and do what you please with them. We deliver them to you with all our hearts, but we will not be carried to jail." Andrew Lycon happened to be away from his cabin, but his children were expecting their father and mother back presently, and the justices continued the rites of officialdom. Next morning, White, Cahoon, and Hiddleston were required to give recognizance and execute bonds for themselves and volunteered those formalities for Lycon, to the effect of their trespass and repentance, and the gentlemen of the law next took into charge the house of the two Galloways.

They emptied it of its occupants' goods and then held a long conference on what should be done with it. Deliberation became mature. It was reasoned that, unless some cabins were destroyed, trespassers would all too soon be tempted back, at their great distance from the Proprietaries, once more prove defiant and continue to provoke the anger of the Six Nations. Mr. Weiser's opinion was that the Indians were certain to fall on such settlers next winter, murder the offenders, and set their cabins afire. There seemed but one thing to do. The Secretary of the Province accepted the conclusion of the justices, authority exercised itself, and on Richard Peters' order, the house of the Galloways was burnt by the undersheriff and his assistants.

Such was the beginning of the emprise of the law. But one example, it was realized, would hardly suffice, and the company of the Proprietors' agents moved on the cabin of David Hiddleston. That trespasser voluntarily removed his household things, gave Mr. Peters possession, and saw the torch applied to his empty and unfurnished abode. Thus was a second, and it was hoped adequate, example set at Big Juniata. Unfortunately, however, as the company next day gathered around Andrew Lycon's house, with intent only to inform him his neighbors had been bound for his appearance and immediate removal and to caution him not to bring them or himself into further trouble, a possessor less mild than Hiddleston made an appearance. Lycon, in fact, presented himself with a loaded gun in hand to the sheriff and magistrates, warning that he would shoot the first man who dared to come nearer. He was disarmed promptly enough, convicted, and committed to custody, but his truculence impelled an unhappy result. A tribe of Indians came along just in time to be offended by the man's behavior. To the Shikellamys, these indicated in vigorous terms that either the commissioners would destroy Lycon's house or they would burn it themselves. So a third fire became imperative at Big Juniata, and Andrew Lycon, more docile in custody, first helped carry his things out before the conflagration and after it in his person was borne off to jail.

Four days later, at Shippensburg, Mr. Peters found himself in a larger circle of magistrates, coming in from several points to report that the people in the Tuscarora Path, in the Big Cove, and at Aughwick were all minded to submit. Mr. Weiser, who had an abundance of business to arrange for at home, asked to be excused from further work of the commission and, granted permission, left the party. Then, after his departure and two days of rain, the justices and their supervisor proceeded into Path Valley, where scenes like those at Big Juniata began to be enacted. In the length of the Tuscaroras' trail, from Sherman's Creek and southwest, eleven log houses were burned, their occupants "cheerfully and a very few of them with reluctance carrying out all their goods." At Aughwick, two more were destroyed by the same means, one of them consisting, before the moment of demolition, of only a few piled logs. Later, similar proceedings were followed at the Big Cove down near Maryland; more settlers of Scotch-Irish names gave recognizance and bonds for their trespass, and three cabins at the north end were burned voluntarily by their own earlier intruding occupants.

Ultimately, Mr. Peters moved with greater precaution, in the southern end of the Big Cove, in the Little Cove and at Little Conolloways, he knew he was close to Lord Baltimore's province. The magistrates from Cumberland County ceased to be aggressive, and the Secretary found it wise to stop at Philip Davies' and let the inhabitants offer petitions to him. These desired to be suffered by the Proprietors of Pennsylvania to remain on their settlements till the line should be extended between the two colonies. Their signatures were not numerous, Mr. Peters was not positive they were north of the temporary line, and he did not wish to risk embarrassment with Maryland if, after all, they should be south of that barrier. So he temporized; he told them of the importance of maintaining the good harmony now existing between the two provinces. If they were south of the temporary line, they should behave as in the jurisdiction of Maryland; if north of it, they should give no umbrage to the governors of that colony.

In brief, everything had been achieved that was necessary to security from Indian ravages and alienation of any of the allies of Onas, and a document of state could be drawn. The Secretary occupied himself with a formal report, reviewing the history of trespassers for a decade, the burning of the cabins, the alertness and integrity of the magistrates, the contrition of the offenders, and their submission to law. With a full narrative of his diplomatic cautions and his exploit, he was able to return to Governor James Hamilton and the Council at Philadelphia and ready to transcribe a complete relation to Mr. Thomas Penn. His account bore with it no sense of chagrin. Rather, the general submission of the people gave its author a sense of an evil effectually removed, and he wrote that he had omitted no kindness in his power to show the offenders. Where they were poor, he gave them money. Where they were able-bodied, he promised them they could go presently into some part of the two million acres recently purchased by Pennsylvania from the Indians. If they wished, where their families were large, Mr. Peters was willing to let them stay rent-free on some of his vacant plantations till they could provide for themselves. And, in view of such lenity and good usage, he warned they must not stay on their present settlements later than the time limits set unless they wanted to feel the full rigors of the law.

By way of conclusion, not to the ousted folk but to his colleagues and superiors, he remarked: "It may be proper to add that the cabins, or log houses, which we burned were of no considerable value, being such as the country people erect in a day or two, and cost only the charge of an entertainment." His mind took no occasion to sentimentalize on the hospitality, the neighborliness, or the good cheer of a barn-raising. Richard Peters' imagination was more city-bred and Philadelphian than that.

Yet, once he was back among the Councillors of the Province, he did not omit certain other points in testimony: at Croghan's early in June, he had met Indians who were trafficking with one Colonel Thomas Cresap, at his post far up the Potomac. They had told they were loath to commit themselves to any land transactions with that trader or his supporters but that he allowed them much better prices on trophies of their hunting than they could have from Pennsylvanians: a matchcoat for a buck, a stroud for a buck and a doe, a pair of stockings for two raccoons. The Secretary knew the burned-out Captain of fourteen years previous had not turned into a friend of the Penns. Cresap's civilities were in the interest of Virginia.

But Mr. Peters did not let that suspicion spoil his relish of the compliments of the Proprietor, which reached him in the last months of 1750. Thomas Penn wrote: "Your proceedings in turning off the settlers on the Indian lands had been very well concerted." If they had been "executed with an hussar spirit, nothing less than that would do with the people." He approved of the whole enterprise, from proclamations read by the Secretary to bonds taken of the culprits. No other method of removal than Mr. Peters' would have answered the design of the Penns so well, as the agent had so justly concluded in his letter. No other measure could have been more truly favorable to the people. It might not have been prescribed by English law, but "where a second people, the Indians, were equally concerned who were not regarded as subject to English law and from whom a war might come because of breach of the treaty with them, the way of military usage was certainly the safe and justifiable way. There came moments when strictly legal modes are insufficient."

So, Richard Peters, the dignities of his public office sustained, the laws of the province enforced, and its frontiers secure could give himself in January 1751 to such services as adorn the private and individual life of man. Indeed, he was very busy then with the affairs of the Academy. For a pamphlet on that institution, now happily become a reality, he prepared a preface addressing the Trustees and describing its condition of forwardness. The Latin and English masters were giving great satisfaction. The boys enrolled, despite the prevalence of smallpox in the province, already numbered above a hundred and were making a "truly surprising" progress. Masters were being provided for writing and French. The mathematical school increased in size daily. Prayers, composed for the schools, were in use both morning and evening. All these advantages were due to the regularity of the visitations of the Board. Those gentlemen were to be congratulated that the Academy now had two good grammar schools—one in the English, the other in the Latin tongue—to the no small benefit of the province.

But there was far more than this preface of acclaim in the pamphlet. Its two other inclusions were an appendix outlining, over Ben Franklin's initials, the constitutions of the Academy and a sermon on education by the Reverend Richard Peters himself.

That Mr. Franklin had been right when he said "money would buy all sorts of learning" seemed fully attested, for the constitutions embraced not only financial arrangements with the Rector, contracts with the masters, and allowances to the old Whitefieldian Charity School but such a comprehensive array of subjects to be taught as might have awed Solomon. From grade to grade, the offerings of knowledge mounted, ever increasing in abundance and dignity, from English grammar to Latin and Greek to the useful living foreign languages, French, German, and Spanish, to history, geography, logic, rhetoric, arithmetic, natural and mechanical philosophy. The best masters were proposed for reading: in English, Tillotson, Milton, Locke, Addison, Pope, and Swift, in translation from the Classical tongues, Homer, Virgil, Horace, and Xenophon in his *Travels of Cyrus*. Beyond these notable possibilities were culminations in moral philosophy.

As for Mr. Peters' sermon, printed midway between "Preface" and "Constitutions," it yielded nothing in radiance to these. It had, in view of its inherent somewhat material purpose, to expand at points on the Corporation, the Rector, the proficiency of the masters in English and mathematics, the several advantages of native and foreign languages, and the plain parts of learning. But it lost no glow on account of those mundane ends. Quite oppositely, it burned in its fervor. For Richard Peters confidently believed that "If slavery be deservedly esteemed the worst and liberty the best state mankind can be placed in, and ignorance certainly leads to the one, and knowledge to the other, then all his fellow Christians and fellow citizens had the greatest reason to expect the approbation of all good men on the opening of the Academy for the instruction of youth in piety, virtue and knowledge." He had, in fact, chosen for his text: "And ye shall know the truth, and the truth shall make you free," and in 1751, he was not ashamed to have either his sermon or his faith in the values of education printed for Philadelphians to read.

He had had the advantage of studying at Westminster College, Leyden, the Temple, and Wadham, Oxford. At his distance from England, he saw no particular reason for coinciding with Thomas Penn's convictions that tradesmen's learning was good enough for the province.

Yet he gave good heed to a request that came to him from the Proprietor late in the spring of 1751. Mr. Penn desired "to have a perspective view of Philadelphia" drawn. He thought almost any painter could draw it from the New Jersey shore opposite Market Street. He confessed, rather forlornly, "Had it some steeples, it would look better." The Secretary became at once sympathetic. He was glad to be instructed "as soon as any proper person appeared, to employ him to do it." On opportunity, he began looking at the waterfront of the city and talking to the Surveyor-General of the Province.

XII

Promise of Beulah

In 1751, Thomas Penn determined to turn his way of life into a new course. Apart from his brother Richard and Richard's three sons, John, Richard, and little three-year-old William, there remained no heirs male bearing the name of the Founder of Pennsylvania, and Richard Peters' patron had come to believe implicitly in the importance of the Proprietary Family, for which a design "in tail male" had been effected even before the late older John Penn's death. Thomas' nephew John was an uncertain quantity who, at the age of eighteen, had got himself involved with a woman. His nephew Richard was but a boy of sixteen, and Mr. Penn could not be too confident about the chances of survival of a boy of three years. So, the active Proprietor began taking steps. An accident with a pistol intervened awkwardly, maimed his person, made a sitting posture uncomfortable for him for a time—so that he could not write many letters, and even threatened his life. But his wound healed presently, he was able to complete proper negotiations with the lady of his choice and her father, and on August 22, he married Lady Juliana Fermor, fourth daughter to Thomas, First Earl of Pomfret. A month later, he could apprise the Secretary of his Province in Pennsylvania of his joy at being now "settled with a companion possessed with those qualities that must render a reasonable man happy" and of his satisfaction at having allied himself with "a family remarkable for their affection to each other."

The sort of news that his letter brought was by no means ungrateful to Mr. Peters. For to him, it signified much to have the Proprietor content—and so obviously well connected, for the Fermors, although their earldom was of comparatively recent creation by George I, had long been Barons Lempster, had many relatives in the peerage, and possessed a noble seat in Easton Neston, Northamptonshire. In correspondence thereafter between his patron and himself were prospects of new and pleasant threads. Other topics than the French, the Assembly, the Indians, and uneasy settlers might offer. Mr. Penn might be less exacting about the sale of lots, less concerned at having trespassers in the Juniata lands returned to fields which they had given their security a year before to leave unviolated. Complaints to Virginia and Maryland might have less to be made. The Secretary could occupy himself with his Council Books more uninterruptedly. He could watch the Academy grow, scheme with Ben Franklin, other wealthy Philadelphians, the master of mathematics in the schools, and the captain of the *Argo* for the discovery of the Northwest Passage, could rejoice in the paths of inquiry, piety, and peace. He approved with whole-hearted sanction Mr. Penn's opinion that a reserve to the Proprietors of five hundred out of every five thousand acres surveyed in the province was the only way to support the Family adequately in its position at the head of affairs in Pennsylvania. Receipts of quitrents would never amount to sufficient to maintain the chartered governors in the respect and dignities due to their position. Complacently, Mr. Peters shared in Thomas Penn's new ambition.

In the first half of the year 1752, there was, however, a slight undercurrent of apprehension in the consciousness of the Secretary and Councillor. In January, he felt constrained to warn the Proprietor of new mischief being brewed by Cresap and wrote of a rumored petition about to go to the King at Whitehall from certain of that rascal's dupes. "Poor, infatuated people" of the frontiers had been "spirited up" by the man to protest to the Monarch against Richard Peters for having burnt their houses. One Andrew Dunlop and his son were to go to London by way of Virginia and, no doubt, would be abetted there by some of the "great men"—perhaps by Lord Fairfax himself—to malign the Government of the Province of Pennsylvania. Yet, his warning sent to Mr. Penn, he composed his fears and awaited eventualities, and the end of the summer confirmed how little he needed to be disturbed.

For the Proprietor wrote comfortingly. Cresap's gull had indeed come to England and offered the bruited petition. But it had caused little stir. The Council refused to admit it and properly, thought Mr. Penn, referred the petitioner for redress to the common legal remedy in Pennsylvania, the courts of the province. Moreover, the refusal had been in no way solicited by the Secretary's friend. Furthermore, when, rejected by the Council, the foolish old Dunlop had presumed to approach Thomas Penn directly, that gentleman had declined him any hearing whatsoever. So Mr. Peters felt trebly vindicated for his forthright and just behavior in 1750: by the deed, by the King's ministers, and by the *de facto* governor of the province.

There was cheer for him accordingly in the winter of 1752, and in April 1753, an urbane cheerfulness still prevailed in his manner as he wrote to Mr.

Penn of what he had just learned of Mr. Tench Francis. That recent traveler in England declared "very deliberately" in Philadelphia, "Your son is the finest boy in the world." And there should be no wonder at that, for Mr. Francis added with great seriousness he had never seen "the peer of the infant's mother for grace, amiableness, and a fine person." Richard Peters himself was delighted that Lady Juliana had done him "the honor to take notice of my mentioning the joy expressed on the happy state of your Family at the birth of your son." He cordially expressed his conviction that "Such news every year would give fresh delight if she should retain her health and you, your spirits."

He did not know that his master's firstborn had died two months before his letter was written. But he was glad to know in midsummer of 1753 that, her health having continued at least so far, the Earl of Pomfret's daughter had borne her husband a second child, even though it was only a female.

He experienced cheer in the second half of 1753 also for another reason. The Academy was prospering. Thomas Penn's attitude toward the institution had been transforming. Colonel Martin had brought his own three boys on from Long Island with their tutor, Mr. William Smith, a young Scotsman now on the eve of a visit to England and the Archbishop of Canterbury and a scholar already deeply interested in the plans for education in Philadelphia.

Richard Peters thought further of the possibility of a charter to bring to the Academy increased eminence and prerogatives, and imaginatively, he thought a plan through. When the tutor went on to England, he had been preceded by a copy of a pamphlet of his own on matters educational sent by the Provincial Secretary, and he bore with him a letter of introduction from that gentleman to Mr. Penn.

William Smith, however, did not hurry at once to the Proprietor with Richard Peters' communication. More shrewdly, he waited upon the Archbishop first and then bore with him, on his visit to Thomas Penn, credentials from the high-officed ecclesiastic. His Grace of Canterbury, in fact, more than confirmed Mr. Peters' prophecy of "a most kind notice" and sent Mr. Smith to the Proprietor of Pennsylvania with a very gracious introduction. The great churchman's letter indicated that he had had an eye on the young Scot until the man had chosen to go to New York as a tutor. There, he said, he had behaved very well. Mr. Penn might well consider his attainments and "the important character he aims at in the conduct of the infant College at Philadelphia." His Grace regarded William Smith as an ingenious scholar and "what was of the highest consequence, of a temper fitted to pursue a plan of education upon the large and generous footing of aiming at the public good." The Scotsman would show no other bias than "preserving his duty to the Constitution of the Mother Country consistently with a warm regard to the service of the colonies." Thomas of Canterbury thought he was not mistaken in Mr. Smith. He was confident he would become "a very useful and faithful servant in a country in whose prosperity Mr. Penn had so strong an interest." He suggested that Mr. Penn question the young man, predicting that he would be pleased with his ingeniousness and all the answers to his questions.

Nothing, as a matter of fact, failed the Archbishop's predictions or Mr. Peters' hopes in 1753. In England, the Proprietor received William Smith very affably, wrote cordially of his approval of the young man to His Grace of Canterbury, and thanked the Primate for the recommendations he had offered. From Philadelphia, late in November, the Secretary to the Province, in his now new function of Chairman of the Board, could applaud by brief letter the conduct of the Penns. "Honored Proprietaries," he wrote,

> The Trustees of the Academy have been so scattered by absences during the summer that they have not been able to meet in so large a body as they thought respectful enough for an address of thanks to the Proprietaries for their goodness in the grant of a charter and their generous grant of five hundred pounds, and I have it in charge from them to make their apology till their address comes, which will now be very soon.

It was a note that he could sign with the elation of spirit. When he sealed it, he used a signet showing the crest of his own family. The two lions' heads, ringed and addorsed, came out sharp and clear in the wax. But Mr. Peters, who would never admit that, despite his activities in lay functions, he had himself become anything else than a clergyman, was glad that the Academy of Philadelphia had favor not only from the Penns but also from the ecclesiastical head of the English Church. He was glad to be a friend to young William Smith. Moreover, he knew he had always wanted a cordial relationship between the clergy and the adherents of the Proprietors in Pennsylvania.

Signs were fair for education, religion, and business at the beginning of 1754. The Secretary could well believe that when George Heap's and Surveyor Scull's perspective view of Philadelphia, now painted and ready to be sent on to England for printing, should be published and distributed, it would adorn no mean prosperity but give rather a right prospectus of a flourishing city and province. Furthermore, trusting in the favor of the Archbishop of Canterbury for the College, Mr. Peters could commit himself without regret to dining with genial Ben Franklin in April and discussing with that printer—in his good dame's absence—the affairs of Mr. Smith and the Academy.

There was pleasure also in May in having Mr. John Penn in Philadelphia at his side. The son of Richard Penn had been sent over to learn something of public affairs and to prepare perhaps to act for the Family someday. The youth struggled manfully to acquire a sense of the meaning of recorded Votes of Assembly and the Council Books, but his admiring gaze from time to time at Richard Peters was such as made that mentor realize that no one in Pennsylvania knew public and private affairs better than he. To have Mr. John Penn's deference gave a lively pleasure.

But the late spring brought responsibility, and a new war with France seemed highly imminent when commands reached Pennsylvania from the Lords of Trade. These ordered that the province participate through commissioners in a conference to be assembled at Albany to consider the general defense of the colonies and their allies, the Six Nations. Governor Hamilton appointed Mr. Isaac Norris, Speaker of the Assembly, Mr. Franklin, and Mr. Peters to serve in that congress, and, with John Penn accompanying them and fortified with gifts for the Indians, the three men set out presently for New York.

In mid-June, they convened with fellow commissioners from New Hampshire, Massachusetts, Connecticut, Rhode Island, New York, and Maryland, and their session at Albany began to be protracted. Mr. Peters stirred himself chiefly in Indian affairs but was not surprised at beholding Mr. Franklin become, in other matters, the chief figure in the conference. That affable politician, while on his journey to the gathering, had developed a plan of union for the colonies, which for some weeks took priority in all discussions. It called for a general government of the provinces to be administered by a president-general appointed and supported by the Crown and for a grand council to be chosen by the representatives of the people of the several colonies meeting in their assemblies. Eventually, the scheme appealed and was adopted by the Congress. Mr. Peters could neither too obviously endorse nor too obviously oppose it. He entertained no illusions about the value of colonial assemblies, few illusions very long about Mr. Franklin—and he had not had Mr. Thomas Penn's opinion.

Yet the Secretary of Pennsylvania was not to let the conference remain without a moment to the province. Whatever the other commissioners might concoct with each other, to be accepted or rejected later by His Majesty or by Proprietors in England, there was no point in failing in negotiation with the Indians. With rumors of a dishonest purchase of Susquehanna lands by a group of Connecticut Yankees penetrating the Governor in Philadelphia,

Richard Peters realized the need for wise and offsetting diplomacy. And indeed, except for the palpable fraud, effects of which could hardly materialize whatever settlements the Yankees might dream of, Mr. Penn's friend could go home easy in mind. For events shaped quite to his wish. For £400 in New York currency and £400 more to be paid when settlements should begin to be made, the Six Nations sold a new tract to the Proprietors of Pennsylvania, a vast territory south of the Kittochtinny Hills toward Maryland and farther west of the Susquehanna, valleys and coves in which Mr. Peters had protected the Iroquois' rights in that progress of justice which he conducted in 1750. More than that, there were clauses of agreement. The Six Nations confirmed earlier arrangements: they would not sell other lands within the Province of Pennsylvania to other than the Proprietors, they pledged themselves to act as brothers to the Pennsylvanians to the latest generation, they vowed they would never part with their land at Shamokin and Wyoming. Those were favorite hunting places. In them lay scattered the bones of their ancestors and kinsmen. In them, they intended to shelter whomever of their relatives the French discomforted from time to time. In them, they had instructed John Shikellamy to let neither Onas's people nor those of New England settle. Rightly enough, in view of such declarations, the cheerful Secretary could feel advantage and protection were assured to the Penns and their wards, white men and red. He thought of old James Logan and half regretted that that good man had died in 1751 and had not lived to appreciate what a capable Indian agent his pupil had become.

But, before Richard Peters had got back to Philadelphia, new problems were facing Pennsylvania. In the midst of other matters, letters from William Peters and Provost Smith of the Academy informed him of the defeat of Colonel Washington in the Meadows westward toward Ohio. His brother was hardly more distressed about his country than about the misbehavior of his eldest son, twelve-year-old Billy, whom ten-year-old Dicky Peters was making worse daily and for whom the father wished his uncle to find some place of apprenticeship (and of reform) ere he returned from his travels. Mr. Smith wrote a sad paragraph on the military disaster only to follow it with a lengthy account of affairs at the College. The Secretary sighed that William Peters, for all his present success and his beautiful house of Belmont with its celebrated plaster ceiling of violins and guitars, viols, and trumpets, bespeaking his love of music and the arts, should be such a poor hand with children. He read the Provost patiently, learned much to his satisfaction of the superiority of the Philadelphia Academy to one in New York to which William Smith feared Colonel Martin might be removing his sons, and he smiled a bit blandly at the compliments sent by the scholar "to our dear Franklin." But his thoughts fastened much on the news from western, unpurchased Pennsylvania.

It was not that the Virginia Colonel had lost. He had lost to the French—not only struck his colors, signed papers of capitulation, and withdrawn on terms of carrying arms and wounded men with him and leaving provisions and cattle but left the enemy free to fortify themselves powerfully at the forks of the Ohio. Indeed, there was little difficulty for Mr. Peters in agreeing with the sentiment of Tanacharisson, the Half-King, set down by Conrad Weiser in his journal at Aughwick and entrusted to the Secretary by that interpreter on his return to Philadelphia:

> The Colonel was a good-natured man but had no experience. He took it upon him to command his Indians as his slaves. He would take no advice from the Indians. He lay by from one full moon to another, and made no fortifications but the little thing on the meadow. Had he taken Tanacharisson's advice, he would certainly have beat the French. The French had acted as cowards, and the English as fools during the engagement.

Yet Mr. Peters felt no pique when September of 1754 brought him a frivolous letter from Ben Franklin, still lingering on in the Province of New York.

> The bearer, Mr. Elphinston, has a secret art [wrote that wag] by which he teaches even a veteran scrawler to write fairl[in thirty hours. I have often heard you laugh at the Secretary's writing, and I hope he will take the opportunity of mending his hand, for, though we are about to have a new Governor and, they say, a new Assembly, I do not desire to see a new Secretary. I only think it convenient that what he writes may possibly be read. [And he postscripted:]
>
> I have heard our good friend Mr. Allen sometimes wishing for a better hand, this may be a good opportunity for him to acquire it. His example and yours would be the making of the artist's fortune.

For Richard Peters was really in a good mood at the end of the summer and could smile indulgently. Governor Hamilton had tired of the Quaker Assembly and resigned. A new executive was on his way to Pennsylvania. Perhaps the new broom would sweep clean. At any rate, when stone walls had been struck, Mr. Peters did not dislike change. Moreover, the Secretary had already had the taste and hospitality of the Morris family of Morrisania, New York. So, having had word of the arrival of Thomas Penn's new deputy from Europe, he wrote on September 19 to Robert Hunter Morris:

> We were really in pain for you, having received accounts of your having left London in June. Be so good as to let me know when you set out, time enough to wait on you at Brunswick, being impatient to make you a tender of my services, which I shall do with infinite pleasure.

Early in October, Governor Morris arrived, and relations with him were at once agreeable. But the faithful Proprietary servant did not forget the Family in England. Their scion, Mr. John Penn, was still at hand to be counseled to wisdom and tutored in the processes of government when he was responsive, and in England was another heir. Lady Juliana had been brought to bed of her third child on July 18, and his father could write proudly to Mr. Peters of a new little Thomas, who was "a fine boy and as likely to live as any I ever saw." Yet there were disappointments in the letter with which Mr. Peters sympathized. Mr. Penn had been grieved by the lack of deference shown to himself and his offspring in the newspapers of the province. He lamented very justly, in his Secretary's opinion, that these had taken no notice of his marriage and announced the death but not the birth of his first son. He deplored the fact that "an event which so much concerns the whole country was not told to the people whereas a hundred trifling things were." He did not like the indifference shown to his family. They did not merit such disregard and would not have it "in any other country." Manners in Philadelphia, Mr. Peters reflected, had hardly improved since Governor George Thomas's time, and the poor Penns, he knew, had their cares.

So, too, had that other good friend of the province, Mr. Weiser.

Conrad wrote from Heidelberg at the end of October. He was concerned on several accounts. The relations of Henry the Mohawk toward the Proprietors were dubious and too dictatorial a hand with that chieftain dared not be assumed. He was afraid Henry might have signed the fraudulent deed to the Connecticut people. The point must be determined for truth or untruth. If the Province of Connecticut should countenance the felonious bargain of Lydius with the Indians, and the Yankees attempt settlement in Wyoming, there would be bloodshed, and any effort of folk from the northern colony to set up in those Susquehanna lands might alienate the Onondagoes and Senecas still more to the French. Despite the prospective near issue of the new map of Philadelphia and the perspective view by Heap and Scull, Secretary Peters could see that the year 1754 was not to wind up in glory.

In fact, he wrote apprehensively in a letter of December 19 to his "Honored Proprietor." He had had a kind letter from Mr. Richard Penn on the subject of his oldest son and had tried in answer to give the father "some present satisfaction." To the uncle, he confided that he really did

> ... not know what to think of Mr. John Penn. He has of late looked as if he was in distress and inwardly grieves much. But he says not a word to anyone. I frankly told him I observed that he was under concern or grief for something, begged he would think me his friend and use me with confidence. I further told him that the Proprietors had heard he was not inclinable to business and did not frequent the company he was recommended to, that they had written me on the subject. And I desired he would enable me to give them an answer. He said he would consult with me—confide in me. But he has not done so yet, and I am loath to press lest I should thereby lose his confidence.

But, as the old year closed and the new one opened, there were items to appeal to his alacrity of spirit.

The engraver Vandergucht had done a fine big piece of work with the view of Philadelphia, and copies of the issue had arrived from London. From waterfront filled with shallops and ships to wharves, streets abutting on the Delaware, houses, public buildings, skyline, and clouds—all was magnificent. An inset at the left side pictured the staunch Battery, really downstream at Wiccacoa. A table at the right identified structures and points of interest. A commodious statement below ranged on either side of a dedication to the true and absolute Proprietors of Pennsylvania and the counties of Newcastle, Kent, and Sussex on Delaware, recited the material glories of the city and the province in a proud tale of population, agriculture, manufacture, shipping, and trade.

Yet prouder even than titles, coat of arms, and prospectus was the array of turrets and steeples in the perspective. Mr. Penn could not have asked for more, and Richard Peters himself took great delight from the drawing of the spires. The cupolas of the State House and the Courthouse were pictured modestly enough, but the steeple of Christ Church soared with mammoth height into the skies, the largest and most beautiful feature of all George Heap's composition. Though not on the shoreline and so cut off by obstructing houses, the crest of its front elevation bulked up huge and imposing above all other roofs, and the spire rose from its basic tower in tier after tier of architectural beauty.

Far less impressive, thought Richard Peters, were the steeples of the Presbyterian and the Dutch Calvinist meeting places to its right, and that of the new Academy building was soberly small. Yet all seemed somehow proper. If the spires of the Presbyterians and the Dutch were mythical representations, at least that of Christ Church now had real existence apart from the "Perspective View"—and bells below in its tower, recently installed to the Secretary's pleasure. That the Church of England should loom larger than the State House or Courthouse was properly parabolic. Also, religion should always have greater eminence than any mere mundane political power. Moreover, the diminutiveness of the Academy spire could be forgiven, seeing that it was so near as to be appropriately within the shadow of the Church. Besides, modesty always beseemed learning. On the whole, Mr. Peters rejoiced in the encouraging interpretation of Philadelphia, which Nicholas Scull had achieved in response to Mr. Penn's wishes.

But just at the time when the view began circulating, an anonymous pamphlet began commanding readers in the city with its shilling's worth of print, and, to belie the grandeur of the commonwealth, *A Brief State of the Province of Pennsylvania* became the talk of the town. Richard Peters read with both sympathy and chagrin. The thing had been sent to England for printing and then been sold both in London and Philadelphia before Thomas Penn had been informed of its being composed, although the author was transparently a friend to the Proprietors. It did not advertise either wealth or security. Rather, it dealt in detail with woe and corruption—with all that was rotten, and all that was dangerous in the province and on its borders. It set out to explain why Pennsylvania, among the richest of the colonies in North America, was the most backward in contributing to the defense of the British dominions.

The chief faults were that the Assembly had acquired, by law from Governor Keith's time, complete power over the disposal of all the public money and that the Assembly consisted mostly of Quakers. Beyond these two misfortunes were the sad history of non-contribution of funds for the public use, or the King's use, in year after year of crisis, and latter-day connivings between the Quakers and the Germans, or connivings even between popish citizens of Pennsylvania and the Catholic French. To counteract such unhappy conditions, various measures were proposed: That one-half of the population, which consisted of "an uncultivated race of Germans," must be reached more by Protestant clergymen and schoolmasters warning them against popery. English Parliament should produce laws requiring all Americans who sit in the Assembly to take oaths of allegiance to His Majesty or to subscribe to a test or declaration that they will not refuse to defend their country against all His Majesty's enemies. The right of voting for members of the Assembly should be suspended from all Germans until they knew the English language and the English constitution. All bonds, contracts, wills, and other legal writings, unless in the English tongue, should be made void. No newspapers, almanacs, or other periodicals should be printed or circulated in any foreign language.

Richard Peters read of dangers and of proposals, feared that those were too true, and knew that these had a small chance of enactment. He continued uncertain that Colonel Washington's defeat last July would influence the Assembly of Pennsylvania toward either the establishment of militia in that province or grants of subsidy to any armies of King George raised in the colonies for their defense. There were hours in January 1755 when the "Perspective View of Philadelphia" contained small promise for him apart from the comforts of religion.

He was, in fact, in complete agreement with the convictions that reached him during the next month from his old friend George Thomas, once Governor for the Penns and now an executive for the Crown at Antigua and St. Kitts. That thoughtful dignitary wrote in a grave strain:

> Your North American affairs are truly in a bad situation. If nobody was to suffer but the Quakers, they would not be pitied. But I am really concerned for my friends and for the general national interest. You are to have two regiments from Ireland, two more are to be raised in North America under Shirley and Pepperell, but unless the colonies unite in raising men, there will not be sufficient to dislodge the enemy after having so much time to collect their whole strength of Indians as well as French. A Quaker government was never calculated to resist invasions, and yet I very much doubt whether the power will be taken out of their hands.

Colonel Thomas explained that the old pain in his breast which had troubled him in Pennsylvania was entirely gone—that at sixty, he suffered from no other complaint than a flatulency in his bowels. Aside from such minor difficulties, he knew no burdensome cares. The people of all the islands were rendering the government extremely easy to him. Indeed, he concluded, "I live in perfect harmony with them, and I govern rather by reputation than by force or policy."

Enviable state!

A South East View of Christ's Church circa 1787

James Logan (1674–1751)

Surgeons Hall at the College of Pennsylvania

Benjamin Franklin c.1746–1750
by Robert Feke

Indian Treaty of 1744 as depicted at the National Wax Museum, Lancaster County, Pa.

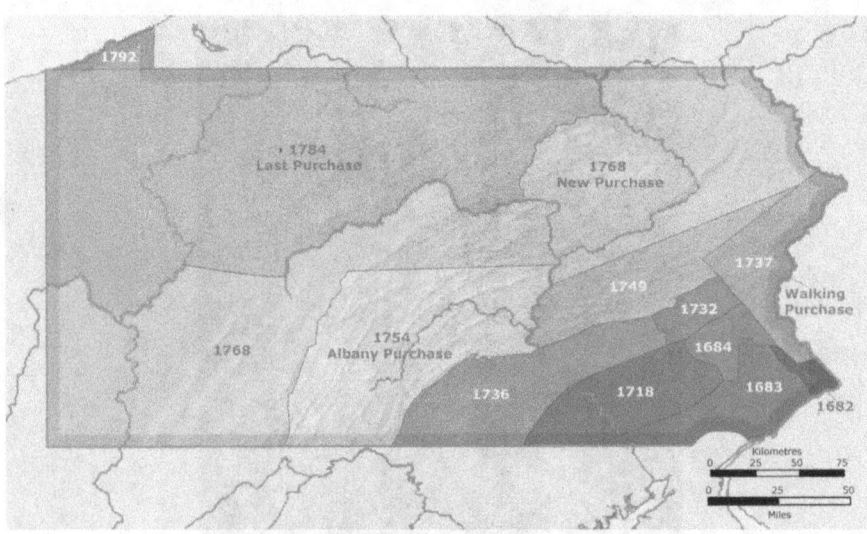

Pennsylvania Land Purchases

Andrew Hamilton (1676-1741)
by Adolf Ulrik Wertmüller

Teedyuscung (c. 1700–1763)
"King of the Delawares"

George Washington (by Charles Willson Peale, 1772) depicted in uniform as a colonel of the Virginia Regiment.

Bishop William White circa 1795

Thomas Penn, son of William Penn

Philadelphia Mayor William Allen

An elderly Conrad Weiser

Evangelical preacher George Whitefield (1714-1770)

Bush Hill, home of Andrew Hamilton and later John Adams

Death of Braddock

General Edward Braddock

Edward Shippen by Gilbert Stuart ca. 1796

Dr. William Smith (1727–1803)

Richard Peters, Jr. (1743–1828)

XIII

Foretastes of Battle

Richard Peters' spirits rose with the advance of spring. In the first days of March, it became known in Philadelphia that General Edward Braddock had arrived in Virginia and that regiments of the King with him, commanded by Sir Peter Halkett and Colonel Thomas Dunbar, were designed for an expedition against the French. From Annapolis, Maryland, an aide of Governor Sharpe wrote to Robert Hunter Morris on February 26 of the eminent soldier's arrival, and two days later, a letter was despatched, by express from Williamsburg, from the General to the Governor of Pennsylvania.

This message was peremptory. It spoke only of a packet to Governor Shirley, which was to be forwarded by Morris immediately and the answer to which, when it came through from New England, was to be sent on to the General with equal promptitude. The brevity of the command carried with it a decisive ring, and a sense of action came into Richard Peters. From March forward in 1755, the campaign of Braddock became for the Secretary, as for one hundred thousand other Pennsylvanians, the chief topic of interest. Every auspice of its success was exhilaration, every obstacle to its performance a cause for apprehension. The significance of the Academy grew momentarily pale in comparison. John Shikellamy's vigilant watch for possible Connecticut intruders in Wyoming dwindled for weeks at a time into a mere corollary to the greater problem of the state.

Yet though General Braddock's and His Majesty's business was surely the business of every councilor of Pennsylvania, it fell more properly to the Governor's portion to act for and with the eminent soldier than to Mr. Peters'. Robert Hunter Morris, rather than the Secretary, had to bear the bluntness of tone in letters which came from Braddock, and it was to him that summons came to attend with executives from other provinces the conference which the General presently called. Toward Morris in his official capacity, the Commander was, in fact, very brusque.

Braddock wrote of his surprise at "the pusillanimous and improper behavior" of the Pennsylvania Assembly. He was indignant to learn of "faction and opposition where liberty and property were invaded." He condemned the Assembly's "absolute refusal to supply either men, money, or provision for their own defense" while Philadelphians, through their shipping, were profiting by the sale of provisions to the enemy, as he declared. He was astonished to see "one of the principal colonies preserving a neutrality when His Majesty's dominions were invaded, when the enemy were on the frontier, nay even at Fort Duquesne, on the undetermined soil of Pennsylvania itself." Out of regard for his subjects in these parts, the King had ordered two regiments and a train of artillery from England and, when it was imperative, to drive the French from their encroachments. His Majesty's General was outraged by the slackness of Pennsylvania. No measures were being taken "to repair roads, to provide horses and carriages to transport army stores, or even to offer subsistence for those troops who were come to restore and preserve the property which the factious councils of the Assembly had suffered to be invaded."

Nor did the General limit himself to complaint. His letter of February 28 from Williamsburg contained a warning also. His commission had empowered him to settle for the next winter as he should think proper. Governor Morris, he counseled, could assure the Assembly of Pennsylvania that Braddock would consider the behavior of the several colonies, decide to regulate the quarters of his army accordingly, and perhaps "repair by unpleasant methods what for the character and humor of the assemblies he should be happier to see cheerfully supplied." So, when ten days later, Robert Hunter Morris received an invitation to convene with the General, Governor De Lancey of New York, Governor Shirley of Massachusetts, and the Governors of Virginia and Maryland, he apprehended that whatever report of the Pennsylvania Assembly he might be constrained to make at Annapolis, he would be dealing there with a man of resolution.

A month of conversations with the Speaker of the Assembly, of addresses to the body, and of visits both from William Shirley of Massachusetts and Six Nations Indians ensued. Yet when in mid-April, not at Annapolis but at Alexandria, General Braddock was in high session with the chief executives of Massachusetts, New York, Pennsylvania, Maryland, and Virginia, Morris had little comfort to bring from the province of the Penns. It was something to be able to testify that the Assembly had passed an act making further trade at sea between Philadelphians and the enemy on Cape Breton impossible. But there was nothing of cheer in the report from the sachem Scarroyady that the French of Canada had been only too successfully soliciting members of the Six Nations. Nor was there any alleviation for that bitter fact in the deadlock between the Assembly and himself upon the subject of support for the King's army, which the Governor had to report at Alexandria. The legislators of Pennsylvania were willing to provide funds by striking sums in bills of credit, a procedure to which the stipulations both of the Crown and of the commission which Robert Hunter Morris held from the Proprietors were opposed. They were unwilling to make other sorts of grants unless the privilege of taxing the Proprietary estates in Pennsylvania as they taxed other properties there was conceded to them.

So the delegate from Philadelphia at General Braddock's council could agree in spirit with all the resolutions taken at Alexandria, but he could not promise effectually that they would be endorsed by the lawmakers of the province he represented. Furthermore, as the deputy of the Penns, he had not been authorized to announce that money could be raised by any infringements upon Proprietary privileges of being exempted from all taxation. When he returned to Philadelphia, he could not bring back to the province and its Secretary, Mr. Peters, anything more than an account of what had been subscribed to in principle in the city on the Potomac.

The colonies were to form a common fund for carrying on the services being promoted under General Braddock's directions. Proper presents were to be paid for to retain the friendship of the Six Nations, and Colonel William Johnson was to act as the responsible agent for all the provinces in that problem. Reduction of the French forts at Crown Point and Niagara was to be undertaken by that same official, aided by forces to be supplied from the colonies. The fort at Oswego, the key to the attack upon Niagara, was to be garrisoned by four companies under the command of Sir William Pepperell. The authority of Parliament in England was to be invoked to find a method of compelling the assemblies to raise the expenses for the King's service or to defray these until the method had been found. When Fort Duquesne should be reduced, if Braddock determined to leave a garrison there, it should be provided for by contributions from the governments of Virginia, Maryland, and Pennsylvania—as should be any possible schemes of defense adopted for Lake Erie.

Such was the stuff of the indefinite entries that Richard Peters could record in the Council Books of his province. It was well, in fact, that, during those days of perfunctory and impotent rule in Pennsylvania, the Secretary could be interested in the Academy, minor in significance though that institution might sometimes seem in the light of the colony's more importunate needs. Until, in some direct and immediate way, Edward Braddock should require his duty,

Mr. Peters could devote himself with Mr. Allen to measures for education. At least he could not withhold ear very long from thoughts on that subject, which were forever occupying the mind of William Smith. For speaking or writing, that sententious young Provost had a way in 1755 of absorbing the Chairman of the Trustees.

Allied with him now in the corps of the faculty was Mr. Francis Alison, a Presbyterian clergyman and no mean scholar in the languages—one, in fact, whom Mr. Smith admitted to be his equal in all respects. Moreover, both the Provost and his friend, the Secretary realized, however much favor its present head had found with the Archbishop of Canterbury, the foundation of the Academy required an interdenominational staff of teachers. Presbyterians, then, were relevant enough figures in the group. Although Churchmen might not care especially to encourage it, preferment of them dared not to be neglected. So, the matter of a colleague and peer had to be adjusted with delicacy, and Mr. Smith enjoyed explaining to Mr. Peters the way to do so.

Mr. Alison, he said, must not be slighted. But philosophy was certainly the appropriate sphere for a provost, and the duties of that office could hardly be added to those of a Latin master. The thing to do was to let Mr. Smith have the provostship and not subordinate Mr. Alison with a vice-provostship but to honor him with the title of rector. The Trustees might lat—Mr. Smith would, in due season, be the advocate of their action—endow Mr. Alison with some less laborious professorship than that of the languages.

A long letter to the Secretary of the Province was necessary to establish these niceties of learning and office, and Richard Peters was not without pleasure at being consulted so formally. It was something to know that honors in philosophy could be granted without questioning the grantor's authority to confer them and something to keep professors in the sciences from being despised by the students because of any inferiority in status or title. Moreover, the ceremonials of education could be depended upon when superintended by the protege of the Archbishop.

So Richard Peters was glad to be at the head of a second lottery for the Philadelphia Academy in 1755. Among his private papers, he was later to preserve three printed tickets, all signed with his name to give them validity. But over a thousand of those sesames to fortune had been sold. There was a proud array of the numbers, and the prizes won, filling the first page of the *Pennsylvania Gazette* on March 25. Most of the purchasers won but five pieces of eight, yet for their support of education, many were rewarded with 62½ and 125 pieces, some fewer with 250 pieces, and four benefactors with 500 pieces.

One pillar of humane culture was lucky enough to have his faith compensated by a return of 1,000. Altogether, the Chairman of its board could be content that the Academy was patronized and prospering, and he did not repine upon understanding from Mr. Smith who had really been the author of that *Brief State of Pennsylvania* which last winter had been so offensive in the nostrils of Quaker Assemblymen and Dutchmen of Christopher Sauer's kind. In fact, Richard Peters smiled whenever the Provost signified to him privately how he had perpetrated that "innocent fraud" by first having it printed and afterward writing to Mr. Thomas Penn about it.

He could not rebuke severely a young scholar who was now doing well not only at the College but in influencing the Venerable Society in London to the founding of schools in parishes all around the province. Religion—and of a proper Church of England breed—was, on Mr. Smith's prompting, doing for the folk what Mr. Penn had not offered to do for the children of the settlers of York Town. Moreover, the little charges of the Society's beneficence were not going to be instructed in the principles of the Friends, nor the Dutch ones of them to be left ignorant either of the English tongue or of the wisdom of adhering to Proprietary policies. The Secretary agreed with William Smith that "to mend matters by the schools was a slow method," but he kept his faith in the power of education and hoped with his younger friend that the full effect might presently be hastened by the enactment of a law requiring all legal documents to be printed in the English language. Too much latitude ought not to be granted in the province either to Roman Catholics or to German speech. Religion and humane culture there ought to be protected with wisdom and fostered with diligence. Mr. Smith at the Academy was a man to be esteemed. Richard Peters was glad to recall that the Provost had been introduced to Mr. Thomas Penn in England by quite the proper methods.

But in the late spring, Mr. Peters' mind had to be occupied less, particularly with the Academy and considerably more with the cares of the state. He had beheld during the six years of Governor James Hamilton's administration the recalcitrance of the Assembly. He was not to behold that body more responsive to Robert Hunter Morris in April 1755. That dignitary got back from Alexandria only to find the old barriers facing him. Despite the conference of the governors of the colonies, the Quaker legislators of Pennsylvania persisted in offering grants only on their unacceptable terms. As much as Morris could obtain in the last week of the month was a promise that, at its next sitting in the second week of May, the Assembly would allow £200 for the cutting of a road westward toward the forks of the Youghiogheny on which supplies might eventually be carried to Braddock's army. So, on Governor Morris' instructions, Richard Peters became an intermediary between His Majesty's QuarterMaster General Sir John St. Clair and a project of road building. On April 25, he wrote urgently to several commissioners who had already been studying possible routes to lend support to the army concentrating at Fort Cumberland, at Will's Creek, in Maryland. George Croghan, William Buchanan, John Armstrong, Adam Hoops, and James Burd were, in the Governor's name, "to clear the roads a sufficient breadth which should be thought by them necessary to be opened, to make causeways and lay bridges, and to set about it with the utmost expedition." The Secretary bade them omit nothing in their power; they were "to get a number of hands immediately," they were "to further the work by all possible methods."

The tone, as much as the contents of the letter, revealed the alertness of Mr. Peters' spirit. He made patent his view that unless flour could be delivered in time to Braddock by the new route, "great blame might be laid with truth at the door of the commissioners." He showed as clearly that he expected more of Sir John and General Braddock than he did of the province. He insisted that what the former had said was true: "Had the army been ready now and then retarded by delays in matters undertaken by this province, all the mischief arising would have been justly chargeable on Pennsylvania." Then, having been severe, he wavered a trifle. In one breath, he questioned whether the military leaders could get their artillery within another month as far as the terminus of the road to be built. In another, he queried what route the army was likely to take. And ultimately, what he was most certain of was that the commissioners were to do everything which he commanded as though it were done wholly by the Governor's directions and under that official's great seal. Morris, he explained, was busy seeing Governor Shirley off for New England. They were to remember that the Secretary "engaged on the part of the Governor and Assembly that they should be paid all their expenses in clearing the roads and making necessary causeways and bridges."

As a matter of fact, while what Morris called his "Quaking Assembly" dallied, and the chief executive for the Penns and the province expostulated, Richard Peters began at the end of April to regard the success of General Braddock's campaign as his chief reason for being. The excitement of the times was in his blood. He wanted to be up and doing. He wanted to superintend to the full capacity of his fifty-one-year-old powers, whether official, moral, or physical. He wished to participate in every spirited association possible during the spring and the coming summer of 1755.

During May came abundant opportunities to participate. A letter from James Burd in Carlisle indicated that the commission for road building had become diligent at once on receiving Richard Peters' letter. Workmen had been advertised for in three counties. On Monday, the first that engineer advised that the work would begin. A communication from Braddock to Governor Morris acted as a spur on the committee of the Assembly to ensure the granting of the initial £200 promised, and the Secretary could dispatch that sum to John Armstrong without any delay. On the third of the month, that commissioner could send back to him a draught of the roads to be built with an estimate of what the cost must finally prove to be. More cheerful as an item of news, Mr. Armstrong reported that spades and pick-axes were a-making in Carlisle, that two merchants there were providing flour and a third one bacon. Moreover, grass for the subsistence of horses promised to be enough in a week. The only thing to mitigate the cheer of the commissioners and of the folk of Cumberland County was that Cresap's son should be receiving contributions from Pennsylvania. Mr. Armstrong did not enjoy the prospect of any discredit to the province arising through "the knavery of that family." Nor did his last mention bring any pleasure to Richard Peters.

But the month advanced, and he was glad to have the opportunity to serve Braddock in a second fashion. On May 12, the Governor informed the Secretary that he was to go to the frontiers not only to expedite the opening of the roads but to act with George Croghan on the matter of adding to the General's army as "large a body of able-bodied Indians as he could." If Pennsylvania was not to contribute companies of its own, at least the province might offer some advantage to the King's service through intelligent handling of its neighbors to the west and north.

Accordingly, Mr. Peters busied himself at once with a long letter to William Shirley, son of the Governor of Massachusetts and now secretary and aide to General Braddock, a young officer with whom he had already been in terms of friendship and with whom he could begin warmly. Indeed, he owned himself to be under no small uneasiness at not having had a recent line from Lieutenant Shirley, and he began graciously.

"The whiling time," he wrote, "is always a disagreeable one, but the good-natured man, the moment he sees a good dinner come in, thinks nothing of what is past, but falls to, eats heartily, and if his entertainer be cheerful and affectionate accepts every future invitation with pleasure." It was in this temper that he had read William Shirley's last communication, perfectly "delighted with his fare, and in high hopes of a continuance of a good table." But, after these initial encomiums, Mr. Peters kept his paragraphs strictly upon affairs, being personal only to the extent of admitting his own experience in Indian problems. He conceded surprise at having had word from Captain John Rutherford of Maryland that no Indians had been employed as scouts and messengers to the several tribes living beyond the Ohio River. He regretted that Governor Dinwiddie of Virginia had not carried out his scheme to have a meeting of northern and southern Indians at Winchester. He was of the opinion that some sort of general conference might have revealed whether a majority were on the side of the French or might prudently have brought the red men into a general neutrality. Such measures would have saved Braddock immense trouble and the Crown a heavy expense.

Yet, now that the General was already on his march, Richard Peters advised his addressee no better method could be followed than to employ Mr. Croghan, Andrew Montour, and others who had influence over the Indians and to get as many as could be got into Braddock's service. That method, however, he warned, would be expensive, for the Indians had been costing Pennsylvania a great amount all winter at Aughwick and, in return, providing no material information. As a rule, they had even declined to attend the commissioners who had been surveying the country to find out good places for roads. Nevertheless, Governor Morris had not omitted, on his return from Alexandria, to send a dispatch to George Croghan to encourage all the Indians with whom the province had intercourse to repair forthwith to the General.

So far as he risked asides, Mr. Peters suggested that Shippensburg would have been a better location for Braddock's camp than Will's Creek, and he implied that, inasmuch as Postmaster-General Ben Franklin was now stirring about finding not only wagons but single horses for the expedition, the ride over the hills would be a pleasant one. In fact, the farther the army got from "that dismal, inhospitable place, Will's Creek," the more grass and finer country it would discover. Finally, reverting from *esprit,* he wound up in a pious mood: "My prayers are for the General and all under him, that they may reap glory and enjoy health."

For two more days, Richard Peters remained in Philadelphia to attend a meeting of the Council on May 14 and hear himself named in that body for a particular service to the General. Then, in his secretarial fashion, he was off to the wars. On May 17, he was in Shippensburg, where his alacrity of spirit began waning again. From that town, indeed, he wrote both punctually and anxiously to the Governor. He had already met with Commissioner John Armstrong, who reported there were but sixty men working on the road, with only Mr. Burd in charge, "who was not, one might well suppose, equal to such a task," however good and well disposed a person he might be. In ten days, the party had cut not more than seven miles, and at that rate, six months would be required for the task, and the expense would become very considerable. Obviously, more laborers were needed at once, but the countryside seemed exhausted; as many as two hundred men had already enlisted in other branches of the public business.

On the next day, still disturbed, he wrote that although a new commissioner might not be necessary and might breed confusion, he could judge better when he got to the point where the new road was being cut, and he lamented that, on Sir John St. Clair's not having discovered another way to the Meadows, the army had concluded to follow the old road which Washington earlier had taken. As for himself, he would not wait upon the General till he had settled the matter of the roads he had come to further-which would take three days at least. Moreover, he had heard poor accounts of the Indians of the province, whereas a report (He doubted that it was accurate!) had come from Carolina that at least four hundred southern Indians would assist Braddock's army.

On May 21, writing from Fort Cumberland, young William Shirley composed an answer to the Provincial Secretary's letter of May 12. He was complimentary and wished it might have been in that gentleman's power to accompany Governor Morris to Alexandria. Had Mr. Peters been there, things might have gone better. Certainly, wiser measures ought to have been taken—at least to the southward. Mr. Shirley feared the army would be deceived in its hopes of assistance from the Catawbas, and the neutrality which Mr. Peters' letter had inferred would once have been possible could hardly be looked for now. Croghan, too, had been able to offer Braddock's secretary no encouraging news of the Twightwees in the Ohio country.

For, altogether, the writer was in no way sanguine. Ben Franklin was about the only person to whom the General was indebted for either wagons or horses. Apart from that assistance, everything else was difficult in camp. Ignorance or insolence irritatingly attended every motion proposed or performed.

The letter was dispatched to Philadelphia, and on the next day, William Shirley had the pleasure of seeing Richard Peters himself arrive at Fort Cumberland. Much business of state ensued, and the distinguished Pennsylvanian had to go through official rounds with both Sir John St. Clair and the General. But the two secretaries had enough association in the two days of Mr. Peters' visit for Shirley to be confirmed in his admiration for the older man, and nothing more pleasing came out of the brief sojourn in the camp of the emissary from Philadelphia than the opinion of him which the young officer set down on May

2 3 in a letter to Governor Morris. "I can't let Mr. Peters go without a line to you. He arrived at the camp yesterday, and I was extremely glad to see him, not only as an intimate friend of yours but as a man of worth and sense and one whom everybody else would wish to be on the same terms with." For, ten days later, the bearer of that private epistle was to be shown it by his friend Robert Hunter Morris and to be instructed, because of a matter of official importance also found in it, to enter it as a document in the Council minutes—allowing no others for a time to be acquainted with its presence there.

Late May and early June of 1755 were, in fact, to contain much more of that strange admixture of experience, official and personal, which was so often in the lot of Richard Peters. Having found a trustful ear in William Shirley at Fort Cumberland, from his stop at Carlisle on his way back to Philadelphia, he wrote a letter to Braddock's secretary, which revealed him still wavering on the subject of Commissioner James Burd. Inhabitants of the frontier town, he said, were like himself dubious as to the capabilities of the builder of the new road. The persons Burd had employed, he was told, did not understand making good, strong, and durable wagonways along hills of any steepness. Since the General had so much dependence on the road, he counseled the aide that Braddock should send an engineer from the camp to direct and overlook the workmen. But, back in the city on June 2, he was ready to offer to the Council a brisk and unshaken narrative of his experiences.

His oral account dealt forthrightly with both retrospect and the situation. The new provincial road being opened at the instance of General Braddock, he reported, had already been extended twenty miles from Shippensburg to Anthony Thompson's. Although the commissioners were under great discouragement from want of ready cash, 108 men had been put to work. Having found rum and carriage set at too high a price, Mr. Peters had summoned the principal men of Conococheague and other places and agreed with them on more moderate terms for supplying the needs of the laborers and the accessories to their work. The road itself he ordered to be reduced from an unnecessary breadth of twenty feet to one of twelve. Moreover, whereas two roads had originally been planned, one to Will's Creek and the other to the Crow Foot of the Youghiogheny, he directed that the former should be given up, as it would have no use after the General's forces moved from Fort Cumberland. Both Braddock and Sir John St. Clair had agreed to his wisdom in that detail and had urged that the other road be opened to its destination with all possible dispatch. The General, moreover, had declared with great earnestness that he would not stir from Will's Creek until he had Governor Morris' assurance that the road would be opened in time.

In response, Mr. Peters had informed that officer that the task could not be managed unless the army would detail an escort out of its own number to protect the road-builders while at work. Without such protection, he doubted whether the workmen could be kept for a single day in the event of Indian alarms. But General Braddock seemed unpersuaded upon that point as upon others, for the Commander gave small heed to Richard Peters' further counsel. He smiled at his opinion "that the General would find his march difficult if Indians could be got by the French to annoy him." He rejected as absurd the Secretary's prediction that "if there should be an army of Indians conducted by French officers, he would not, with all his strength and military skill, be able to reach Fort Duquesne without a body of Indians and several companies of rangers, on foot as well as on horseback." When Mr. Peters repeated his appeal for a military escort to protect James Burd's workers on the new road, he was rebuffed again by the General. All his observations about an attack from the Indians were despised.

On the other hand, Braddock was free of his censure upon others. He complained perpetually of the failure of everybody with whom the Government of Virginia had contracted for provisions, forage, wagonage, and horses. He was of the opinion that "unless the Province of Pennsylvania would hearken to his applications to them by Mr. Franklin, the army would not be able to stir this summer." If that should be the event, he threatened that "he would complain to the King of the remissness of the contiguous provinces."

Then, after complaining, he begged. He besought Mr. Peters most earnestly "to engage Governor Morris to purchase for him a stock of flour and provisions and store them at Shippensburg or the most convenient place thereabouts." The Secretary rejoined that neither Mr. Morris nor himself was a merchant, and the General insisted that at least they could employ the best merchants to procure supplies on the cheapest terms. Indeed, Braddock ventured that he appreciated his obligations to Mr. Morris, and he said: "he would depend on him and on no one else for the future for what he should want."

Yet there were other points than repining and sententiousness in the General's quarters, which Richard Peters observed at Will's Creek. Scarroyady, Andrew Montour, and about forty other Pennsylvania Indians had come on to the camp from Aughwick, bringing their families with them. The men among these were extremely dissatisfied at not being consulted by the General. The squaws were bringing their husbands money in plenty—wealth had of the officers, who, the Secretary remarked, were "scandalously fond" of the Indians' wives. In fact, Mr. Peters' last service to Braddock was his representing to that leader the dangerous "consequences of this licentiousness." And, for once, the General had been amenable to suggestion. He issued orders that no Indian woman should thereafter be admitted into the camp. He insisted with the Indians that their women should be sent home.

So the Secretary of Pennsylvania, before his return to Philadelphia, had done all that he could to promote the safety of the province and the service of the King. He had inspired the building of a road to supply the King's forces. He had conferred with the King's officer. With the Pennsylvania Assembly what it was and Governor Morris powerless to procure subsidies on legitimate terms from that body for the King's use, he could do little more. But he brought letters back with him from Will's Creek, and after the Council meeting, it was relevant for Robert Hunter Morris and him to consider two of them together. One was an official communication from Braddock, the other a private missive from William Shirley.

The first, as might be expected, combined drastic criticism with a request for assistance. With equal vehemence, the General lamented the folly of Governor Dinwiddie of Virginia and the roguery of the Assembly of Pennsylvania. He insisted piteously that "unless the road of communication from your province is opened and some contracts are made in consequence of the power I have given, I must inevitably be starved." He deplored the fact that St. Clair, on the advice of Governor Sharpe of Maryland, had "employed a fellow at Conococheague, one Cresap, who had behaved in such a manner in relation to Pennsylvania flour that, if he had been a French commissioner, he could not have acted more for their interest." In short, in every instance except his contract for Pennsylvania wagons with Ben Franklin, Braddock had "met with nothing but lies and villainy." Then, having expressed those convictions, the writer hoped, in spite of those trying circumstances, that Morris and he should "pass a merry Christmas together."

To his letter were appended proposals that the Governor and Mr. Peters should together find some proper persons who might make one or more contracts for furnishing "bread, or flour, and beeves, or in want of them, salt beef, pork, or fish, sufficient to subsist three thousand men for three months, to be laid in at Shippensburg until any other more convenient place could be proposed and agreed to." And to those proposals was attached a promise to Governor Morris and Mr. Peters that General Braddock would "be accountable for the expense and charge attending 'em."

The two Pennsylvania officials reviewed attitude, data, and proposals thoughtfully. On June 3, Robert Hunter Morris had an answer ready to be posted to the commander-in-chief of His Majesty's forces. He explained earlier measures that he had taken to further the provisioning of Braddock's army, the times for harvests in the province, and relevant places for storage. He estimated that the expense of such supplies as the General desired would be £4,000 sterling—a sum much higher "than a plantation governor, lately returned from Europe, and upon bad terms with his assembly" could easily furnish. He asked that funds be sent to him to that amount and volunteered to manage the problem of purchase to the best advantage once they were forthcoming. He reported that he selected for the undertaking Mr. Charles Swaine. He hinted that such flour as had already been forwarded by the Committee of the Assembly to Conococheague had been packed in casks made of green timber, would inevitably turn sour in such containers, and should be promptly examined and transferred into bags or other casks.

The second letter from Fon Cumberland, written by William Shirley to Governor Morris, was entrusted by the executive to Mr. Peters to be entered into the Council Books and be made, for the interval, one of the secret archives of the province. The Secretary perused it both with appreciation of Mr. Shirley's compliments to himself—and with understanding, he believed, of the young man's sentiments toward Edward Braddock. For in the private letter, he read:

> I don't know what description Mr. Peters will give you of our camp and the principal persons in it, but, as this goes in his packet, I will give you mine, grounded upon the observation of several months. We have a G----- most judiciously chosen for being disqualified for the service he is employed in, in almost every respect, he may be brave for aught I know, and he is honest in pecuniary matters. But, as the King said of a neighboring governor of yours when proposed for the command of the American forces about a twelfthmonth ago, and recommended as a very honest man though not remarkably able, "a little more ability and a little less honesty on the present occasion might serve our turn better."

Richard Peters had no quarrel in June 1755 with Mr. Shirley's opinions. He had seen Braddock himself, and he found it easy to sympathize with all that the young officer said further as he unburdened himself. He hoped sincerely, as Governor Morris' correspondent wished, that the G----- might continue to be influenced wisely by the first aide-de-camp's beloved friend, Robert Orme. But he was not as idealistic in his feelings as the son of the Governor of Massachusetts as to a friend's powers, and there was not much comfort for Mr.

Peters' middle-aged mind in the faith of the writer of the letter that it was "uncommonly fortunate" for the Commander to be "under the influence of so honest and capable a man" as that good captain.

The Secretary's zest for superintendency was hardly as active in him in June, in connection with General Braddock, as it had been in April and May. He could find a truer pleasure, he remarked to himself, in serving the interests of the Academy of Philadelphia. When, in the middle of June, another letter from William Shirley arrived for Robert Hunter Morris, he learned of its contents with more of official satisfaction than of individual enjoyment. The £4,000 sterling were on their way to the Governor for the purchase of provisions, and the march of the army from Will's Creek had begun; a military escort, after all, was being sent from Fort Cumberland to protect Mr. Burd's road-builders.

XIV

Aftermath of Defeat

Other amenities, too, added for a time to the comfort, if not to the immediate enterprise, of Secretary Peters.

Omnipresent Ben Franklin had got on as early as April for a visit with Braddock at Fredericktown, Maryland, a temporary stop for His Majesty's army, and there the Postmaster-General of the Colonies had cemented an intimacy with the King's representative, which promised advantage both to Ben and the province. For the genial and energetic Philadelphian came away from the interview with both funds and a commission, and busily, he set himself to procuring wagons and wagoners for refurbishing as well as transporting the General's stores. With his son, William Franklin, he coursed about Lancaster, York, and Cumberland Counties, bargaining for 150 vehicles and printing advertisements in whatever county newspapers availed.

These had several means of persuasion. They offered detailed and liberal compensation. They promised easy service, exempt from military obligations, and they appealed to patriotism. Only by way of postscript did they predict that if Pennsylvania farmers did not agree to furnish four-horsed wagons and a driver for each at fifteen shillings a day, they might expect Sir John St. Clair to enter the province in a hussar fashion with a body of soldiers and to commandeer whatever wagons Braddock might need. "B. Franklin," the advertisement of April 26 at Lancaster concluded, was very sincerely his fellow countrymen's "friend and well-wisher." So, to Mr. Peters' knowledge, there were signs of other activity than road-building in the province. Wagons were now gathering on the frontiers. And, whether or not Mr. Peters wholly approved the effective but designing Ben, he must agree with William Shirley. In mid-May, that good-natured gentleman had written to Governor Morris that for at least the last clause of his advertisement, "one could but honor Franklin."

Moreover, the agile Postmaster had set another example for the Governor and the Secretary. He had induced the Committee of the Assembly to make a gift of viands and beverages to the General's officers, and a cargo of luxuries, selected by his son William, had gone forward to the camp. Twenty parcels of sugar, butter, tea, ground coffee, chocolate, pepper, a half-chest of white biscuit, rice, raisins, mustard, and a quart of white vinegar, plus a half-dozen dried tongues, two well-cured hams, two gallons of Jamaica spirits, and two dozen bottles of old Madeira wine, laden, as the proponent said, on twenty horses—were the tribute of the legislators of the province to each of Braddock's subalterns. That generosity, Mr. Peters could not but reflect, contrasted with the Postmaster's less complacent temper on June 6, when, on account of "this extreme hot weather," Mr. Franklin was unwilling to go abroad and stir himself with the Committee of the Assembly to find funds for providing Mr. Burd's road-builders with a defense.

Yet it was fortunate that the best graces of the season to date could be rivaled by another instance of benefaction. Robert Hunter Morris was more successful with the lawmakers of Thomas Penn's three Lower Counties on the Delaware than he was customarily with Assemblymen nearer home, and at the meeting of the Provincial Council of Pennsylvania on Friday, June 13, 1755, he was able to have a pleasing letter of June 9 entered into the minutes. That letter modestly begged of General Braddock that he "do the Little Government of New Castle, Kent, and Sussex the honor to accept a small token of their regard for him and the cause in which he was employed." Mr. Morris and Mr. Peters were both highly gratified to know that the small gift consisted of 50 fine oxen already on their way from the three counties, 100 fat sheep to be taken up at Lancaster, and a long list of commodities for General Braddock's aides. The enumeration, sent to Captain Robert Orme, ran pleasingly. Though it contained no Madeira and only two kegs of spirits, it embraced, among other things, a fine assortment of pickles and mustard, spices and currants, sturgeon and herrings, and twelve hams, eight cheeses, two dozen flasks of olive oil, and two chests of lemons. The Proprietary interests in Philadelphia were not to be outshone by Quaker Assemblymen in the offices of hospitality.

Richard Peters also could now look back with less embarrassment on his short visit to Fort Cumberland. A gift sent through Captain Orme to the General was one sent through a very gracious intermediary. From Robert Hunter Morris, he had learned that the one letter that he brought on to Philadelphia for the Governor from Braddock's most trusted subaltern was full of compliments. The Captain indeed had written of the Secretary to the Province and of himself: "Souls congenial will unite." With fervor, he had praised the sense and amiability of his new-found friend and guest at Will's Creek. Thought of Mr. Peters,

Governor Morris reported, would add not a little to Mr. Orme's pleasure at having Philadelphia for his own next winter's quarters. Morris, Shirley, Peters, and the favorite aide-de-camp could be great comrades there. The prospect of an amiable society in the capital of Pennsylvania was enlivening.

Encouraging, in addition, was another more solid and material fact. Charles Swaine was pursuing his duties of purchase and storage of supplies with diligence. Buildings, cellars, some pasturage, and fine ranges of forage in and around Shippensburg were proving available. The Commissioner was making prudent arrangements for the acquisition, distribution, preservation, and protection of provisions. The handicaps and the capacities of the countryside were being properly estimated. Pork and flour to sufficient amounts were in prospect, and fodder for the beasts that should transport these in eventual wagon trains. The £4,000 from the General was being wisely dispensed.

With a grateful heart, Richard Peters could endorse the spirit of the public fast, which Governor Morris proclaimed for Thursday, June 19, to be observed in the province and counties under his government. The Secretary regarded it as entirely right "to keep alive among the people a just sense of their dependence on the Providence of Almighty God." He felt it important "to remind them of the intimate connection between the Divine favor and public happiness, between national calamity and national vice." He believed it right for the people "in all their just undertakings to address themselves for aid and direction to the Supreme Lord of the Universe." On the brink of their dangerous war, he fervently wished them to beseech God's infinite mercies and intercession of His Blessed Son.

But all the while that he meditated as a gentleman upon the urbanites of well-bred companionship or as a Christian upon the uses and the value of religion, Richard Peters retained impressions of the General's camp at Will's Creek. He remembered Braddock's indifference to Indian scouts, the predilection of baser ones of his officers for Indians' wives, the boasts of the talkative Commander, and some few asides of the leader's subordinates. He hoped rather than trusted that the vauntings would be made good. Mr. Peters was not himself sure that Braddock would take Fort Duquesne in two or three days, then proceed at once to Niagara, take the French fort there, and get on from there to seize Frontenac ere the summer's campaign would be over. Ben Franklin might be altogether correct in saying that the General talked a little too much.

June of 1755 moved into July. Provost William Smith was full of information on the Academy at the beginning of the new month. He talked to Mr. Peters about how far £400 received from the Venerable Society was extending

Aftermath of Defeat

education in the province. Fourteen communities in new towns and counties from Easton to Reading, to Tulpehocken, to York, to Lancaster, to Chester were reaping the advantages of culture for boys and girls. A new additional charter was being arranged with Mr. Penn by Mr. Smith for the Earent institution of learning, and more dependable financial schemes for a sinking fund were being established. Governor Morris was considerably more absorbed, as was proper—despite the formal address of welcome which had greeted him from the Academy in November 1754 and advised him that a chief glory of his administration would be "to protect the infancy of science" there—in the material affairs of the province. Letters from the frontiers were not all of them assuring. There were reports of six settlers at the Little Meadows slain by Indians, claims that Braddock, who had left Fort Cumberland on June 10 with provisions for only thirty days, had already got on to the Great Meadows and was approaching the French fort, statements that Captain Hogg's company, sent by the General to protect James Burd's road-builders, was being made futile by lack of food and a swelling number of deserters. Edward Shippen of Lancaster was having problems with pasture for cattle and wage rates for drovers and wagoners. Robert Hunter Morris concluded he might be more useful to Pennsylvania for a time in the back parts of the province than in Philadelphia. He despatched official letters to the Secretary of State in England, to Mr. Thomas Penn, to divers colonial governors, and the General of His Majesty's Army. In the second week of July, he parted from Secretary Peters and set off westward, and on the 14th, was in Carlisle.

From that Cumberland County seat on that date, he forwarded an answer to a letter of June 30 from Braddock. He wrote regretfully of new interruptions that had come to Mr. Burd's road building: several wagoners carrying supplies to that engineer's workmen had been killed by Indians, thirty of Mr. Burd's men had, for the want of arms, left the enterprise at Allegheny Mountain. He wrote hopefully, however, of the new roads being presently brought near the Great Crossing, and he was planning to send by it a parcel of oxen and as much pork and flour as he could find wagons to carry. He promised he would stay "in this part of the province, where he came to forward and secure the magazine, till that should be done." He did not know that he was addressing a letter to a General who had died one day earlier or that on July 9, Braddock had lost a disastrous and unaccountable battle.

Indeed, it took a full week for news of the debacle in the forest beyond the two fords of Monongahela to reach Philadelphia. Then, it came by way of Annapolis and Governor Horatio Sharpe of Maryland. On Friday afternoon of the 18th, the Provincial Council of Pennsylvania sat together considering that executive's letter and its fateful enclosure. This was a tiny missive from Colonel James Innes, despatched from Fort Cumberland on the 11th:

> I have this moment received the most melancholy news of the defeat of our troops, the General killed, and numbers of our officers, our whole artillery taken. In short, the account I have received is so very bad that, as please God, I intend to make a stand here, 'tis highly necessary to raise the militia everywhere to defend the frontiers.

Mr. Secretary Peters read with his colleagues and at once realized his official function: he must transmit the grievous intelligence to the northern and eastern provinces. Dating his letter as of "Five o'clock, P. M., July 18th," he wrote to Governor De Lancey of New York with a cool but intense brevity:

> Sir
>
> We have, in the absence of Governor Morris, who is over Susquehanna, received the melancholy news of the defeat of General Braddock. It is contained in a small bit of paper despatched by Col. Innes from Fort Cumberland at Will's Creek and was forwarded by Gov. Sharpe. It speaks for itself and needs no comment, and you will, no doubt, communicate it to the Generals and Admirals and Governors on the Continent with all possible expedition.
>
> Your Honor's, etc.
> RICHARD PETERS,
> Clerk of the Council
>
> P.S. It is not an hour since the news arrived, and no other particulars are come to the knowledge of the Council.

The Secretary of Pennsylvania had, in fact, become the messenger of catastrophe, and for the rest of the summer of 1755, he was to be its archivist.

His personal papers and the Council Books alike filled up with its annals, and his private records were of one tone with his official entries. He received letters, he read letters, and he made transcripts in his hand of depositions and memoranda. One account reaching him mitigated, another magnified the extent of the defeat.

One early informant spoke initially of "the most shocking blow ever English troops received," told of the General's march within seven miles of Fort Duquesne with fifteen hundred men well equipped and a very fine train of artillery, explained that Colonel Dunbar had been left behind with almost half the troops with orders to bring up wagons with tired horses and to stop until the horses had recruited a little. He narrated a defeat by three hundred Canadians and Indians, the death of Sir Peter Halkett and most of his best officers, the dangerous wounding of the General and Sir John St. Clair, the loss of the artillery train, all provisions, baggage, and ammunition, and the fact of the retreat of the second division "very little strengthened by the remains of the first."

A second writer "on good authority from the forces" believed that the General was not killed, as reported at first, but was wounded in the body, although not mortally. He vouchsafed Braddock had had three horses killed under him, that Captain Orme, aide-de-camp, was wounded in the thigh, Sir Peter Halkett and Secretary Shirley both killed, and that all the artillery was taken, and the whole division "put to the rout by a few Indians."

In Governor Morris's absence from Philadelphia, Secretary Peters perused a letter from Colonel Thomas Dunbar, posted from his camp near the Great Crossing on July 16. That communication acknowledged the Colonel's receiving of the Governor's letters to the General and, because of Braddock's and Sir Peter Halkett's deaths, his opening of them as next in command. It recounted briefly the engagement with the French near Turtle Creek, six miles from Fort Duquesne, and the fact of defeat. It explained that the remnants of Braddock's force had joined the writer at four miles distance from the battle, that Colonel Dunbar now had with him three hundred wounded officers and soldiers. It announced the new Commander's intentions.

He was going to leave the wounded at Fort Cumberland with the Independent Company to garrison them. He designed to send the members of the Virginia Company home to their respective provinces. He was instructing Captain Hogg, defender of the new road, to retire immediately. As General Braddock had intended to quarter his two regiments in Philadelphia during the coming winter, he was now on the march for that destination. Indeed, he begged Governor Morris to be so good as to provide quarters for about a hundred officers—and, he believed, twelve hundred men. A hospital would be absolutely necessary, he added, as if by way of reminder.

Richard Peters realized that he was not reading the letter of a particularly valiant soldier. Nor was his smile altogether a pleased one as he noted the last sentence of the document: "I can't say when I shall have an opportunity of kissing your hand, but it shall be as soon as my situation will permit." Neither was the Secretary very sympathetic to the Colonel when he read from Dunbar's postscript to Morris: "I never underwent such hardships as of late."

A letter from Robert Hunter Morris in Carlisle, which reached Mr. Peters at much the same time, related misgiving but exhibited considerably more mettle. The Governor was trying to sift facts from rumors on the battle beyond Monongahela. Three frightened wagoners had struggled into the frontier town with diverse narratives to offer. It was averred by one that Braddock had not been killed instantly but been wounded, put into a wagon, and borne away only to be cruelly butchered later by a party of Indians with their hatchets. Another reported that Halkett and Orme were both killed, that the military chest and all the artillery had been taken, and that scarce a hundred of the General's advance party had escaped. Governor Morris would not accept as authentic the tale of a third wagoner of the panic that had seized upon Dunbar's camp on the news of the defeat. Fortunately, an express from the Potomac reached him just as he had concluded his investigation of the wagon men. According to it, "Our army was beat and the artillery taken, but the General and the rest of the army were making a good retreat."

So the Governor was awaiting clearer and possibly better news—an account from Braddock himself or, in the event of that leader's death, from the commanding officer who survived. He was, however, alert in Carlisle, steadying the morale of the back inhabitants, helping the townsmen to form themselves into bodies for their common defense, and making them a little more regular by issuing commissions. He had, too, engaged two trusty Indians to keep the news of the defeat secret, if the news should prove true, and to fleet with the message of it to General Shirley in New York as soon as facts could be determined. Meantime, the Governor instructed Mr. Peters to notify members of the Assembly that they were to convene on Wednesday next in Philadelphia and that he would be in the city by that time.

Before Mr. Morris returned, the Secretary posted other more detailed accounts of the disaster to General Shirley and Governor De Lancey, written in the light of the several relations he had received, and, within a few more days, the Governor of Pennsylvania and Mr. Peters had their clearest report of the catastrophe direct from Robert Orme. That aide-de-camp phrased himself with the coherence and the candor of a gentleman, if not with the unbeatable resolution of a soldier. His two friends in Philadelphia remembered that his words, put down on paper for him by Captain Dobson, came from a man who was racked by suffering in body and mind.

He was extremely ill in bed with a wound in his thigh, but he feared that every officer whose business it would have been to inform the governments of the colonies had been either killed or wounded. The distressful situation of those who survived had made it impossible until now to send full a relation.

> On the 9th [he said], we passed and repassed the Monongahela, by advancing first a party of 300 men, which was immediately followed by another 200. The General, with the column of Artillery, the baggage, and the main body of the army, passed the river the last time about one o'clock. As soon as the whole had got on the Fort side of the Monongahela, we heard a very heavy and quick fire in our front. Immediately we advanced in order to sustain them, but the detachment of the 200 and 300 men gave way and fell back upon us. This caused such confusion and struck so great a panic among our men that afterwards no military expedient could be made use of. The men were so extremely deaf to the exhortations of the General and their officers that they fired in the most irregular manner all their ammunition, and then ran off, leaving to the enemy the artillery, ammunition, provisions, and baggage. Nor could they be persuaded to stop till they got as far as Guest's Plantation—and there only in part, for many of them proceeded as far as Colonel Dunbar's party, who lay six miles on this side of the river.
>
> The officers were absolutely sacrificed by their unparalleled good behavior, advancing sometimes in bodies and sometimes separately, hoping by such example to engage the soldiers to follow them, but to no purpose. The General had five horses killed under him and at last received a wound through his right arm into his lungs of which he died on the 13th instant. Poor Shirley was shot through the head. Captain Morris was wounded. Mr. Washington had two horses shot under him and his clothes shot through in several places, behaving the whole time with the greatest courage and resolution. Sir Peter Halkett was killed on the spot, Colonel Burton and Sir John St. Clair were wounded.

Having got so far in his narrative the invalid aide-de-camp resumed earlier details of the campaign:

> Upon our proceeding with the whole convoy to the Little Meadows, it was found impracticable to advance in full force. The General therefore advanced with twelve hundred men, and the necessary artillery,

ammunition, and provision, leaving the main body of the convoy under the command of Colonel Dunbar with orders to join him as soon as possible. In this manner we proceeded with safety and expedition till the fatal day I have just related. And happy it was that this disposition was made, otherwise the whole must either have starved or fallen into the hands of the enemy, as numbers would have been of no service to us, and our provisions been all lost.

Then Captain Orme explained the consequences of the defeat. The horses of the beaten vanguard were fallen or taken, and those left were extremely weak. Many carriages were wanted for the wounded men. It was necessary to destroy the ammunition and superfluous part of the provisions left in Colonel Dunbar's convoy, lest they fall into the hands of the enemy. With the artillery all lost and the troops weakened by deaths, wounds, and sickness, it was impossible to make further attempts, and Colonel Dunbar was returning to Fon Cumberland with everything he was able to bring up with him. The aide-de-camp was forwarding as full a list as he could obtain of wounded and killed officers and men. He believed that five hundred more than the number it embraced had also been lost by injuries and death. By the particular disposition of the French and the Indians, it had been impossible to judge what numbers they had had in the field on that day of disaster.

Finally, the patient at Fort Cumberland broached his plans. He would remain where he was until he could be removed to Philadelphia. Thence, he would proceed to England. Governor Morris might direct commands to him in camp. He requested the Governor to hire a house or lodging for him in the city and for wounded Colonel Burton and the Governor's kinsman, Captain Roger Morris. Last of all, Robert Orme sent his compliments to Mr. Peters.

To the end, his was a gracious, if not a heroic, narration.

During the last week of July, to supplement it and to piece out further for Secretary Peters the dismal story of the battle, came other letters. Commissary Charles Swaine twice wrote brisk and cogent accounts. In the first, of July 19, he said:

> They were unexpectedly attacked ascending a shelving hill. Polston and some few were shot, but the enemy were not seen. This caused some confusion, and they immediately repaired to the cannon and drew up the people twenty deep, fired in platoons, but could see nothing to fire at, the enemy never appearing, but firing from the bush and retreating

as they discharged. Croghan, Montour, and Washington applied to have the command and let the men spread. But Braddock would not consent. The General had two horses shot under him and a third wounded. He also was wounded and put into a wagon.

In his second, from Shippensburg on the 25th, Mr. Swaine wrote of Dunbar's being now chief in command and that he was for repairing to winter quarters in Philadelphia. He commented: "What adds to the misfortune of the defeat is that the General's instructions and all of his papers are taken." He explained that there was squabbling at Fort Cumberland. In the great differences among the officers there, Colonel Dunbar was complimenting "Captain Orme with the name of General Orme." He believed the whole army was "intending" for Philadelphia. If that intention was carried out, he predicted, "the army once passed, the whole people will also come in, leaving behind all their grain and their household stuff." He requested, therefore, that Dunbar be instructed to quarter part of his troops in Shippensburg to keep some defense on the frontiers against the French and the Indians.

A letter of the same date and from the same town concluded for the Governor and Mr. Peters the history of the new provincial road over the Alleghenies. James Burd wrote crisply, without a parade of spirit but with simple force. Having had news of the battle and instructions from Colonel Innes to retreat, he marched his provisions and cattle back eighteen miles to a house, begged for assistance there and horses to carry his supplies to Fort Cumberland, where they might serve in good stead, and was refused aid. So he employed seventeen of the carrying horses of his road-builders, loaded them with all the flour he could manage, and continued his march with them and Captain Hogg's company to the camp at Will's Creek. There, he remarked, he was told he had done right, and there he had waited for further instructions from Colonel Dunbar.

Other communications, and from loftier officialdom, had to be weighed in the last days of the fateful month by Robert Hunter Morris, the Secretary, and the Provincial Council. James De Lancey of New York was skeptical of Mr. Peters' hurried letter of July 16 and Colonel Innes' "scrap of paper" and expected—as he wrote Governor Phipps of Massachusetts, sending a copy to Pennsylvania—other reports to be better. He was of the opinion that the affair might perhaps make it necessary to reinforce the troops of the colonies under Major General Johnson. If regiments were recruited soon enough, they might win a campaign before October, before which month the French would have to recross their St. Lawrence ere it became impassable in the rough winter weather.

George Baynor, clerk to the Council in the same province, thought the thing to do was to keep Braddock's disaster a secret from the Six Nations and to have the American forces in New York take and secure Niagara.

Governor Belcher of New Jersey was more affable. He hoped that things with General Braddock might not be in as bad a posture as was feared. But he congratulated Mr. Peters on the promptitude of his messages. He was right to convey them, whether their news was good or bad, that everyone might form his judgment. He prayed that the wise and brave General might yet do the best services of his King and Country. He observed, "with much pleasure Mr. Secretary Peters' fidelity and great vigilance in the service of our common Royal Master."

Writing from Albany on July 23, General William Shirley offered neither implied reproach nor compliment to Mr. Peters. He doubted the full accuracy of Colonel Innes' brief account, knew from a letter sent him late in June by Braddock that only a picked force of eleven hundred men were to be marched in the van, trusted that Dunbar, then, had not joined the General at the time of the action. He announced that he was setting out the next day for Schenectady with the last division, but one of his forces, that he expected soon to be at Oswego or Niagara. He asked that the Pennsylvania Government order be transmitted to him at once any new intelligences coming from the General's camp.

Writing again on July 28, Mr. Baynor read the possibilities of a fortunate event in the disaster of Braddock. He hardly expected the colonies ever to unite themselves, but the defeat might soon bring the union of them before Parliament. Union effected through that body seemed to him the only means to save America. But, more than forecasts and eventual hopes, he suggested policy also. Virginia, Maryland, and Pennsylvania had men and money enough. Why should they not be fired with a generous resentment and animated to proper use of their strength? The way was now open almost to Fort Duquesne; a new train, "confined to a very few things," might be soon procured. At least Mr. Baynor would indulge himself in the hopes of a second attempt. Indeed, that clerical strategist saw farther than his nose. He knew that it was unwise to abandon the thought of taking the fort on the Ohio and to let the French detach part of their forces to Niagara. He declared it best to reduce the enemy's strength on the frontiers before their problems of supply compelled them to withdraw across the St. Lawrence into Canada. Moreover, he saw in his clear-sighted fashion other important military points. If Braddock's papers had been captured, the French had now the secret plans of the English to help them. If Braddock was dead, the command of His Majesty's Army in America devolved upon General Shirley.

Aftermath of Defeat

Mr. Peters read Mr. Baynor's sentiments with great interest. But he remembered that fact sometimes had little to do with sense and realized that the Governor and Council in Pennsylvania had both the Assembly and Colonel Thomas Dunbar to deal with. He knew, too, of military stores, unpurchased, undelivered, undeliverable in a season of desperation—and of provisions lost at Monongahela, of provisions, ammunition, and wagons destroyed at Dunbar's camp this side of the Great Meadows.

The Associators of Ben Franklin had disappeared. There was no militia in Pennsylvania. The back inhabitants of the province were critically without weapons or powder. From the frontiers began to sound voices now of anxious importunity, now of desperate alarm. Indians were slaying here and there, and massacres were more and more anticipated.

Mr. John Elder of the Presbyterian Meeting House in Paxton brought Mr. Peters a letter from John Harris reporting the flight of the settlers at Mahanoy on Penn's Creek down the Susquehanna past Harris' Ferry, and that good minister, in a few minutes of interview with the Secretary, told on the one hand how he and Mr. Harris were endeavoring to spirit the men of their community to defend themselves, and on the other of hopes of protection for all from the Government in Philadelphia. The Reverend Mr. Thomas Barton, Missionary for the Venerable Society at Huntington in York County, sent an urgent appeal for small arms for the men of his congregation, told of gathering folk to his own house to lay plans of self-defense for the flock, and described a pitiful situation. The poor back inhabitants whom he was serving were almost all of them weaponless. They had had neither locks nor bolts to their doors. "It would grieve any person that was not void of fellow—feeling to see those poor creatures, at the bark of a dog in the night or at the least noise, jump out of their beds in the utmost consternation—not being able to make the least resistance, but to rush at once into the arms of the most shocking and cruel death."

The needs of the back counties were imperative needs of rest, freedom from fear, mercy, and protection. The security of the whole province of the Penns was critically threatened. Yet, as Mr. Peters knew, the reconvened Assembly had met only to resume their quarrel with Governor Morris. They had doubled the amount which they were willing to raise for the King's use. They continued inveterately opposed to exempting the estates of the Proprietors. To tax those properties, as well as all others in Pennsylvania, they insisted was an inalienable privilege they possessed as free men. They would not forego it, Richard Peters sadly predicted, if their own houses were burned down over their heads and their infants slaughtered by Frenchmen or Indians. For, although they were willing now to admit the feasibility of a remunerated militia, they were resolved to surrender none of their vaunted liberties.

As July ended in political deadlock, the Secretary saw only one ray of light on the provincial horizon. Thomas Graeme contributed a suggestion in which Mr. Peters saw a solution toward which he could work. The gentle physician and master of Graeme Park expected no new measures of any promptitude from General Shirley. He knew the mettle of the Assembly. He knew that English law exempted the Penns from taxation in their province, and he knew the Proprietors would not abandon their prerogative. The thing to do was to have Mr. Peters and others advise a gift from the Family, perhaps double what a tax on their estates would amount to. Then the exigency could be got round, and money be found for the King's service. Moreover, Dr. Graeme's scheme "would take the thorn out" of Mr. Peters' foot and place it in shoes where it more properly belonged and where the writer "should see it with pleasure." He was writing, he remarked, strictly *entre nous,* and he hoped he could have the Secretary as his guest on Friday or Saturday night to talk matters over.

Richard Peters did not remain silent upon the subject of the physician's proposal with the persons most concerned by it. He continued to be anxious in August. The Governor and the Assembly remained in dispute and burdened him much secretarily with their debate. It seemed more definite, too, that Thomas Dunbar would retreat all the way to Philadelphia in another month. Petitions and laments from the back inhabitants were increasingly importunate. Richard Peters thought it a malign diversion to have to read a confidential letter that he received from John Rutherford of Annapolis and kept among his effects. The first paragraph of that Maryland official's communication bespoke its quality:

> I was resolved not to write to anybody on the subject of our scandalous, and worse management, which exposed us to it. But the public good obliges me to give you a few hints without respect of persons that will easily explain the whole. Sir Peter Halkett had no sooner calmly and regularly put all in good order at Will's Creek than the General arrived and spent the month idly, whoring and feasting till our men debauched with rum. No more order or discipline. Thus we marched out, the Knight swearing in the van, the General cursing and bullying in the center, and their whores bringing up the rear. What need I to say more to you but that, to crown all, he divided his army, leaving us who were with Colonel Dunbar 40 miles behind him, and kept advancing, though he had information of the French reinforcements arriving at the Fort.

From the height of presumption, he fell into the deepest despair and fled; he and his managers, though no one pursued, in fear of scalping every minute—until they arrived at Dunbar's camp, where the General lived long enough until he or those who used his name scandalously destroyed prodigious quantity of powder, balls, cowhorn shells, in short, most all the train stores, hospital stores, heaps of wagons, and provisions.

Presently, Captain Rutherford remarked unctuously that he needed to add no more, then switched into praise of Colonel Dunbar and his prudence and management, then insinuated that he was not writing to Governor Morris, lest he offend him by railing "at his Tunbridge acquaintance."

Mr. Peters had his memories of conditions in headquarters at Will's Creek. Doubts and suspicions were moods which often clung to his mind. He had not forgotten poor young Mr. William Shirley and his thoughts on the "G-----." He studied the clandestine letter of the aspersive gentleman from Lord Baltimore's province. He was not unimaginative about that human and mortal phase of experience, which sums up in the Latin *Sic transit gloria mundi*. He wondered. Was it not possible that John Rutherford was lying about both General Edward Braddock and Colonel Thomas Dunbar? Did the slur "Tunbridge acquaintance" refer to the dead Commander or to Governor Morris' friend, Robert Orme?

XV

Moods in a Province

The Autumn of 1755 was not a universally happy one in Philadelphia. Merchants and wealthier citizens shook their heads over Braddock's defeat and resented with more active anger the behavior of Colonel Thomas Dunbar, who by September had retreated the entire way to the city and in that month busily begun recruiting his depleted regiment from their scapegrace apprentices and runaway indentured servants. Ben Franklin was disturbed by demands of reimbursement for wagons bought from folk all over the province at his behest and lost or destroyed in the Great Meadows before the £800 that the General had allowed him for them could be stretched to cover the cost of even wages and hire for their owners. Robert Hunter Morris was harassed not only by the obstinacy of his Assembly but by the truculence of Dunbar, now retorting to the protests of the burghers of Philadelphia, complaining to the Governor about the polluted food being supplied to his soldiers. The commoners were troubled no less by the Assembly's refusal to raise funds for their defense without gaining a new prerogative to tax the Penns than by the accounts of horrors on the frontiers which threatened to penetrate even to the Delaware. Richard Peters remembered disagreeably the wild mob which had formed on the afternoon of July 18, soon as the dismal news of the rout before Fort Duquesne had reached the city, and thronged toward Willing's Alley to destroy "the Roman Catholics' Mass House" until peaceable Quakers had persuaded them that all religions had privilege of existence in Pennsylvania, he meditated gravely upon the frequent promises of violence in the town, and the numerous letters from the western counties which were swelling his secretarial rolls.

The Receiver-General, Mr. Richard Hockley, was distressed by another problem, which, inasmuch as it was of concern to the Family, bore relations also to the province. On October 5, in fact, he sat writing to the older Proprietor. He began his letter diplomatically, congratulating Thomas Penn on the birth of another son in early July—a happy event, as it were, on the very threshold of disaster. But he moved promptly to his real subject, which was Mr. John Penn, on whom his friend at Braywick had commanded him to be explicit.

The truths of Mr. Penn's nephew's conduct were sad. Although the writer had a tenderness for that young man "as a branch of your Family," the duty that Richard Hockley owed to the Proprietor required him to be candid. The anxious uncle, he declared, did not need to be under the least apprehension that Richard Penn's son was making remittances to Mrs. Maria Cox in England. Indeed, the youth, if he had to speak of that female at all, now called her "with great emotion and indignation the woman." But Mr. John Penn was undoubtedly spending a great deal of money. He had had £1,600 from the Receiver-General, spent he did not know how, and he was, according to his uncle, Mr. Lynford Lardner, £300 in debt.

The dutiful writer did not think that Mr. John Penn had been gaming. But the saddest truth of all was that he had become the unfortunate dupe of an insinuating Italian musician, a fellow of debauched principles. Common rumor was not only that Mr. Penn paid the man's house rent and found him his necessaries but that he spent his time at his house until two or three in the morning in quite unsuitable company. Moreover, the fellow was constantly tagging after him. Mr. Lardner thought the Italian had got most of the things he had brought from England. The young man's servant, the faithful creature Pierre, had wished again and again that Mr. Thomas Penn were in Philadelphia for his master's sake, for Mr. John hardly knew one piece of gold from another and let all money slip through his fingers.

Yet Richard Hockley thought there were extenuating circumstances. Mr. Penn had not been advantageously situated. Governor James Hamilton's reservedness and his devotion to reading had irked the Proprietor's nephew, "the former at his books and John Penn at his violin in his chamber for hours together." Governor Morris' turn for gaiety and fondness for sitting up late suited the young man better but did him no benefit. In sum, the youth was very unhappy. His travels on the Continent had given him a distaste for both America and England. Apparently, the only thing to do for him was what Mr. Thomas Penn was doing—summoning his brother Richard's son home.

Mr. Hockley sent his letter to England, and some seven weeks later, toward the end of November, it was known to him in Pennsylvania and to Secretary Peters and Governor Morris that Mr. Thomas Penn had been busy at Braywick on October 4, 1755, composing an important triad of letters. Indeed, on that date, he had written information first to Mr. Peters, then to his Lieutenant Governor, then to his Receiver-General—to the effect that the Proprietors were making a gift of £5,000 to be paid by Mr. Hockley out of arrears in their quit-rents, to whatever committee on disbursement the Assembly of the Province should appoint, and then to be used for the defense of the colony. Mr. Richard Peters had the satisfaction of knowing in November that Dr. Thomas Graeme's hint had worked; however "freely" the present of the Penns was announced. Robert Hunter Morris had to his advantage a sudden new means of reconciling the Assembly. The Receiver-General could respond with the money of the Proprietors to a more warrantable use of funds than the maintenance of Mr. John Penn's violin and his Italian friend. The future of a province could be more adequately provided for.

The later autumn in official Philadelphia and the beginning of winter were more happy than had been the month of September. The Assembly proved responsive at once to Thomas and Richard Penn's generosity and forewent a political principle without further demur. Fifty thousand pounds, to be raised by a tax on properties, exclusive of the Proprietary estates, were voted, and plans could be laid for restoring the security of Pennsylvania. Mr. Franklin could entertain rosier hopes of having some allowances for meeting obligations on the lost and troublesome wagons come to him from His Majesty's new Commander-in-Chief in America, General William Shirley. Citizens of Philadelphia could reason that better times were in store for the province. News of General William Johnson's victory over Dieskau at Lake George had come to Pennsylvania, and that blow to the French meant that invasion of the northern colonies by the enemy had no longer to be feared. The £50,000 voted by the Assembly and the £5,000 gift of the Penns were earnest of organization of, and support for, militia in 1756 and a program of fort-building to protect the back inhabitants. There were signs, too, of stiffened authority in the executive branch of the Provincial Government.

Mr. Secretary Peters, appalled rather than bewildered by the stories of massacred families and houses and harvests burned, could prepare to be as coolly assiduous as ever in the year at hand in the interest of Pennsylvania and the Proprietors. He began the labors of 1756 with energy.

In January, with Governor Robert Hunter Morris, Mr. James Hamilton of Bush Hill, other notables from Philadelphia, and Conrad Weiser, he sat in council with Six Nation Indians at John Harris' Ferry in Paxton and later in the same month beyond Susquehanna at Carlisle. In April, back in the capital, he affixed his signature to Governor Morris' proclamation of war upon the Delawares, once the allies of William Penn but many of them of late years renegades who had disregarded their duty of obedience to their uncles, the Six Nations, and gone over to the French interest. Having made official with the seal of the province a document of the state that offered bounties for the scalps of enemy Delawares, male and female, twelve years of age and over, he added to it as automatically as became his office: "God save the King." Better to serve the colony now by letting the back inhabitants have their reprisals than to listen to the pleas of the Friendly Association, latterly formed by the aides of Israel Pemberton and still offering the ubiquitous warnings of the Quakers against sowing and reaping with the sword. If marauding Indians were to go so far as to fall on burial processions—as they did in the summer of 1756 at Salisbury Plains on Conococheague—to seize corpses away from Christian mourners and scalp both corpses and living mourners, it was best to arm frontiersmen for both protection and revenge. So, if Mr. Peters was as competent as ever, during months of crisis, in making up accounts of surveying expeditions and rendering them with proper charges for ferriage, lodgings, dinners, stabling of horses, and the like—he could in September at least let himself, tender as he always was to missionaries of the Anglican Church, romance on the valor of one pastor militant. To Thomas Penn, he enclosed copies of letters that he had received from two apostles in the field, serving the Venerable Society in foreign parts, and fervidly he penned his praises of the author of one of these:

> But Mr. Barton, in a more particular manner, deserves the commendations of all lovers of the Country, for he has since November last put himself at the head of his congregations and marched either by night or day on every alarm. Had others imitated his example, Cumberland County would not have wanted men enough to defend it, nor has he done anything in the military way but what has increased his character for piety and a sincerely religious man and zealous minister. In short, Sir, he is a most worthy, active, and serviceable pastor and missionary, and as such, please mention him to the Society.

But the second half of the year 1756 was to contain little rapture for the individual experience of Richard Peters. His elevation to be the President of the Board of Trustees of the College of Philadelphia was an honor that compensated his scholarly tastes, but it did not lessen his responsibilities or teach him that perfect moderation in all things could be his only secure defense against the successor of Robert Hunter Morris. In Governor William Denny, who in August succeeded the resigned chief executive of Pennsylvania, he was to meet effective foil to his equanimity, and the armor of his peace went down before the eccentricities of the new lieutenant of the Penns.

Other obstacles to composure were to loom in the figure of "one Teedyuscung," a noted Delaware Indian and the author of all the attacks on the settlements east of the Susquehanna, in the machinations of the Quakers all too sympathetic to the claims of the Indians that they had been cheated in land transactions by the Proprietaries, and in the person of the now implacable Mr. Franklin.

Indeed, it was bitterly disappointing to have to contend all in one season with an imperious Indian "much on the Gascoon," an Assembly that was once more at odds with the Government in the matter of amounts to be raised by tax or excise to support the King's cause in America against the French and Indians, and a Governor who made indiscreet admissions to such opponents of the Proprietors as Isaac Norris and Ben Franklin. In August, he had the chagrin of writing to Thomas Penn in full about the affronted Delaware, whose "miff" was so great at the neglect he had had the year before in negotiations with the Six Nations that he could be appeased only by having the notables of Pennsylvania come on to Easton to treat appropriately with a potentate so rightly to be honored as himself. Off to the point of the conference, they had gone with £300 allowed them by the Assembly for expenses and a present, only to find Teedyuscung alternating between a drunken boastfulness that those who took sides with him would stand while the others fell and a tearful gratification with the goodness of the Governor of Pennsylvania and his people.

Lusty, rawboned, fifty years of age, the meteoric chieftain drank his three quarts or his gallon of rum a day; crudely, he responded to the ceremonies of welcome which the diplomats from Philadelphia, long trained in their deportment by Conrad Weiser, accorded him, impudently he kept them in the hollow of his hand. In a year when devastation and massacre were separating them from a completely tacit communication with the Six Nations, Governor Denny, the Council, and Secretary Peters did not dare risk refusal to treat with a braggart who declared that the Iroquois were waiting to determine what they should do until they heard from him the results of his mission with the Governor of Pennsylvania. These first overtures from Teedyuscung were only a preparatory fire. He would influence large numbers to come down later and effect a treaty. He was poor. He would need an abundance of wampum from the Philadelphians to effect his purpose with his ten allied Indian nations. The negotiators looked on helplessly at the raiment worn by Indian women in Teedyuscung's party—apparel made from Dutch tablecloths stolen from the massacred folk of Gnadenhiitten and Northampton County.

With considerable apprehension during the next month, back in the capital of the Penns, Mr. Peters kept an eye alike on the Executive and the Assembly. In mid-September, he was sent posthaste by Governor Denny to inform that body verbally that his superior's confidence and candor had been abused: the bill they had sent him would not be ratified. As there was no judge here between the Governor and the House, he would immediately transmit to His Majesty his reasons for his refusing to pass the act.

This abrupt denial had the transient effect of surprising and confounding the Assembly and was so far consoling to Mr. Peters. The proposed excise of four pence a gallon on retailed spirits to be applied for twenty years and to raise £60,000 had been obviated. But a week later, after an abundance of altercations and Mr. Denny's indiscretion of admitting to Ben Franklin, the Speaker of the House, and to Mr. Norris, that the Governor, by information had of Mr. Penn in England, might extend for five years the tenor of the recent Act of Parliament for the Eastern Colonies in the raising of subsidies in Pennsylvania, the Secretary was again made anxious. The passing of an act for striking £30,000 in bills of credit to be sunk by the usual excise of four pence a gallon on retailed liquors, applicable for five more years than Richard Peters approved—ten years to come—had ruined the chances of an election in October favorable to the Proprietors. Messrs. Hamilton, Allen, and Chew went into conference with the relentless Franklin, and a ticket of candidates was agreed upon for Philadelphia. But the ticket was "extremely disagreeable to the town in general," and the servant of Thomas Penn feared what the Quakers might do to it if, in their public meeting, they determined to participate in the voting.

The election that followed more than revealed that Richard Peters' concern was justified. Such exemplary contestants as Messrs. Coleman, Duche, and Parlin went down to defeat, and for the County of Philadelphia were returned a set of the "veriest partisans against the Proprietaries and moderate measures as could be picked out of this town." Their names would confirm the interpretation of Mr. Penn: "Isaac Norris, Joseph Fox, Thomas Leech, John Hughes, Daniel Roberdeau, one Dr. Byrne, an insolvent, and Mr. Galloway, a young noisy Quaker member of the law." At Chester, too, results had been distressing. All but three of the men returned there were Quakers, and the excepted three were one Presbyterian and two Churchmen "of no sense or weight." Everything indeed culminated sadly in October for the Provincial Secretary, and his tone in letters to his friend and master in England assumed a tone of desperation that they had never before evinced. On the second, he wrote:

I wish I could suppress the information, but truth and justice will not conceal from you that the hatred of and opposition to the Proprietaries increases and will be irretrievably fixed by this election. The Quaker plot is, as I imagine, to show the Ministry that it is not the Society of Quakers but the Proprietary instructions that obstruct the King's business. I know not what to say about the Governor. He sometimes talks in a sensible manner so indifferently as to the Proprietors and expresses such unfavorable sentiments of their measures and particularly the unseasonableness of trying for the appropriation of the public money by act of Legislature that I am at my wit's end with respect to his future conduct. He is a trifler, weak of body, peevish and averse to business-and, if I am not mistaken, extremely near, if not a lover of money. I know him not enough to pronounce positively about him, but I see so little of judgment, and difficulty of access, and such a dread of visits, though from men of influence and character, so little inquiry into the nature of the matter before him and such a fear of disobliging the Assembly that it does not appear to me that your affairs will be put upon a good issue in his administration.

But to crown the sorrows of his melancholy epistle, Mr. Peters had another item of news for Thomas Penn on that arid early October day. Just before Governor Denny had set out for Carlisle with Mr. Hamilton and Mr. Franklin to plan at that frontier town another expedition against the Indians west of the Susquehanna, a letter had been handed to the Executive, brought by express from Lord Loudoun. It was a communication of the most extraordinary nature ever written to a chief administrator. In it, Secretary Peters discerned the dictation of Mr. Pownall, close confederate to Ben Franklin. In effect, it informed Mr. Denny of a change in state policy for the colonies; presently, authority to treat separately with the Indians would be taken from the several provinces in America, and all such business be transacted directly by an agent of the King. As he enclosed a copy of the document to Thomas Penn, the anxious Clerk repined: "If Indian affairs are to be taken out of the hands of the Government so as neither to suffer the Governor to confer nor treat with the Indians, all our friendly Indians will turn against us, and we shall have a most lamentable winter." Lord Loudoun, he believed, could not, would not, spare Pennsylvania either men or time to help. It was as though an ominous handwriting on the wall was threatening the Family of the Penns in England. Mr. Peters did not quite dare to think or to express himself fully.

Four weeks later, he became more candid in phrasing his apprehensions. "Whilst Mr. Pownall has an influence with Lord Loudoun or the Earl of Halifax, let this poor province do what it will," he wrote, "it will be blamed, and the warmest endeavors be used to dislodge the Proprietary Family." He hoped against hope that that gentleman might not prove as bad as the report made him, but Thomas Pownall and Ben Franklin were exchanging letters every post, and it was well for Mr. Penn to have an *eclaircissement* upon the subject with Lord Halifax and not be blind to the something more substantial than the promises and thanks which he suspected Israel Pemberton and other Quakers were to employ to abet the machinations of the two confederates. Franklin's passions against Mr. Penn were in the extreme, the Secretary averred, and that malcontent was the more angry for having the less reason for his grievance. The Proprietor would do well, should Mr. Franklin come to England, to take measures to make the man show an open hand and then, if possible, disappoint or convert him. If he did come, Mr. Hamilton would plan to accompany him, acting as a foil to his scheming. Only the jealousy of the Speaker of the Assembly would avail now to keep Franklin in Philadelphia.

The end of October indeed brought little comfort to Mr. Peters. He was generous enough to admit that the Governor's visit to Carlisle had borne some fruit. On his return, that dignitary had engaged an engineer to investigate the condition of the township forts among the back inhabitants and now had a full account of the necessities for improvement or reconstruction at all of them. But Mr. Denny, generally ignorant of business and difficult to approach, cross, and peevish, continued to require a dancing attendance of the Secretary to the Province and, much to his revulsion, would do nothing without him. Moreover, Teedyuscung had once more loomed up at Easton, and, an additional cause for apprehension, Mr. Peters found that in Northampton County, the Moravians were now dabbling both in an election and Indian affairs as the irrepressible Quakers had long before them had done. His only solace as the month closed was the prospect of going off presently with the surveyor, Mr. Edmund Physick, to collect the abundance that was due the Penns in New London Township. They were to have that earnest of gain, he reasoned, when three months of drouth in the province had stopped the mills, and other farmers everywhere were finding it hard to convert their stock into ready money.

November was as little gratifying. Governor Denny concluded upon a second conference with Teedyuscung and started for Easton with a diminished escort, only one member of the Council choosing to attend him and some representatives, including the Speaker, Ben Franklin, from the Assembly, and two military men. Mr. Hamilton, the Secretary insinuated, stayed away not so much by reason of the indisposition which he pleaded as of his dislike for the Governor's pettishness. Other folk were notable in their absence because they would not form themselves into an uninvited entourage, for the ungracious Mr. Denny would not consent to invite anyone whose official connection was not immediate. Yet still more embarrassing than the lack of the best men of Philadelphia from the excursion was the press of Quakers who attended, with Israel Pemberton leading—obstructionists all of them and designing deliberately Mr. Peters was confident, to get the Indians to complain of injustices done them by the Proprietors.

But, chagrined as Richard Peters was by the course of affairs in 1756, he was blind to really very few of them.

Little as he liked either Governor Denny or Teedyuscung, he kept his eyes open. He beheld with interest the minority of Six Nation Indians, the few Shawnees and Mohicans and the group of nondescript Jersey Indians who arrived in the potentate's train, an insignificant band that numbered not above forty in all, and he observed how small was the increase which joined these coming with Jo Peepy and Nicodemus from Bethlehem. But in their fewness, he saw no disdainful reason for not treating with them. They were certainly of the men who had caused the first attacks upon the province and must be reckoned with as powers. As long as they were Indians into whose minds notions about land claims might be put by the Quakers, they must be regarded as equal nations. He was glad, then, to note the now dignified behavior of Teedyuscung, to estimate the abilities of that leader to keep the Indian "riff-raff" gathered at Diahogo from going over further to the French and doing other mischief on the frontiers to counsel measures which would keep the Delawares in line again with the Six Nations. He was relieved to see at the end of the conference that the two great rocks that might have hurt had been avoided: Pennsylvania had not made a particular and separate peace, and no act had been committed contrary to His Majesty's new appointment of Sir William Johnson to be sole agent in Indian affairs. All these points he concurred in or influenced with his usual shrewdness. If unhappiness remained, it must be borne with a courageous insight.

It did, of course, remain. At Easton and broad in the province, the names of the Proprietors continued to be much impugned. The Indians complained of the sales of lands into which they declared they had been deceived. Though they would not insist that the war upon the English had come by reason of fraudulent transactions at the Forks of the Delaware, they expressly observed that that blow had come from them quicker and harder because of misunderstandings arisen there. The result of that declaration was that the Quaker party triumphed, shifting off from themselves—as Richard Peters wrote to Thomas Penn—the cause of the war and bloodshed by their refusal to support taxes for military defense and attributing it to the Proprietaries.

For such malignity, Mr. Peters could compensate himself only by writing at the utmost length to explain to Thomas Penn how unjust were the accusations that, in 1737, the boundaries had been unfairly determined. He had no memory of the Proprietors' getting strong and able people for the purpose, or of their running instead of walking out the lines or of their exceeding the natural day and a half allowed in the earlier deeds of purchase. He was sure that a walk moderately gone for a day and a half from the place of beginning would have carried a man to the foot of the Kittochtinny Hills. Moreover, the Delawares had had no right or pretensions in 1742 to the lands which they were now claiming, those having been sold as early as 1700 by Orytagh and other lawful owners and again to the Proprietors in 1736 by the Six Nations. It had been an error, perhaps, that the matter of the Walking Purchase of lands from Neshaminy Creek to beyond the Blue Hills had not been fully explained to the Six Nations in 1742. But certainly, Mr. Peters knew of no unfairness in Benjamin Eastburn's draught of its sixty-mile west and northwest line. And whether or no it occurred to him to inquire if a man walking moderately could walk sixty miles in a day and a half over hill and dale and two mountain ridges, he was convinced that not the Delawares, but the Six Nations, had reason for complaint if the surveyor had carried his line without due right beyond the limits of the mountains into Northampton County. Mr. Weiser might think—as he did—that when the purchase was made of the Six Nations in 1742 north of the Blue Hills, the Delawares were much neglected, and Mr. Peters might have transmitted that comment to Mr. Penn at the time—yet the fact remained that Mr. Nicholas Scull (who by chance was with Richard Peters in November 1756) had been present at the running of the line and avowed the walk had been strictly within the interval between sunrise and sunset at a fast walk, but never a run, on October 19, 1737, and the morning of the next day, Edward Marshall of Bucks County had done the walking, with five Indians at his side who left off indifferently at Bethlehem. Furthermore, Mr. Scull doubted Benjamin Eastbum's estimate of sixty miles and was certain the northwest line was not more than fifty miles in length. The wrong done in the Walking Purchase, in brief, Richard Peters regarded as a main fabrication of the Quakers. In essence, it was an invention to undermine the already much-undermined Proprietaries.

But perforce, he acquiesced when Governor Denny promised the Delaware chieftain his party should have satisfaction on the subject of the Walking Purchase provided that the next time they came down, they should bring with them the Indians who claimed they owned the lands at the Forks. Another visit, he apprehended, would result in more mischievous counsel from interlopers that the red men demand a large price. But to offset that emergency, the commissioners were already thinking of offering five hundred pounds, and Conrad Weiser had been directed to sound the Indians in the matter. For the present, that overture had only brought the flamboyant response from Teedyuscung that if mountains of gold were offered, he had no power to take it for land that belonged to others. In conclusion, Richard Peters hoped that Thomas Penn had copies of all the Indian deeds, particularly of the Release of the Delawares in August 1737, with its ratifications of all previous transactions. But the all-competent Secretary would take no chances of complicating problems by any omissions of his own, and he forwarded to the Proprietor a new and complete set of copies. His assiduity, if not his peace of mind, was once more perfected.

Finally, having got himself so far back toward the recovery of his spirits, he informed Mr. Penn of the "very sensible pleasure and the honor done me" in your kind manner of communicating the knowledge that Lady Juliana had had another increase of family. To that noble person, he sent his prayers and compliments. Her husband, he reminded the recipient of his letter, with so much new felicity at home, would be more able now to endure afflictions.

But his assurance that the swelling number of his offspring would arm the Proprietor with ample patience did not put the Secretary himself at full ease in 1757. The war between England and France dragged on, with its ineptitudes continuing in the American provinces, and politics in England and Philadelphia raged as always. In February, Richard Peters was anxious both about Dr. John Fothergill in London and Governor Denny in Pennsylvania. He was concerned that the eminent Quaker physician should have become the conduit pipe in England for conveying all the foolish and passionate scribble of Israel Pemberton. That meddler had been gleaning too much misinformation from weak and dishonest Indians like Moses Tittany (whom Conrad Weiser called "Moses Deedany") and Jo Peepy, two renegades who extracted from their fellows all manner of charges against the Proprietaries and retailed them to Israel, who swallowed all as sacred and posted his discoveries by the first vessel to his friend in England. There, the weight of the good physician's character sanctified a sort of correspondence by which Mr. Thomas Penn was "cut down, aspersed, and proved to be the cause of the defection of our Indians." At home, Mr. Peters could look only with misgiving upon an executive who frankly told the Secretary that the English Ministry was now commonly suspicious that the present Proprietor had cheated the Indians. He, Mr. Denny, had been warned by several great men at the time of his accepting the appointment to be Governor that all was not right, that, notwithstanding the Proprietors' declarations of having always been kind, they had abused the Delawares. Such an admission from a nominal superior was like a worm at the very seat of the bud. An administrator for the Penns ventured the opinion that "it would all come out some time or other"! Treason never had troubled a clerk more.

Yet again, efficiency remained with the Secretary. In the same month, he forwarded to Thomas Penn a report of wise additions made by the Governor to the minutes of the Council at Easton, recording the gift of more goods to the Indians than they had expected, a generosity which had had the greater effect of having been unsolicited. And in his letter, he set forth clearly a new plan of Conrad Weiser, already aired with Teedyuscung, to assign new lands to the Delawares at Juniata, Wyoming, or between Wyoming and Shamokin. This he begged Mr. Penn to consider well and to "send proper powers with full instructions." Then, having for a digression indulged sentiments upon "envenomed rancor in the infected spirits" of certain Assemblymen, including "B.F.," he wrote that Lord Loudoun was presently expected in Philadelphia to study the situation there with Governor and Assembly, and after that proceeded to a forthright account of the truth about Teedyuscung.

> You have a wrong notion [he remarked] of his Ten Nations and of the extent of his authority. It is, I believe, truly set forth by Newcastle in his report after he came from Sir William Johnson, which is copied and herewith sent. Teedyuscung is, in fact, a poor Jersey straggling Indian who went to Wyoming for trade and who, at the time the war broke out, thought himself neglected and that he might advance himself by hostilities. After he had committed the ravages, he began to be afraid of the English revenging their injuries on Wyoming and so advised the Indians, Delaware, Mohicans, Shawnees, and Nanticooks, together with some of each of the Six Nations then living on Susquehanna at Shamokin, Wyoming, Neskopecka, and thereabouts to fly their habitations, which they did, and afterwards settled in a body at Diahogo and there lived, making a considerable force of Indians. These he calls Ten Nations, and over these, he has power. Tohiccon, situate at the mouth of the Cayuga Branch in Latitude 41°: 45', within the Connecticut Claim, is the same

as Diahogo. Teedyuscung, I say, put himself at the head of these Indians, went to the Six Nations, and, on his return, pretended to be ordered and empowered by them to make a peace with Pennsylvania.

All that boasting, Mr. Peters reasoned within himself, could eventually be mined. But for the present, it must be tolerated—at least until means were discovered for discountenancing the Friendly Association, which Israel Pemberton and men of his like were now building up further with subscriptions from wealthy Quakers totaling to five or six thousand pounds! When the operations of that insidious group were disposed of, the Proprietary visage might once again shine in splendid honor.

Yet the truth was that, as the year 1757 drew to a close, the Quakers' faculty for slyness was not to be left unrivaled in the Province, for there was a diplomatic innuendo in a November letter of Mr. Secretary Peters, weightily sealed with the arms of Mr. Peters' family and addressed to Colonel Conrad Weiser of the new Pennsylvania militia, which could hardly have come from an innocent heart.

Mr. Weiser had grown elderly. The experienced interpreter had not been brilliant as a military officer. Executive eyes were on another personality to command the companies whose northwestern focus was on the Susquehanna at Shamokin, now protected by the new Fort Augusta built by Mr. James Burd. Under Mr. Peters' seal and his signature went to Mr. Weiser as inexplicable a message as was ever conveyed to a faithful servitor. On a return from Newcastle to Philadelphia, its author professed surprise that the conversation there was mostly upon the sad state of Colonel Weiser's battalion, and its author dilated quite fully on the variety of the surprising comment. It seemed that it was said that the Colonel's men were left to themselves; two or three were by themselves off in farmhouses, their captains were continuing to enlist men for more than their company quotas for three years, whereas they were keeping in service men who had enlisted for only one year and whom the Governor had ordered to be discharged. Other bad features reported were that, though several men were left without weapons, Colonel Weiser had fifty good ones in his own house and that the powder and lead were being suffered to remain at Easton and Reading instead of being at the advantage of the companies at their posts. Moreover, a number of old, unfit men had been enlisted, and, reputedly, the Colonel's company was worst of all handicapped by such enlistments. In short, Mr. Peters remarked he had learned that Conrad Weiser's officers were under no command. They did not scout or range. The battalion was almost useless.

So, Colonel Weiser's friends in Philadelphia were grieved and did not know what to say.

Yet other points the Secretary had to confide. It was reported that a man was kept in Weiser's house to make shoes and that these were sold to the rangers. It was even rumored that Conrad had grown into a great lover of money. There was, too, a matter of military punctilio which had not been carried out with the officers of the battalion. The captains had never been given explicit, clear enlisting or beating orders. The copies of instructions in such details had not been dispensed by their Colonel.

Mr. Peters could not help saying what had been said. He regretted that the Governor was so much displeased in the matter. He concluded warmly: "I am, Dear Sir, Your Affectionate 'Humble Servant, Richard Peters."

Conrad Weiser did not respond with any slyness; rather, he answered with spirit, and the Secretary could read no warmth in the reply. Nor did any apologetical sense run in its veins. The writer began directly. The complaints against him and his battalion, he informed Mr. Peters bluntly, had sprung either from malice or ignorance. He would not trouble the Secretary "with an answer to some of the charges." Colonel Weiser was unaware of men having been put into farmhouses, although—as Governor Denny had already been informed by their commanding officer—Captain Wetherholt's company had been distributed in the neighborhood. As to the matter of enlisting, every captain in the battalion had been ordered to recruit for three years, making up their complements to fifty-three men, including two sergeants, two corporals, and a drum. If any captain had enlisted more, he had suffered for it. Conrad Weiser himself had suffered for raising his own company to above the recommended number, the Commissary having refused pay to the supernumeraries, and the Colonel having had to remunerate them to the extent of £40 out of his pocket. Perhaps, he remarked tartly, that was what Mr. Peters' informants meant when they said he was a lover of money.

As for there having been more men in the battalion than its right complement, that would not have happened except for some verbal encouragement Colonel Weiser had had from the commissioners. Those gentlemen, upon being told his battalion was too full, had assured him that they would pay 1,400 men. Besides, they knew that neither the Augusta Regiment nor the Second Battalion, but particularly the Augusta Regiment, had its full complement. Moreover, if the Commissary had paid the Colonel's men monthly and kept the Governor's promise, Conrad Weiser would only have had to lose the pay of the supernumeraries for only one month. He felt wronged that he had had to lose that pay for five months.

He remembered no orders from William Denny to discharge all the men enlisted for only one year. He understood such men should be dismissed only as their companies filled up. As to the ammunition in Reading, it was deposited there "as in a safe place in the keeping of an honest man, who distributes or delivers it out on the Colonel's orders."

"That my own company is the worst of all and that the officers are under no command," Conrad Weiser denied absolutely. As for enlisting old and unfit men, although he had engaged some elderly men, he had been replacing these with younger ones whenever they could be obtained. The commander of the battalion could not see the uselessness of companies that he had assigned to such vital points of defense as Cumberland County, Fort Augusta, and Wyoming. Any captain in the battalion who says he has not received instructions from his Colonel about recruiting "is a liar." As for the charge of his keeping a shoemaker in his house, that was "scandalous, malicious, and undeserving of notice." He would not undignify himself to respond to it.

If the Governor had charged him with disobeying orders, Weiser was aware of having punctually obeyed his commands in all instances. Indeed, he remembered obeying orders from Denny to maintain two saddle horses at each fort, one to alarm the neighborhood in case of an Indian attack, another to bear intelligence from fort to fort or commanding officers. On the Governor's instructions, he had provided the horses only to have the Commissary refuse later to pay for them and thereby was out of pocket for another £100.

That the Colonel was capable of punctilio, a late paragraph in his letter revealed: "I hereby send the journal of the several captains and commanders of forts in my battalion, as also the return of the battalion which I desire may be laid before his Honor the Governor, in order to justify my officers."

In conclusion, he had of himself only to say:

> I have constantly endeavored to give the back inhabitants all the protection in my power and always understood that it was for that end that the battalion was raised, and, if that does not please, I have only one offer more to make, which is my resignation, which shall be immediately on their doing me and my battalion justice.

His complimentary close was devoid, too, of all ingratiation, and an abrupt dignity characterized its words:

Moods in a Province 185

I have nothing further to add at present, but,

Sir,

Your humble Servant,

CONRAD WEISER.

Then, to explain the fact that his long letter was in the hand of an amanuensis rather than his own writing, he appended a postscript: "I have a lameness in my hand, and can scarce hold a pen."

Nothing, when he wrote his communications of November 17, 1757, suggested any lack of power of composition or firmness of mind in the long-tried and faithful Provincial Interpreter. But on January 2, 1758, Secretary Peters realized, with the peculiar satisfaction that was often his own, that his friend Ned Shippen's son-in-law, Mr. James Burd, road and fort builder, had been appointed to succeed Colonel Weiser.

XVI

Peace and War

Henry Bouquet, born Swiss but Colonel in the Army of His British Majesty George II in the American Colonies in 1756, did not at first have an exactly easy time in December of that year in Philadelphia. He was one to succeed with gentlemen, being facetious in manner and fluent in two languages, but, as a foreigner by birth and a man in his second tongue French, he hardly dared assume vigorous measures with mistrustful burghers or recalcitrant assemblymen. It was but natural that citizens should desire the King's protection both for themselves and the back inhabitants against the French and the Indians, it was human nature in them not to want the King's soldiers billeted in their own houses. A man whose native speech was that of the enemy had to behave with prudence.

So Colonel Bouquet, as the subordinate to His Excellency the Earl of Loudoun, acted with a proper indirectness, taking his problems to Governor Denny and Mr. Secretary Peters. With these two, he made his protests masculinely enough to instigate the former to motion and to challenge the latter, always subject to affability and hearty respect for his standing as a person of quality. Mr. Denny could not comply with the officer's demand that he issue a warrant to the sheriff to assign quarters for Colonel Bouquet's men in the private houses of Philadelphians. But he could see that the military gentleman's points were true ones: that the keepers of the public houses of the city and county were miserably poor, without adequate beds or necessaries, and incapable of supplying either of these, that hospitals were required and unavailable, that an examination of the public houses was essential, and a refurbishing of them imperative to the comfort of such companies as had been quartered in Philadelphia before they could be turned into an army of deliverance on the frontiers. Moreover, Mr. Peters could see that Colonel Bouquet had been cruelly and barbarously treated. So Governor Denny committed himself to a week of wrangling with the Pennsylvania Assembly, Captain Tulleken, sent as a timely aid by Colonel Stanwix of the King's Army, helped toward the end of December with an articulate and specific list of demands, and the Assembly in due time arranged for the comfort of Henry Bouquet and his men.

Months afterward, when the Swiss officer had been established with his companies in South Carolina, and his return north during the prospective year of 1758 had been hinted at, he thought fondly of Philadelphia. Indeed, he was charmingly condescending as, in late October of 1757, he composed a letter in Charles Town to Richard Peters. He had not written to his new friend before because he knew the Secretary, among his multiplicity of affairs, had no time left for an insignificant correspondence. But, now that he wrote, he let his feelings flow with full fervor. He was by no means indifferent to what happened in Pennsylvania. Rather, he looked upon that province as his mother country in America and was highly prejudiced in its favor.

It was not that the soil there had any share in his affections. He had never seen anything but dirt and dust in and about Philadelphia. Certainly, too, with regard to prospects, Charles Town had the advantage. But the South Carolinian city was hot; for the whole summer, the thermometer had never fallen below 86 degrees. The whole countryside had been sick. If he had kept his health, his men at least had died very fast—more of them in one month than in a whole winter in the city on the Delaware.

In short, when nature was so gracious in a territory, Colonel Bouquet could but sympathize the more with a man who, in that domain of good health, had so to put up with the petty squabbles of other men. He regretted much that, as newspapers coming south kept informing him, faction subsisted still in Pennsylvania. He assured Mr. Peters that his immersion in those unhappy affairs made Colonel Bouquet even more sensible of the vexation which they were to private gentlemen and of the hurt which they did to the public. He hoped the deputation of Assemblymen from Philadelphia to London would bring matters to a crisis and put an end to the present divisions. Luckily, he was not himself exposed to political storms in South Carolina, but circumstances in that province were also ticklish, and there was only one point with regard to it in which he was perfectly clear: he would like to be away from it to Pennsylvania—nothing in South Carolina pleased him at all.

He had, as had almost all correspondents of his epoch, to subjoin obligations to compliments, and he asked Mr. Peters to arrange to forward to him by ship the feet of a theodolite and an astronomical quadrant which he seemed to have overlooked at the Surveyor-General's house. But knowing to whom he wrote, he could not, when he was framing both admiration and sympathy, omit waggishness altogether. So, when the good Secretary was forwarding things, would he please send on Colonel Bouquet's servant's little dog, unfortunately, left behind in Philadelphia—the one "which used to go at Mr. Allen."

Richard Peters smiled as he read the affable epistle. It took his mind back pleasantly to a brief one that he had had a month earlier from Colonel George Washington of Mount Vernon in Virginia. He recalled that gentleman's friendly recommendation of Colonel Fairfax, cousin of Lord Fairfax, whom General Braddock's recent aide-de-camp wished him to show courtesy to, on his passage through Philadelphia for New York and England. He remembered his guest of a day in early October. He did not forget that Colonel Washington, in sponsoring my Lord's kinsman, had remarked, "To whom can I better introduce him than the agreeable Mr. Peters?" He thought for a second of the grave Virginian sponsor, whom he had once seen at Fort Cumberland fleetingly. He was sorry that that young officer had in him so little of the charm of Colonel Bouquet. But then, Mr. Washington was only an American, after all—unacquainted with the polish of England and the Continent. One must not expect too much of a mere provincial belonging to a southern colony.

Yet, despite pleasure to be found in the condescension of gentlemen, Richard Peters could not contemplate the new year at hand with an untempered hopefulness. The affairs of Thomas Penn were not shining too splendidly in December 1757. He knew Mr. Penn was still smarting from what he called "the atrocious charge which Teedyuscung was induced publicly to make against the Proprietors at the late Treaty of Easton, of having forged a deed and altered courses." He must go on pitying a master who could not rest, as he declared, under such accusations. Sir William Johnson, now under Lord Loudoun's agent for His Majesty in Indian Affairs, and his deputy had both declined to inquire into the vagrant Delaware's arraignment of the heirs of William Penn. Matters must rest for a time longer between the accuser and accused.

On the whole, however, matters went better for Mr. Peters and the Proprietor in 1758 than was anticipated. In the first months of the year, Mr. Thomas Penn could keep his eye on Mr. Franklin, who was in London, and, with James Hamilton also there as a check, supervise the malcontent's activities at the English capital. The business of reporting these, then, was shifted from the Secretary's shoulders to the Proprietor's. For the time, Richard Peters could read rather than recite, and in the letters which Mr. Penn composed was evinced a proper caution. The Assembly definitely intended now not to lay the complaint of Teedyuscung before the King. There would be no ministerial investigation of the reported fraud. Teedyuscung could later be shown by the authorities in Pennsylvania independently that he had been misinformed about the deeds.

As for Mr. Franklin, that emissary had been told firmly that the Proprietors would not consent for the present to withdraw instructions from the Governor and let him act entirely upon his counsel with the Assembly. The Penns were weighing "B.F.'s" proposals that approval be given to an act of the Assembly which would grant £60,000 to the King's use, strike £55,000 thereof in bills of credit, and provide a fund for sinking the same, but they did not find it advisable to give a more general power to Governor Denny to agree with the House if they should agree to revise the bill in any particular. Moreover, the exceptions provided for in the bill and affecting the Proprietary estate had been agreed to not from any desire of Thomas Penn to render less, in proportion to the Family income, than other people to the necessary protection of the Country in time of war. If, after a just method of taxation for all in the province had been worked out, the Proprietors were found to be contributing less than their proper share, they would willingly make up the deficiency.

Furthermore, it was satisfying to Mr. Peters to note, beyond the generosity of Mr. Penn, that that astute gentleman had discovered that whenever he agreed to a law that the Assembly pronounced just and equitable, the House quarreled with its proceedings and found it neither just nor equitable.

The month of April brought communication from the Proprietor in a fashion even more personal and particular, for William Peters' son, Jemmy, now grown up and into difficulties of his own in Liverpool and Lancashire, arrived unexpectedly in Philadelphia, bringing letters. In them, Mr. Penn informed the Register of the Admiralty that the gentleman with whom James thought himself fixed had begun to entertain scruples about sending that young man on errands to receive money. James was not himself in the best standing with his creditors. English Raphy Peters thought it better, under the circumstances, that his brother "go abroad at least for some time."

But, whatever apprehension such news afforded when carried to him by the sanguine Jemmy, the uncle read with characteristic pleasure Mr. Penn's acknowledgment of early inquiries about the Proprietary Family's health. He was indeed elated to learn about the little son of his patron, a child whom his nephew knew.

> He has a very good constitution, never having had any illness, is well set, not tall for his age, but by no means short. Very likely and sensible, he has a very good memory and knows every country in Europe, its capital, and

the rivers that flow through it. This his parents taught their son at play, by pasteboard maps divided into the several kingdoms. Thomas Penn's friends regarded the boy as sensible and promising. He would be four years old in July next.

Such felicity was finely satisfying to the affections of Richard Peters. Yet the Secretary savored quite as much the intimate fashion in which the Proprietor told him of Lady Juliana's sorrow and his own at the loss of two children, one of them born dead, in 1757. Both parents had submitted quietly to the dispensations of Providence, and the Earl of Pomfret's daughter had borne her grief with resignation rather than in the common way. The example of her good behavior made it more possible for Mr. Peters to endure the temper of William Denny.

Except for a sudden display of that explosive at a Council meeting, the end of April was to be as gratifying as its beginning. Affairs had taken a favorable turn with respect to the Delaware complaint. It was commonly thought that Teedyuscung was going to be deposed by the Susquehanna Indians. The commission that Mr. Penn had sent could probably be executed. Even Israel Pemberton said all ought to sleep at present. The sudden heat of Governor Denny might, therefore, be met with equanimity.

That administrator had stamped his way out of an executive conference declaring he would no longer sit in any company where Mr. Peters was, but the Secretary's friends and colleagues in the Council had rallied to his support, concurring in his just claims for reinstatement and the privilege of attending meetings, and the hot-headed Governor was "mean enough to declare he had been under a misapprehension" and received the victim of his wrath back into favor without apology. In the interest of charity, Richard Peters bore the affront with a right reserve. To be sure, he wrote in detail of it to James Hamilton in England. But his letter so brimmed with other news that no deep cherished anger might be inferred.

Brigadier General Forbes, with Captain Halkett, his Brigade Major, and Sir John St. Clair, Deputy Quarter Master, were in Philadelphia waiting for their regiment and, by rumor, destined for a western expedition. Good Colonel Bouquet's four companies had marched into the city from South Carolina by way of New York. Three-and-twenty additional companies were to be raised in Pennsylvania, two of them of light horse. The leaves would be out in a fortnight. May, June, and July would all be good months. Three thousand men from Pennsylvania, 2,000 from Virginia, 1,000 from Maryland, and 1,500 regulars could proceed then to the conquest of the Ohio. The Cherokees and the southern

Indians had received Major James Burd with great affection, and 1,100 of their warriors would join the expedition if only General Forbes could collect his forces before those Indian allies disbanded. Everything promised well. The city had gained great credit for fitting out eighteen as fine vessels as ever were seen in the transport service. These had already sailed to Halifax and the Capes. As for the land army—forage, provisions, and wagons in abundance were already purchased and on their way to the magazines west of Susquehanna. The name of the province of the Penns was being fast redeemed. The energy of spring glowed again in fifty-four-year-old Richard Peters, and the summer of 1758 occupied him richly with preliminaries for the military campaign that should restore the honor of the province. For General Forbes, he labored tirelessly through Indian agents in the west and, as his emissaries in 1755, had built roads for General Braddock; now the Secretary's aides produced all the explicit information of conditions around Fort Duquesne of the specifications and construction of that French stronghold, of the attitude of the several Indian tribes, of the numbers of the enemy, which the most exacting commander-in-chief might require.

In early August, the brisk Secretary could even be complacent about such trying personalities as the Quakers. Teedyuscung had favored the Government of Pennsylvania with another conference in late July, and for his visit, the unaccountable Assembly had, as usual, made mean preparation. But members of the Friendly Association had arrived more adequately provided with goods worth as much as £120. The Governor, eager to appease the acquisitive Indians and too adroit to let the Friends achieve that purpose in his stead, took the position that no separate gifts must be made by any society to the Ten Nations guests. The Quakers, bent on peaceful measures, yielded to the Chief Executive's wishes. So, for the time forgetting the maledictions he was wont to heap on Israel Pemberton's head, Mr. Peters beamed with pleasure on the "good luck of having a large subscription from the Quakers." The gifts from the Assembly and the Association were put together, and Governor Denny assured the Indians frankly that a large part "was given by the Quakers, a peaceable and good people, the descendants of those who came over with the first Mr. Penn." In fact, the scribe was generous enough to quote the Executive's words to the Proprietor and to add that, had it not been for the Quaker's lucky gift, "we should have been ruined."

But the geniality of the summer denoted no lasting change of heart in Richard Peters, and in October, when the last of the conclave in Teedyuscung's and his Ten Nations' interest occurred at Easton, the Secretary played his old game of frustrating—so, far as was possible—the arrogations of the Friends.

Benjamin Chew, like himself no great lover of Governor Denny, proved in that enterprise a ready, though somewhat inglorious ally. Indeed, for a time, the Attorney-General and the Secretary of the Province were almost oblivious of the diplomacy by which Conrad Weiser and his Six Nations friends kept taking the wind out of Teedyuscung's sails, so intent were the two upon the character of the Governor and the confusion of Israel Pemberton. When William Denny chose to dine alone or with such members of his Council as he chose to invite to be his guests, they were not averse to being absent. When the Executive ordered Mr. Peters never to let his nephew, Dicky, come into his sight, remarking that he was "no companion for boys," they concurred, convinced that the irate dignitary was no fit companion for anyone. The Six Nations held aloof from Teedyuscung, questioning the sovereignty that he had claimed and hinting at the wisdom of his becoming once more the nephew every Delaware should be. The conference closed, as ever, in compromise. Later, Ben Chew and Mr. Peters regaled each other with their accounts of how Israel Pemberton had behaved.

Prompted by his colleague, who had intelligence of all things, Mr. Chew chose one day to stroll down the Easton street and by the Lutheran Church.

By chance then, as it were, several companions of the Council and he heard voices in that edifice, and the Attorney-General put his head in through a window, idly curious. There was Israel, pipe of peace in his mouth, sitting at a long table with Isaac Zane, other Quakers, and a number of Teedyuscung's followers. One Indian was speaking the tone generally assumed at public treaties. All were very solemn. Israel was in a great state. The spectator took full benefit of his innocently fortuitous gazing.

Then Israel Pemberton espied and accosted him. "Walk in by the door," he said, "and smoke a pipe with us, thou'lt hear the Roman oratory revived in Tom King's speaking."

Mr. Chew excused himself. He was only taking the air, he insisted, and happened to hear voices which he could not understand.

"We are about no harm," answered the Quaker, "in fact, we are upon the best subjects in the world: love and friendship." "Those are truly noble subjects," Mr. Chew replied, "and I heartily wish success to all men *sincerely* disposed to promote and cultivate them."

"Would it be unlawful," Israel Pemberton persisted, "for us to send for a glass of wine and drink with our brethren of the Ten Nations?"

"Upon that point, you must judge for yourself," said the visitant.

"But I want the Attorney-General's opinion."

"If you are applying to me as a lawyer for my advice, I cannot give it to you without a fee; advice for nothing is worth nothing."

Mr. Peters and Mr. Chew were themselves satisfied that Ben had come off best in the dialogue. What Israel Pemberton might conclude about the honors of the Attorney-General's prying minds, which despised that Quakers were not too urgent to inquire. Furthermore, personal rivalries were of little moment to persons of right spirit in months, which brought accounts of the success of John Forbes and his adjutant Henry Bouquet at Fort Duquesne on the Ohio and of the breaking of the French and Indian power in Pennsylvania to the west of Susquehanna. Even William Denny might almost become a tolerable figure for the Secretary of Pennsylvania in such hours of good omen.

On January 22, 1759, Mr. Peters sat writing to his familiar Bouquet. He had always desired the favor of General Forbes, he said, to communicate to his friend whatever personal news he had had to convey in his official letters of the previous season. Properly during that interval, he had written to no other officers. But now the victory had been won, and the General was in invalid health and inactive, the Secretary could tender the Colonel his correspondence directly. He hoped his past silence had not been construed to his prejudice. He and Bouquet could exchange confidences with full freedom. He would be glad for any relevant hints that His Majesty's military representative might care to offer on the subject of the officers of the provincial troops. The Secretary might find such intimations serviceable in choosing or avoiding men for appointments in the Pennsylvania companies. Having ventured such suggestions, Richard Peters transmitted what news he had of poor Haldimand in vile Fort Edward and begging accounts of his brother officers almost like an alms, then told of the most recent purchases of majors' commissions in Forbes' regiment in Philadelphia.

Mirthfully, then, he turned from narrative to banter and innuendo. "Did you, or did you not," he challenged facetiously, "intend an attack against the French fort when you began your march towards Duquesne from Loyal Hannen?" (For he remembered how punctually the redoubt at the Forks of the Ohio had been blown up and abandoned by the French on the approach of His Majesty's army in November 1758.) Scornfully, he reported that on February 5, the Pennsylvania Assembly would convene—actually, he wrote, "the province's politicians will meet and make a hog or a dog on it." Then suddenly, he allowed his ink to flow to an effect altogether unprecedented in his letters. He required a pair of phrases to interpret Thomas Penn and Thomas Penn's deputy to Colonel Henry Bouquet. To his amazement, his words somehow ran free: "Our pilot is asleep at the helm, and the present master of the ship is at Athens among some curious antiquities."

It was a strange sentiment to express of his patron—hardly one to be lightly risked. But he wanted to break the ice with his friend of the past two years, and there was no surer sign of his trusting of Colonel Bouquet—who might presently be succeeding the ill General Forbes—than to indulge him with a quip at the expense of a great man in England. Then, in February, he was the sorrier for having ventured the remark when Ben Chew told him of a letter just come to the Attorney General which indicated that Mr. Penn was looking for a new Governor to supplant Denny. "After all," Mr. Peters reasoned with himself, "the Proprietary does respect my opinions. I should not have been so open with Colonel Bouquet on the subject of him."

The year which followed January 1759 added no particular exhilaration to the Secretary's life. He was occupied but in no sense long exalted. The war dragged on, and business continued dull in every branch; even for good Mr. Weiser's sons, Mr. Peters saw little chance of present employment. It was too late that Conrad, now happily out of all military service, applied for a plantation for one of them at the Forks. Mr. Peters read rather listlessly the old Indian interpreter's inquiry as to what Mr. Penn and the Ministry in England had thought of his conduct lately at Easton. He gave no great heed to reports that, since his taking up with his one-time colonelcy, Conrad had perceived the Six Nations transferring their affections from himself to George Croghan and Sir William Johnson.

Furthermore, conditions at the Academy were not encouraging. Although, as President of the Board, Richard Peters wrote occasional letters recommending young men who stood among the first scholars there and "carried all the learning that was taught in Classics and mathematics," he was sometimes doubtful of the general success of the institution. The sums which had been subscribed at its founding and the annual subsidies from Mr. Penn and Lady Juliana were not in themselves sufficient to create a new era of civilization. Even Benjamin Weiser, from whom, as Conrad's son, deference to the Chairman of the Trustees might have been expected, openly preferred to attend Mr. Dove's. Although Mr. Weiser wrote in June inquiring whether it was advisable to let the boy study in an "opposition" school, that ever-frank correspondent wrote bluntly that his offspring had "provided not much" in his last attendance at Philadelphia's proudest center of education.

Nor was Mr. Peters so confident as Provost William Smith, who had gone to England to solicit funds, that contributions for the Academy could readily be raised in London. Moreover, he disliked it so much that, while that master was abroad, the College had to be left in charge of the Presbyterian Francis Alison as chief guardian and instructor. With funds running low, he did not relish his responsibility of dismissing unneeded tutors. Also, at the distance at which he was from London, he could not especially rejoice with Dr. Smith when Benjamin Franklin was "mortified" by being omitted from invitations into the counsels of the committee there.

Communications that Mr. Peters received in August from Colonel Bouquet at Fort Bedford were, in general, devoted closely to affairs and rather too full of protest. When sentences of facetiousness occurred, he was rather less responsive than usual. As a Secretary, he could hardly smile at two of his friend's witticisms: "All private letters are delivered unopened to every individual," and "Those addressed *on his Majesty's Service* are all opened." The cordial close, "I am entirely yours," was an appreciated tribute rather than a greatly esteemed one. Nor did Richard Peters wholly like Bouquet's berating in a mid-September letter of the injustice of the people of Pennsylvania or his frank confession that his patience with them was at an end. He could sympathize with an incensed remark that the power invested in the Assembly was invested in hands "still full of the dirt of their former mechanical and base trades." But he could not cherish the brusque statement that his familiar had had "particular and personal proofs that no gentleman could dream of living in your province." And quite too aspersive appeared to him two other insinuating phrases: "If your Proprietor *will* submit to the encroachments of his Assembly, I think he has a right to do it," and "If he continues to doze, his thin attendance of friends will fall asleep." Indeed, such items of innuendo made Richard Peters remorseful that he had been so hazardous last January as to describe Mr. Penn to Colonel Bouquet as sleeping at the helm.

In brief, the Secretary of Pennsylvania lacked much of his old cheer in the autumn of 1759. The news of General James Wolfe's glorious victory at Quebec reached Philadelphia in October. By commission from Thomas Penn and Richard Penn, Mr. James Hamilton supplanted William Denny as Lieutenant-Governor of Pennsylvania on November 17. But, as winter came on, more than the capture of a Canadian fortress and city and more than the displacement of a "peevish trifler" was necessary to bring back to middle-aged Mr. Peters his old exuberant zest for living.

XVII

Recovery of Function

Among the few papers which Mr. Peters had brought on with him from England in 1735 and which he still treasured in 1762 were two miniature diplomas of ordination. Little manuscripts in the Latin tongue and embossed upon vellum, they bore episcopal seals almost as large as themselves. By the presents contained in them, Richard, by Divine permission *(Divina permissione)* Bishop of Winchester, testified that he had found Richard Peters endowed with such morals, virtues, and knowledge as warranted his being admitted to holy orders. To their pious owner in Philadelphia, they had signified for thirty-two years what was of right his proper calling. Never had he failed to prize either the privileges they accorded or the ecclesiastical phrases which they exhibited. There was a fine ring in *sacros ordines Dei Omnipotentis;* there was eloquent tribute to his learning in *bonarum Litterarum Studio et Scientiarum Eruditum, ac sufficienter Intitulatum.* He knew by their authority that he was suited to doing service to Almighty God and that he was sufficiently learned and qualified in letters and knowledge to perform his function with credit. Ordained deacon and priest in 1730 by Bishop Richard Willis before he had assumed his curacy at Ormskirke, during all the years he afterward held secular office in Pennsylvania, he had never ceased to regret that Bishop Gibson of London had kept him in 1742 from continuous practice of his ministry. When his eyes fell on the tiny yellowing documents, his mind would go back fondly to two ceremonials at Chelsea and Winchester, which had made him a clergyman, and sometimes he would dream an old dream.

In the closing 1750s, the Reverend Mr. Jenney of Christ Church became ill with palsy, and more and more thereafter, his duties must be assumed by his assistant, Mr. William Sturgeon. For five years, that hard-working clergyman found his responsibilities and burdens heavy. He had a growing family and was glad to have the Venerable Society increase his salary from £30 to £50. But more than family was the obligation to watch new St. Peter's building as a chapel to the Old Church, to preach twice on Sundays, to read prayers, manage all other administrative and ecclesiastical duties of the parish, catechize the white children on Wednesdays, the Negroes on Friday, do a sermon every Tuesday at the City Alms House, and, once in every three weeks during the summer, go to some shepherd-less church in the country to read prayers, preach, and baptize. And always there was the necessity of keeping an observant eye on fractious William Macclenachan, who had unfortunately been admitted to Christ Church pulpit in an interim and had promptly set the whole congregation on fire—before ever the body of Pennsylvania clergy had found ways of discarding him. It was painful to Mr. Sturgeon to note how Macclenachan drew a throng from the combined flocks for a time afterward to hear his railing sermons at the State House on Chestnut Street. It was an ordeal to be oneself in danger of one's life from the anger of an incensed mob of rebellious communicants. It was trying to be aware of the machinations of Mr. John Ross, too inclined to the rant of the wild Irish preacher and altogether too influential with restless elements in the United Churches of Christ and St. Peter's. The Reverend Mr. Sturgeon could hardly picture anyone, in fact, envying him and his onerous duties and cares.

But, when death came to invalid Robert Jenney in January 1762, there was one man in Philadelphia to whom the vacancy in Christ Church and St. Peter's spelled the working of Providence rather than unrewardable labor. To Richard Peters, the release of the feeble old Rector from the illness and cares of mortality came like a sacred summons to reassume a once cherished and favorite trust. Sorrow for an old hurt in his own heart could be assuaged if dear friends in the united parish wished him to minister to the good of their souls. He dared not refuse to return to his function as a priest.

Perhaps, he meditated, the persistent condition that had debilitated him in 1761 and had led actually to his resigning his Secretaryship in January of the new year was not so bad a case of the gravel as he supposed. He had been in a better state since he surrendered that arduous office. His remaining on Governor Hamilton's Council had been, he knew, a compromise. He sincerely wanted less of the weight of political labor. He did not wish to forego all his usefulness to the province when his advice should be desired in matters of government. In the first months of 1762, he was confident he was once more improving in health. There would be satisfaction, possibly even healing, if, once again, he were to be toiling for the good of souls.

Moreover, if such opposed persons as Mr. John Ross—who rather too, unfortunately, had been a follower for a time of William Macclenachan—and the Reverend Mr. Sturgeon both were willing to endorse Richard Peters' appointment to the Rectorship of Christ Church and St. Peter's, it would seem ungrateful to Heaven and almost perversely unwilling to do Heaven's work for him to disincline from the office of minister. Richard Peters liked nothing better than effecting union where there had been disunity, achieving harmony where dissent had broken the peace of the Church. So he could not spurn the advances of the churchwardens and vestry of the two United Congregations of Philadelphia in the early spring, and, though intermittently he was troubled by a lax, it was like a renewal of youth in May of 1762 for him to begin busying himself again with sermons and preaching. Ned Shippen's son Joseph had taken over his records and clerkly duties at the State House, except for occasional sittings with the Provincial Council and consultations from time to time with his brother William in the Land Office, the former Secretary of Pennsylvania was free to carry on the dignities of the pulpits of Christ Church and St. Peter's.

On the first Sunday of the month, he excused himself early from breakfast with Governor Hamilton and by ten o'clock was on his way to his pulpit, where he preached from Ecclesiastes 12:13: "Let us hear the conclusion of the whole matter: Fear God, and keep his commandments: for this is the whole duty of man." After morning service, he dined with Governor Sharpe of Maryland and discussed the possibility of more amicable solving of boundary disputes between the province of that executive and Pennsylvania. Then, the world of business and the frailties of the spirit and the body renewed cares for him for the two months which followed. His brother came in on the following Sunday, quarreled with him about salary and allowance of fees for himself in the Land Office, and left him with a severe pain in the breast, which made him resort to Dr. Graeme, who kept him for supper. On the second Sunday of May, Mr. Sturgeon officiated for him while he sat listening, with a sermon on I John, 3:11: "For this is the message that ye heard from the beginning, that we should love one another." His breast still aching, he remained home at noon but was at church in the evening to hear Mr. Duche from James 2:20: "But wilt thou know, o vain man, that faith without works is dead."

In the next mid-week, William Peters argued again with him much out of temper, and on the same Wednesday, Dr. Alison came to blows with him on the matter of prayers for Commencement. The new Rector had only had his thoughts on the subject of delivering them and had spoken to none else on his secret wish, but the Presbyterian took the brusque position that it was the privilege of the faculty of the College to choose their speakers for the ceremony and quite obviously intended no imposing of any participant whatsoever upon them by a member of the Board. Richard Peters presumed that the faculty would have asked for him, and the omission of regard, coming after the difficulty with William, piqued him sensibly. Indeed, he was so moved that he declared with a sudden roundness both that there was nothing new in prayers for Commencement and that he would himself have nothing further to do with the Academy. The remark was an error in strategy, but at least it had the immediate effect of Dr. Alison's assuring him of how invaluable, in many instances, he was to the College. That assurance mollified him until Friday when he was distressed to hear from Mr. Allen that a proposal had been made for introducing the Liturgy into Commencement. He knew that such a rumor was untrue, but he also knew that there was a Presbyterian will in Philadelphia—he thought of it as an obstinate one—to keep all Church of England color out of the Academy. And he thought the less of Alison for talking of the new rect"r of Christ Church.

Again, on the next Sunday, assistants took his place in the pulpit. The Reverend Mr. Philip Reading in the morning preached on John, 14:27: "Peace I leave with you, my peace I give unto you," and Mr. Sturgeon in the evening on Mark 12:34: "Thou art not far from the kingdom of God." And all those points Richard Peters entered into his journal. Then, whatever might be the motive for his conduct—remembering the sermons of Sunday or mastering his pique at not being asked to contribute prayers at the program—he praised in his Tuesday entry all the performance of Commencement, rejoiced in the fact of a crowded audience, agreeably told Dr. Alison he must write Dr. Smith about it, and afterward had tea with Colonel Thomas White.

By July, he was ready to read prayers and preach twice a day, and sermons began flowing more easily, with a new energy of health, even during the hot weather. Throughout September and October, likewise, he continued in the same vigor, now delivering two sermons on one Sunday at the Old Church, now delivering only one at the Old and another at the New. But the pleasure of delivery to large and responsive flocks at Christ's and at St. Peter's during those months became, on occasion, only a supplement to other forms of delight. The popular Reverend Mr. Peters went out much to dinner and supper in that happy autumn of 1762, and, indeed, his diary kept recording the complacency of hosts who heard pre-readings of his sermons. Alexander Stedman, Richard Hockley, Colonel White, Governor Hamilton at Bush Hill, Dr. Thomas Graeme—all were obliged with his company. If Mr. Stedman said little of his message for the fifth of September, being in an ill temper because the Stedman supper was cold, at least the day of his preaching, "For through him we both have access by one Spirit unto the Father" (Ephesians, 2:18) went very agreeably. There were congratulations at the end of the service, there was tea afterward at Mr. Duche's, and supper with Colonel White was an affable experience, with a droll wag present telling of an escape from the French fleet at Newfoundland. Moreover, six weeks later, on a Saturday afternoon, Alexander Stedman listened interestedly to a new sermon for the morrow, and on the same day, after supper with Mrs. Thomas Graeme and a second reading of the manuscript for next day's service, his good hostess returned his kindness by telling him the history of her daughter Betsy's ill-starred love affair with young William Franklin. Then, on the Sunday which succeeded, he made fervent use of his text, "Now, therefore, ye are no more strangers and foreigners but fellow-citizens with the Saints, and of the household of God" (also from Ephesians, and a verse coming immediately after his choice of Scripture for September 5th).

To be forearmed, he began a funeral sermon for Mr. Evan Morgan, but that invalid rallying from his sickness, fortunately did not have to use it. The two autumn months, as they receded, in fact, did little to dampen his ardor. Although during one week, his lax tried him severely, he continued to be the guest of other gentlemen and listeners. He had few burials to make, usually had much notice taken of his preaching, and generous attendance at service. For he would not let rain and lightning, chancing as he read prayers, disturb him, and he was repentant that on one Sunday, when he let another minister substitute for him, and a report came of a great congregation in church, he should have had no good thoughts for the whole day afterward. Yet even then, he had resolutely read his New Testament at night until composure of mind returned.

Apart from his pulpit and the selection of texts, there were other satisfactions also in the winter of 1762–63 for the genial clergyman who had been separated from his function by the deplorable conduct of Mr. Archibald Cummings twenty-five years earlier in 1737. To support him in his new happiness at being restored to his priesthood after that long deprivation, Richard Peters had several causes of encouragement.

In January, a most obliging letter came from good Dr. Samuel Finley, President of the Presbyterian College of New Jersey at Princeton. Its writer had heard with pleasure of "your being chosen Rector of the two congregations." Indeed, he would have been most surprised "had it been otherwise appointed." For Dr. Finley had long ago fixed on Mr. Peters for that office, even though, of course, he could have only private opinions in such a matter. He rejoiced, indeed, that his friend's sincere desire "to be an instrument in the hand of Divine Providence" had been granted. He was glad Mr. Peters was to have the opportunity "to promote the establishment of real piety, upon the faith of our Lord Jesus Christ." "For," declared Dr. Finley, "such are my views of the Kingdom of Christ, as not confined within the limits which narrow minds of all denominations have prescribed, that I cordially rejoice in the advancement of true and substantial religion in a different society as in my own. I know Jesus Christ loves the pious of whatever name or nations, and unless I do the same, I am not agreed with him and so far cannot be approved by him. But let His Kingdom come!"

All that expression of felicitation and faith from a Presbyterian was very gratifying.

Yet greater than the pleasure from it was the recognition, which at length took formal shape for Richard Peters early in February. On the fourth of that month, the two assistant ministers of Christ Church and St. Peter's, Mr. Sturgeon and Mr. Jacob Duche, testified in an address to the Lord Bishop of London that they concurred heartily and sincerely with the churchwardens and vestry in "their appointment of the Reverend Mr. Peters to the Rectory." More than that, they wrote, "They could not but express their approbation of a measure which had been unanimously agreed upon for the maintenance of good order and government amongst them." In addition, they insisted, "From our long personal acquaintance with Mr. Peters, we cannot be strangers, my Lord, to the reputation he hath universally acquired for his learning, piety, and exemplary conversation." On reading their words, the recently chosen Rector not only felt the truths of his old ordination diplomas coming at last into acceptance, he felt there was now no unfortunate division between missionaries and parish, as there had been in 1742, on the subject of his choice. It was as though a quarter-century of forbearance had triumphed. The old ambition and the old hope had come into grateful fulfillment.

To add also to the measure of Richard Peters' joy at being back in ecclesiastical orders, he was inducted, ten days later in February, "into the number and society of his domestic chaplains" by William Alexander, Lord Stirling, a distinguished peer then visiting in Philadelphia. By virtue of a document imposing as any charter, he was to "obtain, have, and enjoy, all and singular, the privileges, benefits, liberties, preeminences, and immunities, whatsoever which have at any time been granted to the chaplains of the nobility by the Statutes and Laws of the Realm of Great Britain," and, although both the office and the emoluments were nominal rather than actual, the Rector of the United Churches esteemed the favor which the obliging nobleman had conferred upon him. Nor did he look with too critical an eye into the validity of the title that his lordship was now wearing in America with so affable an importance. Indian warfare was still waging on the western boundaries of Pennsylvania, but the spring of 1763 promised to be a happy one in the personal life of Richard Peters.

But not all of the renewed clergyman's time then could be devoted to religion. As a member of the Council and as President of the College, he continued also in secular responsibilities. Provost William Smith was in England. A guardian eye had to be kept by the Provost's friend on the problems and the amenities of education in Philadelphia. Difficulties between scholars and masters had to be weighed if not adjudicated, and the observance of right forms had always to be counseled or maintained. So, the month of May did not quite fulfill for Reverend Mr. Peters the spring's promise of happiness.

The season of Commencement was one, of course, for rejoicing-doubly so, now that news had come to the city of King George III having made peace with both Spain and France and by the terms of a treaty acquired all Canada for the British Crown. Yet, it was not an interval of complete gratification. On the eve of the ceremonies, the Chairman of the Board of the Academy was called away to Newcastle to settle an administration account in the estate of the father of Hannah Cookson, wife to Mr. John Galloway of Maryland. When he got back to Philadelphia on the day before the exercises, he found a hubbub of Presbyterians in town, and during the program on the 17th, he was often more aware of the elements of the audience attending than he was of the parts taken by the graduates. At most, he could listen with but wry inward mirth to "A Dialogue on Peace" pronounced by one of these. The declaimer's rhymes glided facilely:

> Hail smiling Goddess! in whose placid Mien
> Celestial Bliss with ev'ry Grace is seen,
> O'er thy smooth Brow, no rugged Helmet frowns,
> An Olive-Wreath thy shining Temple crowns.

But only the last of them moved Mr. Peters to full sympathy:

> Hail! Happy Britain, in a Sovereign blest,
> Who deems in Kings a virtuous Name the best,
> Guardian of right and sacred liberty,
> Rome's glorious Numa shall be seen in Thee,
> Beneath thy Smile fair Science shall increase,
> And form one Reign of Learning and of Peace.

Indeed, more than that, they awakened in him a purpose of his own, and the end of the month proved a richer experience than had proved its middle. On May 27, he gathered around him the Trustees of the Academy to adopt an address to the English monarch which he had composed during the week after Commencement, and on the next day, however much his mind was troubled by conditions at the College, he could write with more quiet heart to Dr. Smith in London. One ship, in fact, carried away to England for the Academy of Philadelphia congratulatory phrases to the King from Richard Peters and for the President of the Board his confidences and compliments to William Smith. The author of the humble address anticipated a double pleasure. Some day, he would see his carefully selected words printed in Philadelphia after his Sovereign had been presented with them. Before next winter, he would have thanks from the Provost for his interest in both little matters and great at the institution of learning.

He was relieved that he could say so much to his friend—so busy there in London collecting funds for the Academy—on the subject of Commencement, whatever chagrin had attended the performance. The celebrations, he wrote, had occurred in Whitsuntide when all but two of the Church of England clergy, Messrs. Thomas Barton and Charles Inglis, were busily preparing their congregations for Whitsunday communion, and unable to leave their missions to attend. So, with the town full of Presbyterian ministers coming to a meeting of their Synod, the function was thronged by the visiting colonists, and only three Episcopal divines, including himself, were present. Yet worse, perhaps, than the absence of proper people, he confided, was an unfortunate grammatical squabble being waged between the faculty and good Mr. Francis Hopkinson. That gentleman had tried to expose Stuart for a printer's error in an Academy prospectus and so added unhappiness to the dullness of the program, which quite brimmed the cup of collegiate woe. Then, to further the infelicities of the occasion, Robert Jones, a well-taught candidate who had gone through all the schools with distinction and could speak very well indeed, would make no acknowledgments in his thesis to Dr. Smith's Vice-Provost. Rather than that, the youth, to the dudgeon of both Dr. Alison and the Jones family, and despite Mr. Peter's intervention as a peacemaker, had quit the Academy.

Such things and other unpleasantnesses which he refrained from mentioning, he was conscious, would give the Provost pain. But he recommended that the distant Professor of Philosophy let them rest in his breast and keep silent; all could be set right when he returned. Then, knowing that the brilliant but oftentimes erratic and irascible William Smith had enemies not only in Philadelphia but at the College, Richard Peters did all that he could to smooth the troubled waters ahead. He assured the seeker of funds in England that he could depend, when he got back to Philadelphia, on the favor of Mr. Chew and Governor

Hamilton. His "extraordinary merit and success were amply acknowledged by those two, and he would find them real friends of the Institution." Richard Peters prayed for the restoration of Dr. Smith's health, predicted he should find matters better than he expected, and promised to help get them on a good footing.

Moving finally into his own affairs, he regretted that he could not this year go to the succor of his invalid sister in Liverpool, feared that her disappointment at his not coming might have a further bad effect on her weak state and spirits, hoped that Mr. Smith, on his visit to Liverpool, had done what he could to satisfy Mrs. Statham of the present impossibility of her brother's journeying to her. Also, he felt constrained to admit that he was himself at times dispirited. There were moments, in fact, when, for all his zealous intentions, he quite despaired of doing the least good. "Everybody in Pennsylvania was in a scramble for wealth and power, and there were so many jarring and opposite interests and systems that no real comfort could continue long in any mind which was obliged to act in concert with men of such worldly tempers." His chief solace under such trying circumstances was that Mr. Alexander Stedman and Mr. Jacob Duche were ever his faithful friends, giving him every assistance in their power in conducting the Academy. Another authentic, although lesser, joy was that the new buildings of the College were finished.

But, as he closed his letter of May 28, he was happy to report that Mrs. Smith and her children were all enjoying perfect health and that Mr. Sturgeon regarded Dr. Smith to be his very best friend. Nor did he, for all his seriousness, omit gossip. Rather, he appended the facts that Thomas Willing was marrying Nancy McCall next week, "a sweet young lady but low in stature," though prophesied to be one who would shine in household economies and the management of a family, that Mrs. Tench Francis, lately Nancy Willing, "was expecting her time every moment," that Mr. Cox was so busy courting in Jersey he could not attend Board meetings of the Academy.

Four days later, on June 1, although his May letter had been a long one, Mr. Peters had an afterthought and addressed Dr. William Smith once more. This time, he acknowledged gratefully the kind notice that the Provost had taken of his being appointed to the rectory of the Church. By this and other letters, he remarked, his friend would see what entire confidence he reposed in him. He would certainly not have chosen any other person to manage his affairs in England. He knew that all of Dr. Smith's "trouble" had been very great and that the unforeseen choice of a rector might increase it. Yet he was sure that "affection makes all this easy, and I can pronounce boldly that you have as much for me as one friend can have for another. I measure your breast by my own towards you."

Later in June, the cup of content filled less troublously again for the Rector of Christ Church. A letter that had been written in April by Mr. Thomas Penn came not only to signify the Proprietor's gratification that his old friend and servant had been invited to return to his calling and had accepted but also to assure Mr. Peters that both the Bishop of London and the Archbishop of Canterbury inclined favorably to his appointment. Dr. William Smith, the same message made clear likewise, was doing more than successfully raise funds in England for the Academy of Philadelphia; at Fulham and Lambeth, he was prospering Richard Peters' cause with the two most important ecclesiastics of the English Church. Indeed, the Archbishop had found only one fault with the address earlier forwarded to him by the new Rector: it had said too many fine things of His Grace. All, in brief, looked fair for the summer of 1763.

The former Secretary to the Provincial Council could conclude now that he was to have both the spiritual office, which he prized, and the full approval of laity, clergy, and government. In the exaltation of his experience, it seemed almost idle for Richard Peters to be anxious about periodic physical illnesses. He could not repine if Mr. Penn wished him on occasion to lend secular aid to William Peters in the mundane work of the Land Office. It was only proper for him to remain on in Philadelphia and prepare for the arrival of Mr. John Penn in the autumn. If Thomas Penn said that he wished him to be at the side of his nephew when that young gentleman came to replace Mr. Hamilton in the government, it was foolish to continue thinking of going to England to seek relief from pains and aches, which had now disappeared anyway. There were, perhaps, other ways of having a more youthful health than travel and English physicians. Who knew but that when the prospective Governor should be set up in office next October or November, there would be good news from Colonel Bouquet's campaign in Ohio to add to the joy of the peace with France and bring in a happy era for the Penns, the people of their province, and Christ Church and St. Peter's. Let, as the Presbyterian Finley had wished in his friendly letter, Christ's Kingdom come!

So, knowing that there is something impossible about both eating your cake and having it, the amiable clergyman put cherished wishes aside. He could not at the same time visit England and preach two sermons on Sundays in Philadelphia. He could not be at the side of his one remaining sister, Hannah, invalid wife of good William Statham in Liverpool, talk with her of her children, or review fond memories of his parents and those other sisters, dear Esther and sweet Maria Helena, dead every one of them so long ago—and serve for the good of souls also in his two churches. He would have enjoyed seeing his namesake, Richard Statham, now grown up in the family circle. It would have been agreeable to talk with William Peters' English son Raphy, now flourishing in the law, so able and so circumspect a young man—to become acquainted with his niece, pretty Nelly Gartside, married now and said to be a most comely young matron.

But those were hopes, pleasures, and duties which must bow to other obligations. At least they would have to wait until Mr. John Penn, reported to be reformed and "eager for business," should be installed in his state. The Proprietor was undoubtedly justified in his reminder that, while Dr. Smith was in England, Richard Peters was needed in Philadelphia no less as Minister of the United Churches than as the President of the College. And even so prosaic and material a prospect as the running of new divisional lines between Pennsylvania and Maryland would make important his being in the province next autumn. So the new Rector of Christ gave up all thought of going to England in the summer of 1763, devoted himself to his clerical function, and waited for Mr. John Penn.

But the satisfaction of greeting a scion of the Family was, happily, preceded for Mr. Peters by two other instances of pleasure. In October came an August letter from Thomas Penn, and after its arrival, the Address sent last May from the College to the King could be published for the province to read.

The Proprietor wrote he was very pleased that Mr. Peters had written congratulations to Mr. John Penn on his being chosen as Governor for the province. He depended very much on the good advice which the long-experienced Secretary could give his nephew and was glad the old friend's visit to Liverpool was being postponed until after William Smith returned to Philadelphia and the College. He was happy to report through that gentleman that Mrs. Statham was well and content her brother should remain in America until Dr. Smith was back there.

There were, too, other touches of kindness in that communication of August 10. Mr. Penn said he was conscious that Mr. Peters' "ministerial function" would not only make those under his care better men in a religious sense, it would make them better subjects as well. Of course, a minister should be very cautious about how he engages in political matters, but there were, the Proprietor thought, moments when it was well so to engage—and at such moments, the greatest men of the church were always wont to serve in the interest of their country. Furthermore, it was pleasing to the Reverend Mr. Peters to learn from the letter not only that Dr. Smith had delivered the Pennsylvanian's Address to King George but that Thomas Penn much approved it for the effectiveness of its drawing up and its appropriate mentions both of the Prince of Wales and the peace itself. And also, the writer confided, an intimate of his—a man of the best judgment—who had read it in the *Gazette* was praising it highly.

Altogether, too, the newly installed priest of Christ Church esteemed Mr. Penn's complete disinclination to agree with what Mr. Peters had earlier written he feared was true of himself: that decay was coming upon his judgment. The Proprietor was certain such impairment of mind seldom occurred to men of his friend's age. He was sure Richard Peters' suspicions were not at all well founded. Indeed, if there was any regret in the recipient as he put away the long, gracious letter, it was that, in the nature of things, it could not detail what the Monarch himself had thought of the "Peace Address."

But there was a means of compensating for so minor (and expected) a shadow of disappointment. The manuscript, Mr. Penn's letter had revealed indirectly, had been printed in the official Court paper in London; the Throne had accepted it. It could be spread now before the eyes of Philadelphia. From the issue of the *Pennsylvania Gazette* of October 20, 1763, the Reverend Mr. Peters read the eloquent phrases of his composition of the previous May—as he knew the whole town was reading them. Pleasantly, words of them fleeted again beneath his cordial gaze:

> Amid the joyous acclamation of a grateful people, exulting in a happiness derived from your Majesty's most wise, just, and gentle administration. . . . It is with the warmest glow of gratitude that we reflect upon the princely condescension with which your Majesty vouchsafed . . . of your own royal munificence. But whilst we are thus imperfectly expressing our unfeigned acknowledgments of your Majesty's royal goodness, permit us, most gracious Sovereign, to embrace this opportunity of presenting our hearty congratulations to your Majesty and your royal Consort, our gracious Queen, upon the increase of your royal Line, by the auspicious birth of a Prince of Wales. Long may your Majesty be preserved to bless your affectionate people. . . . Situated as we are in the centre of a territory, which has long been the theatre of desolation and bloodshed, we cannot but feel a large share of that general joy, which is now diffused throughout rour Majesty's American dominions, upon the conclusion o a peace so honorable to our nation, so peculiarly beneficial to us. By this

auspicious event, we are prompted not only to look upon your Majesty as a conqueror, triumphing over your enemies, and giving strength and increase to your subjects and dominions, but to revere you as a blessed instrument, in the hands of Providence, of planting at once the Christian and the British banners, the banners of liberty and true religion, in the remotest corners of the western world. . . . Heaven seems to have reserved it for your Majesty, not to conquer and civilize only, but, by spreading throughout your wide extended conquests the knowledge of Christ's kingdom, even to bless millions of mankind with the comforts of true religion, and the gospel means of salvation. . . . Encouraged and animated by these prospects and considerations . . . it shall be our earnest endeavor . . . carefully to provide that the principles of true religion, good government, and useful learning, together with a love and veneration for the British constitution and an unshaken loyalty and affection for your Majesty's person, and your illustrious house, be constantly inculcated in the minds of youth placed under our inspections. . . . Signed by order, and in behalf of the Trustees, at a meeting held in the College Hall, at Philadelphia, the 27th of May, 17631 and sealed with their Public Seal.

RICHARD PETERS, President of the Board.

The swelling periods, the rounded sentences, rose and fell to the reader's ever-ebullient fancy, like chords of sacred music. Nor was there any suspicion of decay in his mind as the author of the Address reperused his own paragraphs.

Far away seemed the bleak truth of the reports that had reached Philadelphia last July, a half-year after the treaty of February had been proclaimed, of the enemy's retaking of their former forts of Presque Isle and Venango. Forgotten were the sad accounts of frontier disasters that followed the loss of those two strongholds. Out of Mr. Peters' mind faded all consciousness of what his friend Thomas Barton had written in the summer of the miseries of the back inhabitants: of thousands of acres of fine wheat abandoned in Cumberland County as settlers fled from Indian savages let loose again, of no barn, stable, or hovel in Shippensburg and Carlisle, that was not crowded full with panic-stricken refugees, of scalpings, ever incessant scalpings.

When the failure of the French in the west and the north had made impossible the bestowal of mollifying gifts by that race upon the savages, the Ottawa Pontiac had risen into a great chieftain. Under his influence, Wyandots,

Shawnees, Mingoes, Chippewas, and the Delawares westwardly settled—all had resolved to destroy whatever English settlements should venture into the Ohio country. He was known to be seeking to alienate the Six Nations, despite Sir William Johnson's vigilance, from the British cause. The back counties were all in a confused terror of his incitements. Demands for "scalp acts" were commonly voiced. Now, denunciations of the Assembly came throughout summer and early autumn from pioneer communities. Intruders from Connecticut were known to have set up cabins and farms in Wyoming, challenged the sovereignty of Pennsylvania, and increased the menace from the Indians. There was no interpreter left in the province like good Conrad Weiser, now dead for three years, to intervene for the safety of the western counties.

All these facts receded from the mind of the Reverend Mr. Peters as he reviewed his own words to the King. However much the "voice of Vengeance" kept crying aloud to Thomas Barton's world at Lancaster, only the dullest recollections of it murmured within the ears of that valiant preacher-warrior's Anglican brother in Philadelphia at the close of October.

Then, within a fortnight of Richard Peters' reperusal of what seemed his masterpiece in the *Pennsylvania Gazette,* the awaited Mr. John Penn arrived in the Delaware. With him was his younger brother Richard, but no sign of Italian musician or fiddle, and the Rector of the United Congregations deplored not at all the fact that Mr. Joseph Shippen should be doing the honors to the new Deputy Governor.

Rather, he was delighted that young Mr. Penn should have his commission published with such solemnity at the Courthouse, should be attended with so great a concourse of people, and be greeted with a royal salute from the Battery guns. When the finale of compliments to the scion of the Family of Penn came in the pealing of the bells of Christ Church, something like beatitude filled Mr. Peters' heart.

After that, in mid-November, it seemed anticlimactic for the former Secretary to be introducing to Philadelphia the surveyors, Charles Mason and Jeremiah Dixon, who had just arrived in America with a commission jointly made in London by the Penns and Lord Baltimore and approved by His Majesty's Council, for running a final and authoritative line between the two provinces of Pennsylvania and Maryland—although that service should admittedly prove an important duty and enterprise.

XVIII

Riot and Respite

Neither Christ's Kingdom nor the white-breasted, gentlehearted dove of peace came to Pennsylvania in 1763. Nor was the arrival of Mr. John Penn in the late autumn an augury of happy days. Rather than bask in prosperity and quiet following the defeat of France in North America, that young Lieutenant Governor was to face acute problems in the internal affairs of the province.

The end of the fighting with the French did not bring composure to the frontiers; it did not cleanse the minds of men of suspicions. Everywhere, instead, back inhabitants suspected the "friendly" Indians watched over by the government or sheltered in Moravian missions—as army officers had suspected them in the days of Braddock. Few common folk questioned the fact of their constantly conniving with foes in the forests hardly more malignant than themselves. Every sudden swoop of native warriors from the woods on isolated cabins and families, every murder and scalping achieved by the almost invisible and always unanticipated enemy, had a dual effect. Troubled Scotch-Irish folk in Cumberland, Lancaster, Berks, and Northampton Counties were prompt to blame go-betweens near at hand, and they were eager to exact reprisal. In October, Colonel John Elder, fighting pastor of Paxton Church in Lancaster County, hearkened to the appeals of two of his captains, Lazarus Stewart and Asher Clayton, to lead two companies of the Paxton scouts, defenders of the Susquehanna, to Wyoming. Their reconnoitering in that valley beloved of the Delawares discovered to them far worse matters than fields of corn rumored to have been abandoned (to the comfort of the Indians) by the intruding people from Connecticut. It discovered the massacred body of many a rash New Englander. In pity and horror, unmindful of Proprietary convictions that the men from the eastern province had no right to be there, the Rangers buried the mangled dead of a dozen Yankee families and returned anxious to their cabins and kinsmen in Paxton, Derry, and Donegal Townships. In them was a new consciousness of the vengeful natives and old doubts of every aborigine who might be a secret ally to his malice and cunning. Expostulations had been going all summer to the Provincial Council and the Assembly. Warnings kept advising that no Indians protected by the Government or nurtured as converts by the Moravians should be left in positions where they could traffic with the foe. Neither the Assembly nor the Governor gave effectual heed.

In vain, the Reverend Mr. Elder, fully informed of conditions through his command of the Paxton Rangers, had written in September to James Hamilton: "I suggest to you the propriety of an immediate removal of the Indians from Conestoga and placing a garrison in their room." No attention had been given to his proffered guarantee: "In case this is done, I pledge myself for the future security of the frontiers." Nor was consideration granted to others who warned similarly. Yet Paxton scouts were sure they had traced marauding Indians to the wigwams of the "friendly" Conestogoes on the manor set aside for their use in Lancaster County and to the huts of proselytes among the Moravians of Northampton, and Indian crimes against lonely settlers continued. Appeals and revilings went on through November.

Then, in December, came action, rude pioneer justice, amazement, outcry, grim approval, stern condemnation.

In the cover of night, a band of Paxton "Boys" rode off to Conestoga, dismounted, tethered their horses, and crept on the village. One Indian detected them coming, fired, and charged toward them, tomahawk in hand.

"Mark him," cried a first Paxtonian, "he's the villain who murdered my mother."

Scotch-Irish blood ran into a sudden, unstayable frenzy, and children of the followers of John Knox became violent slayers. Four men and two women died under the shots of the youthful frontier assailants—in their number the old chief Sheehays, whom that responsible member of Mr. Elder's congregation, Matthew Cowden, had so often warned against harboring strange Indians at Conestoga. Then, their angry and hasty deed done, the rangers remounted and rode homeward. On the heels of their raid, excitement ran through the whole province.

A day of black memories entered into the annals of Pennsylvania. News of the outbreak against the friendly Conestogoes and government sped to Philadelphia. Assemblymen spoke in bitter condemnation, Quakers grieved for the slaughtered Indian wards of the Commonwealth and the ruthlessness of back inhabitants murderers, Presbyterian ministers like Francis Alison, Gilbert Tennant, and John Ewing, and Presbyterian communicants were shocked but not precipitate to denounce their fellow Scotch-Irish. Fourteen of the Conestogoes, rescued by the magistrates of Lancaster, were removed from the ruins of their town to shelter in the workhouse of the county seat. Mr. John Penn, the Reverend Mr. Peters, and other members of the Council met promptly in the capital city to review the outrage and act upon measures.

Their combined wisdom resulted in a ringing proclamation on the 19th. All judges, justices, sheriffs, constables, officers, civil and military, and all other of His Majesty's liege subjects in the province of Pennsylvania were to search out, apprehend, and secure in public jails the perpetrators of the violent act until their trials could be proceeded with. Further by his December manifesto, the young executive "strictly forbade" all Pennsylvanians in any way to molest or injure such friendly Indians as were because of the Government's desire to preserve and continue the old friendship, being cared for at the public expense of Province Island or elsewhere in the neighborhood of Philadelphia.

Five days afterward, the Assembly, responsive for the time being to a Governor's will, conveyed a message to Mr. John Penn by its Quaker speaker, Isaac Norris. "Extremely concerned" by reason of "the unprovoked cruelties committed on the peaceable Indians at Conestoga," the legislative body thanked the executive for informing them of the horrid and barbarous affair. Further, they volunteered to provide funds for such friendly Indians as had escaped the fury of their lawless assailants and could be gathered together and sheltered into "the interior parts of the province."

Then, on December 27, direct action was taken for a second time by the frontiersmen of Paxton—more daringly than on the 14th, more openly, in the fullness of day. As Edward Shippen wrote of it from Lancaster several hours later to the Governor, "upwards of a hundred armed men" rode into that town between two and three o'clock in the afternoon, turned their horses into Mr. Slough's inn yard, and proceeded to the workhouse with the greatest precipitation. There, they "stove open the door and killed all the Indians." So brisk indeed were the movements of the followers of Lazarus Stewart and Matthew Smith that, before Mr. Shippen had got halfway down to the scene, they had returned to their horses, mounted, and ridden off again. The mayor of the city could gather little more from sheriff and coroner and others, who had got to the workhouse as soon as the rioters, than that these could not prevail with the Paxtonians to desist and that the Conestogoes were dead. Also, he reported to John Penn several persons had heard the marauders say they would proceed next to Province Island and destroy the Indians there. In brief, as audacious and vigorous a deed as had ever occurred in Pennsylvania history or would again occur had been performed. The enduring horror of life in the back counties had turned wild the blood of even white men.

Before the slaughter could be told of in Philadelphia, the Reverend Mr. Elder, who had pleaded with men of his congregation in the morning not to ride into Lancaster as they threatened to do, had learned the tale of their horrible excursion. Scottish-born, a graduate of the famous University of Edinburgh, proud as any English peer of his breed, forced by the hardships of his congregation to become a soldier as well as a pastor in Paxton, he knew he must also now be not only spiritual guide but judge and advocate as well to his people. On the night of the second slaying, he wrote gravely, defensively, not apologetically, to Governor Penn. "The storm, so long gathering," he remarked, "had at length exploded. Had the Government removed the Indians from Conestoga, as was frequently urged without success, this painful catastrophe might have been avoided." "What could I do," he challenged, "with men heated to madness? All that I could do was done. I expostulated, but life and reason were set at defiance." "Yet the men," he declared, "were in private life virtuous and respectable, not cruel, but mild and merciful." He predicted that the time would come when every "palliating circumstance would be calmly weighed." The deed, now certain to be magnified into the blackest of crimes, should someday "be considered one of those youthful ebullitions of wrath, caused by momentary excitement, to which human infirmity is subjected."

It was a strange letter for the shepherd of a flock of Christians to write, and neither Mr. John Penn nor members of his Council inclined, when they read it, to accept "palliating circumstances" or "youthful ebullitions" as a warrant for the destruction of fourteen more Indians at Lancaster, men, women, and children. When three Indian fathers, three squaws, and eight children, according to the official list of names furnished by Sheriff John Hay of Lancaster, had been slain in a second atrocity, they would bow to no excuse for "human infirmity." All that they could conclude was that the Government must apprehend the perpetrators of the heinous offense, guard against any further repetition of the massacre, and shield the province from any new wrath of the Six Nations while Colonel Bouquet was still occupied in the west with Indians made restless by Pontiac. So in the last days of that fateful December, the Governor, the old Secretary of Pennsylvania, Mr. Peters, the new Secretary, Mr. Shippen, and the other Councillors were much occupied with conference, correspondence, and proclamation. Mr. Penn was advised to write to Colonel Armstrong at Carlisle and to Mr. Elder at Paxton to urge these to exert themselves by all means in their power to discover and detect the rioters and for the future to suppress all such insurrections among the people under their influence. Letters on the subject were dispatched to General Gage, Commander-in-Chief of His Majesty's forces in America, and Sir William Johnson practiced intercessor with the Six Nations. Plans were matured for protecting the Indians being cared for at public expense on Province Island. Rewards of £200 each were proposed for the detection of ringleaders in the riots at Conestoga and the Lancaster workhouse. To add to the weightiness of the Council, whose meeting of Thursday, December 29, was better attended than had been any meeting for years, a new member was elected into the body—with "particular satisfaction and pleasure" to all—in the person of Mr. Richard Penn, younger brother to the Governor.

On the same day, Mr. John Penn wrote austerely to Mr. Elder. "For the preservation of peace and good order in the Government," he observed that it was absolutely necessary to put a stop to riotous proceedings. He begged the pastor to discourage and suppress insurrections among the people over whom he had an influence. He enjoined him "to take all the pains in his power to learn the names of the perpetrators of those barbarities and to acquaint me with everything you can discover concerning them." Moreover, he informed him that decision had been made yesterday to retain thereafter only one commander of the troops on the east side of Susquehanna, that thereafter the pay of himself and Mr. Seeley, as officers of the companies in Lancaster and Berks Counties, would be discontinued, and all the men of those parts and Northampton be placed under the direction of Major Clayton. In closing, he directed Colonel Elder to deliver over to the new commander all arms and accouterments and records, and he thanked him "for the care and the prudence with which you have conducted your military command from the beginning." In fact, after Conestoga and Lancaster, the commission of the fighting parson of the back-inhabitant Presbyterians had been canceled.

The first months of the new year, which followed hard upon the resolved but anxious deliberations of the Provincial Council, were replete with unrest and argument in Philadelphia. Rumor and angry debate permeated streets and taverns, Quakers' gentle persuasions met stony hearts in Presbyterians, and all parties in the city exonerated their souls of guilt. Councilors blamed Assemblymen for never having given due regard to the care of the frontiers. Assemblymen reiterated the perennial weakness of the executive branch of the Government for never effectually enforcing the laws of the Commonwealth. Private citizens deplored the incapacities of both Assembly and Council. Some condemned the Indians, some the ruthless Scotch-Irish. Wags and apologists, whose fervor was left unquieted by forensic ardors on street corner, at the till, or in the public house, resorted to contributions to the printing press, windy polemic and scoffing satire began to flourish, and their mushroom growth ran into prompt publication. Less articulate and more timid folk feared frankly that the Paxtonians' insurrection might presently turn into a rude pioneer judgment upon the whole metropolis of Philadelphia. The defense of the city was thought of seriously by both commoners and officials.

The situation sobered Mr. John Penn; his Councillors argued their wisdom one with another, perused in their conferences the responses that came to their letters or demanded new funds from the Assembly for strengthening the hands of Government. General Gage sent word from New York that he was ordering immediately to Philadelphia three companies of the First Battalion of the Royal Americans, then on the march from Albany, who should be entirely at Governor Penn's command when they arrived. Until they should be at hand, he had sent instructions to the commander of His Majesty's troops at Carlisle to support the civil authority of Pennsylvania in the execution of the laws. Governor Cadwallader Colden wrote his regret that His Majesty's Council of New York could not approve the admission to that province of such Indians as Governor Penn wished to send there for protection; coolly, he offered his opinion that the Indians on the east side of the Susquehanna were the most obnoxious to New York, and had done the most mischief. He even cited the fact that for some time, he had been forced to dissuade men of his province from going out against them to give them the due of their cruelties and perfidy.

The Assembly, through Mr. Norris, recommended repression of such dangerous insurgencies as had occurred in Lancaster County and suggested to the Council to order the Sheriff and the coroner of that part, together with the magistrates of the borough, to come down to Philadelphia, and to require of these the best information possible on the offenders. Mr. Benjamin Kendall, a Quaker merchant of the city, made a solemn affirmation that he had heard from one Robert Fulton of Pequea, Lancaster, that if Captain Coultas raised the five hundred men in the city intended for the protection of the capital, then fifteen hundred men from the frontiers would march down and destroy the Indians sheltering there. He affirmed as solemnly that, should Mr. Coultas assume the said responsibility, Fulton had advised that "he make his peace with Heaven, for he would not live two weeks longer." Governor Penn, acting on his sanction from General Gage, sent orders to Captain William Murray at Carlisle to transfer his company from there to defend the city of Lancaster. Sir William Johnson wrote more sympathetically than Governor Colden, but he wrote apprehensively. He had conferred with the Six Nations, representing the goodwill and cordial intentions of the Government of Pennsylvania, explaining its intention of punishing the rioters, and deploring the incident, but he feared that "would stagger the affections of the Five Nations who had continued most well affected." Gratifying as was Mr. Penn's suggestion of sending the endangered Indians at Philadelphia into his protection, Sir William had, unfortunately, been informed by Governor Colden that they could not be admitted to New York. Round the Council tables, day after day, sat other members and the Reverend Mr. Richard Peters with the young Commander-in-Chief of Pennsylvania, pondering the problems of the state. Outside in the square, at the Courthouse, along Jersey Market, the rumor of citizens persisted. Thousands of infuriated back inhabitants were said to be marching on the metropolis. Volunteer organizations like the Associators of 1748 were springing into being to ward off the new sort of enemy threatening peace and security. And no one, official or obscure, had sent in from the back counties the name of either ringleader or participant in the insurrections of Conestoga Manor and Lancaster. So far as the Presbyterians and Scotch-Irish of the west were concerned, the identity of the rioters had been as indistinguishable in the daylight of Lancaster on December 27, 1763, as it had been in the shadows of the night on December 14 at the Conestoga town.

In early February, the young scion of the Penns, who was being tutored in government by his Uncle Thomas' friend, Mr. Peters, received a letter from Mr. Elder which revealed, for better or worse, the temper both of that minister and of the frontier inhabitants. There was no humility for Richard Peters to find in its phrases. No longer Colonel Elder, the writer bowed graciously to Governor Penn's commands in military matters. He had resigned to Major Clayton the whole of his charge, accounts and stores remaining at Harris' had been resigned to that officer. He was obliged to his Honor for his kindly approving his proceedings in the discharge of the trust lately reposed in him. But, beyond that point, John Elder was a pastor and man. He intended to use his endeavors to promote peace among all people with whom he had any connections. He was concerned that the rash proceedings of a few inconsiderate persons were likely to be attended with fatal consequences. However much the facts committed by these had been, and were, disliked by thinking and judicious men, he revealed quite patently his conviction that there was a small absence of guilt from a government that "caressed" friendly Indians while it let hundreds of frontier families, "His Majesty's loyal and faithful subjects, be driven from house and home, and reduced to poverty and want." He hoped thereafter for a more prudent legislation in Philadelphia. His concluding paragraph burned with the proud fire of his breed and the solemn dedication of his calling:

> Were it in my power to learn the names of any concerned in the late riots, I should think it advisable, on many accounts, to use silence in that case. The character of an informer is one too odious for a gentleman to bear. Besides, the office I have the honor to be invested with in the Church requires that I should do nothing that may have a tendency to mar my usefulness in that station, but anything else that may be thought necessary to promote His Majesty's service, or beneficial to the Province, may at all times be expected from your Honor's most obedient and most humble servant.

For, whatever else they might know them to be, Governor Penn and Mr. Peters knew the Scotch-Irish were not a race of informers.

Indeed, there was something almost fanatically open in the behavior which was exhibited by even certain of the rioters in February 1764. Some five hundred men out of back counties congregated about them, failed to be intercepted by magistrates of Lancaster and Berks Counties, to whom John Penn sent instructions to hinder them, camped peacefully on the bank of the Schuylkill near Germantown, made no motion to penetrate to the barracks in which frightened Indians were housed in the city, and no offer to sack Philadelphia. The bustling of citizens prepared to defend the capital was in vain. No assault was attempted on their persons or their property.

Only a throng of silent men waited in mid-February for the fathers of the city and the executives of a province to take note, not of their rebellion against their governors but of their statements of grievance. Excitement died down. No white man, and no Indian, was threatened or murdered. Quakers who had grown militant in self-defense could lay aside weapons with which they were unfamiliar. Presbyterians could smile more genially, assured that their back-county brethren were not plunderers. Refugees from the ravages of ten years in western settlements could sympathize frankly with the poor folk on the borders of the city.

Assembly and Council acted in fashions characteristic of themselves. There were instructions, conferences, and refusals. Commissioners waited upon the visitants on the Schuylkill. Matthew Smith's and James Gibson's written and signed statements of grievance for the frontiers were received and read. Through a committee, the Assembly proposed that Governor Penn and members of the

Council arrange to collaborate with a group of the House, meet with some of the remonstrants, and show them the fallacies in their claims of neglect by the Government. Mr. John Penn took the position that it was not consonant with the dignity of the executive branch to enter "into any argument or justification with the petitioners on the subject of their complaints," let the representative branch determine what was, or was not, a real grievance and act. The Assembly recorded the clauses of the Paxtonians' protest and took no further measures.

As for the protestants, having said what they had to say to white men in peaceful spirit, they dispersed again to their homes, retained their convictions, set their hopes on what Colonel Bouquet might yet do against the Indians in the Ohio country, looked more to their own right arms for security than to lawmakers in Philadelphia, and anticipated fewer ills from the Indians nearest them amid their own rivers and mountains. In the city, persons who were well-to-do enough began buying and reading the pamphlets and broadsides of critics, apologists, and wits.

Promptly seizing the opportunity to endorse not only the sentiments of the Quaker Assembly but also those of the Councillors of the Province, Mr. Franklin led off with his *Narrative of the Late Massacre of Indians in Lancaster County*, and, besides punctually alienating all other stalwart Presbyterians from his interest, aroused the blunt rejoinder of the Reverend Mr. Ewing in *Conduct of the Paxton Men Impartially Represented*. That second pamphlet, fortified with a quotation from the Latin of Lucretius on truth and falsity and fired in its patriotism by a passage in English from Cato's *Letters*, tempted a retort that pretended to "manifest" the "Ungenerous Spirit" of its author and claimed to pluck away from him his "Spotted Garment." To the energy of the diatribe against John Ewing was opposed *The Quaker Unmasked, or Plain Truth,* and in rapid succession, the censor of that divine was replied to in *Remarks on the Quaker Unmasked, or Plain Truth to be Plain Falsehood* and *The Author of the Quaker Unmasked Stript Stark Naked, or the Delineated Presbyterian Played Hob with*. Those two redoubtable instances of argument evoked, by way of a new exercise in print, a proffer of *Clothes for a Stark Naked Author,* and that latter ironic generosity was countered with *A Looking Glass for Presbyterians*.

Presently, the pamphleteers, after the pungencies of their wits, as well as of quotations from Cicero, Horace, and Alexander Pope, had come near exhaustion and turned into original rhymsters. Farces "out of the original French" were translated into heroic couplets by "natives of Dunnegal," and publication of such parodies was made in the "New Hegira Secundus," a brave young epoch just introduced by "the Paxtonian Expedition." To round out satire and polemic, Christopher Gymnast composed "The Paxtoniade," in what he (rather wrongly) supposed he caught the heroic-comical air of the great writer of the *Rape of the Lock*. Finally, to consummate the vogue of mock epic, a series of copper-plate caricatures made an appearance. One of these, more virile than the rest, pictured the defense of the Friends' Meeting House on the south side of Market Street. Armed men, stationed as it were against an imminent attack by the Paxton followers of Matthew Smith and James Gibson, defended that usually peaceful conventicle. A label below the engraving wished "Success to the new barracks," while Quaker guards leaning from second-story windows of the edifice portrayed called, "Bring the grog upstairs." A last graphic broadside presented Israel Pemberton embracing an Indian Squaw, and, in the rhyming legend below, flaunted its conviction:

> When danger is threatened 'tis mere nonsense
> To talk of such a thing as conscience.
> To arms! to arms! with one accord,
> The sword of Quakers and the Lord.

Philadelphia, in brief, had its nine weeks of alarm and then, following them, its protracted nine days of wonder. The former Secretary of the Province, Mr. Richard Peters, was not certain that the town had lost its old giddiness. But quiet, if not discipline, had returned. Governor Penn could report, to the relief of his uncle in England, that the anticipated assault on the capital had materialized in only a remonstrance. Whatever might be the opinions of Matthew Smith and James Gibson and their back-inhabitant followers in the affair, Mr. Ben Chew could assume credit to himself for having induced the remonstrants to return to their counties. Moreover, happier news had at length come from the Ohio country. The troops of Colonel Bouquet had penetrated to the heart of the settlement of the Shawnees and the Delawares at the heads of the Muskingum, defeated the Indians, and obliged them to deliver up all their white prisoners and to send deputies to Sir William Johnson to arrange for and accept such terms of peace as that dignitary might determine to impose upon them. In the spring of 1764, the good folk of Paxton, Carlisle, and Conococheague could look forward to having children and mothers brought back to them from years of wandering with redskin conquerors.

And in that same spring, the friends of the invalid Rector of Christ Church and St. Peter's could hearten him for taking his long-contemplated voyage to England. Mr. John Penn had been launched in government. Celebration of peace in the province had become a more justifiable sort of activity. Provost William Smith had returned from his long visit abroad not only to take immediate charge of the Academy but to rejoice in the £10,000 and more which his labors of preaching and soliciting in the three kingdoms of George III had won to be shared by the two Colleges of Philadelphia and New York. Mr. Sturgeon and Mr. Duche were at hand to carry on the offices of minister and preacher at the two United Churches. So every material cause and every person coincided to encourage a visit to England. Assistants and fellow Councillors urged it. Mr. Peters' health, intermittently bad and endurable between February and May, might well be improved by reunion with his relatives in England and restful sojourns at the watering places of Britain. No harm could come to the province by Mr. Peters' visiting in person with Mr. Thomas Penn. The cause of Christ Church might be helped by its Rector's waiting upon the Bishop of London and the Archbishop of Canterbury when he got to the metropolis.

With Elizabeth Graeme, the daughter of his old friend and physician, on the same vessel with him, he sailed for Liverpool on June 18. It was good to know that that gifted and aristocratic young woman would be near him during the voyage, to realize that she too was traveling to be inspirited by contacts with her kinsmen in Scotland and the numerous connections of her mother's people, the Keiths, and of her father's in Great Britain. Moreover, Richard Peters had never inclined to shun the society of a female of virtue or charm.

Naturally, he bore letters with him: to the Proprietor, to ecclesiastics, to friends' friends. John Penn wrote to his uncle, apprehensive that Mr. Peters "could not have got through the summer" in Philadelphia but predicting at the same time that the former Secretary would be capable of acquainting Thomas Penn with the situation in the province far better than he could write of it. More precious were the tributes among his papers to which he had access. The Provost, the Vice-Provost, and the professors of the Academy expressed in fulsome terms not only their private regard and esteem but their "public sense of the many obligations he had conferred on this Seminary." His name, they assured him, "stands among the first of those who set this pious design on foot." His zeal for "its advancement had shone conspicuous in his sermon preached at the opening of it." His services as a trustee for fourteen years had suffered no remission. Constantly, the faculty had had friendship and assistance from him and scholars' kindest advice and countenance. He had witnessed and fostered the great progress of the institution. Their prayers for his health went with him to England and for a safe and speedy return to his friends and connections in the province. Treasured, too, was the address of the ministers, churchwardens, and vestry of the United Churches of Christ and St. Peter's to their beloved leader. In it was gratitude for his long and faithful services both as layman and rector. In it was praise of the prudence of his conduct. His "liberality, piety, and other good qualities had endeared him to all of them." Their sincere prayers were offered to Heaven that he might be preserved from the dangers of the seas. They prayed he might speedily be restored in health to exercise his ministry among them. All the words of his friends and his congregation brought Mr. Peters a warm sense of the beauty in unity.

Arrived in Liverpool, Miss Graeme took the stage from there to her relations in Scotland, and the Rector of Christ Church for a time renewed ties with his English kinsfolk. Near at hand were faces not seen for thirty years and new younger faces in the Statham and Peters families. All around were familiar scenes and streets. The affection of his delicate sister, Hannah Statham, comforted him. Her son Richard, his namesake, was all youthful cordiality. His oldest nephew, Ralph Peters, was intelligent and responsive as he was gravely kind, and Ralph's wife, Elizabeth, was as charming and well-bred as any young woman in Philadelphia might ever dream of being.

Yet Mr. Peters had not disembarked into the happiness of Zion. His physical disabilities kept him uncomfortable in person. Fitful recollections of old days came back painfully in Liverpool. Ormskirk and Lathom, places of his early ministry, lay not far to the north in Lancashire. Within a two-hour ride of Liverpool was Knowsley Palace, with all the Stanley kinsmen of the tenth Earl of Derby gone long ago from it. Troubling memories of an unfortunate and rudely broken alliance at moments haunted the mind of the visitor from Philadelphia. Although Mr. Thomas Penn was awaiting him in London, London in August was a hot city, and Richard Peters had come to England for the recovery of his health. The metropolis was hardly a town- to resort to in the summer.

He determined, therefore, to regain all that he could of strength before journeying on to see his friend, the Proprietor of Pennsylvania, and to that end, chose to try the old reputed spa of Scarborough on the east coast. An arduous journey carried him thither. But the mineral waters proved not to agree with him, and he gave up early the drinking of them. Moreover, the chill winds from the North Sea made impossible the refreshment he had hoped for from air and sunlight on the sandy bays of the Yorkshire center for treatments and fashion. So he was glad when September came, and he could repair southwards. Mr. Penn welcomed him late that month for what turned into a visit of six weeks with the Proprietor and his family at their town house in London and their country seat in Bucks.

The Rector of Christ Church could have come into no environment more tonic for him at the time. Host and guest had been in close correspondence for more than a quarter of a century. With an ocean between them, their tastes and their interests had become one. The two men were almost of an age, the older having the advantage of only three years over the retired Secretary and recently reinstalled priest. One topic absorbed them: the right government in Pennsylvania and the Penns as the chief agency to it. Upon that, they talked, whether they dined or supped, whether they walked in the gardens of Stoke or rode together in the Buckinghamshire lanes. Always, the subject was more in their minds than the simple grave of William Penn at the Friends' Meeting-House at Jordans, so near, after all, to the proud old Tudor manor that the Family had recently purchased to increase their aristocratic, not their Quaker, prestige. The melancholy yews and the moldering graves of Stoke Poges might have stirred Thomas Gray to his famous "Elegy" some fifteen years earlier, for Richard Peters and the Proprietor, when the two men regarded them at all, these were but shadows passed ere the Family made their way up the aisle of the church to worship in a paneled pew both ample and august enough for a royal duke, his duchess, and their whole ducal progeny to occupy.

For to libraries and offices crowded with letter books, dossiers of lawsuits, packets of correspondence, prospectus volumes on city and province, maps, plots, globes, shelves and files of duplicate warrant and patent books, the Penns had been adding all the perquisites of wealth and venerable race. The manners, the privileges, and almost the responsibilities of the peerage in England toward folk of the lesser breed had become theirs; everywhere at Stoke were the signs of their graciousness and gentility. And beyond—or, perhaps, in spite of all—was something of natural kindness, care for a loyal servant, love for a friend. When the mind was not too engrossed in business, government, or perpetuation of stock and line, the affections stirred simply. In rich moments, not the past, and not poetry, appealed, but human interchange between persons long acquainted and no more at odds in their selfishness.

Richard Peters was, in fact, for the interim happy. Politics in the province seemed far away: troublesome elections to the Assembly, Mr. Franklin's machinations, even that renegade's rumored intentions of coming again to England to urge on the Ministry the conversion of Pennsylvania into a Crown colony. For at hand were Mr. Penn's friends and solicitors to protect the Family with the Board of Trade, and at Court, the Archbishop of Canterbury had received Mr. Peters graciously at Lambeth Palace, apart from churchly and business hours, two lovely women were interesting themselves in the welfare of the guest from

America. Lady Juliana and her husband's niece, Miss Philadelphia Hannah Freame, whom Richard Peters remembered from her babyhood in the province as tiny Miss Phil, had grown into the greatest of friends and were devoting their lives together to Lady Juliana's present brood of five children. While Thomas Penn's wife cared for the infant Sophia, born only a few months earlier, Miss Freame presided over games, lessons, bedtime, and diet for the other four. But both wife and companion and kinswoman guarded over Mr. Peters' health, and he, in turn, shared with them fondly their solicitude for, or joy in, eleven-year-old Juliana, eight-year-old Louisa, four-year-old John, and three-year-old Granville—wards to be shielded by parental and Christian love, a living promise of the maintenance of a tradition. The kindly Rector looked with affectionate eyes at their play. He conversed with his amiable hostess on their traits of body and mind. He found he pleased Miss Freame no less when he talked of her pretty charges to her than when she showed him her gifted drawings. He was at peace in the autumn of 1764, and he rejoiced that Mr. Penn could write to his friends in the province, to Dr. Smith and Richard Hockley, and to his brother William, of how constantly he was improving in health. That was both earnest of his welcome in England and of the Proprietor's solid respect for him. He had had a close friendship with his master and patron and was ready in December for a second visit to Liverpool. At Christmas, he was again with the Stathams.

The year 1765 remained generally auspicious for him. He continued to grow stronger, and other good reports of him went back to Philadelphia. In February, he rejoined the Penns and once more enjoyed the society of Miss Freame, Lady Juliana, and the children. But there were problems of state to review with his host, and the two men had much to talk about during the next two months in the Proprietor's town house in Spring Gardens, Westminster. Contested lands on the Maryland boundary drew rather less on their time, now that the work of Mason and Dixon was progressing so capably, but much to the fore was the topic of Mr. Franklin, and new Parliamentary measures applying to America could not relevantly be disregarded.

Mr. Penn was himself, on the whole, cheerful. The Paxton affair at Conestoga and Lancaster had by now brought more disrepute upon the "squabbling" Assembly than on the Government in Pennsylvania. Sir William Johnson had written informatively to the Lords of Trade on the fraudulent purchase by Lydius for Connecticut, and that matter could now be truthfully represented to the English Ministry. The Presbyterians in the province had rallied to the Proprietary party, and letters and petitions had come to London from such leading ones of their divines as Dr. Francis Alison and Mr. John Ewing and from their flocks appealing for the continuance of Proprietary government. The eminent Philadelphia lawyer, Mr. John Dickinson, despite family connections with the leaders of the fractious Legislature, had published a weighty speech which, though it showed no regard to "the Family," argued that no advantage could come to Pennsylvania by a change in government. Thomas Penn did not believe that Ben Franklin was going to be received well when he came to London to present whatever petitions the Assembly might frame to have the King take the administration of the commonwealth under the direct charge of his Ministry. The Reverend Mr. Peters was himself satisfied that the old inveterate partisan against the Proprietors would soon cease, will he nill he, being a plague to them. Nothing comforted more the absent Rector of Christ Church and St. Peter's than that his great friend could write assuringly to the Presbyterians of Philadelphia that they would not have withdrawn from them the protecting care of the Penn Family. Indeed, persons close to His Majesty George III had, he knew, averred the royal will would sanction no such withdrawal.

Pleased with prospects for the province, Richard Peters could more cheerfully part again from his hosts in Spring Gardens and at Stoke. In April, avoiding the more rigorous social life of Bath, he took up residence for a season of more comparative quiet at Mr. Speed's in Albemarle Street, Bristol, to avail himself of the hot well at that city. There, while the Penns suffered an incursion of smallpox on their two little boys in Buckinghamshire and won a victory over the ordeal, he kept on mending. And there, while Mr. Penn had reluctantly become involved in plans for the effectuation of Parliament's new Stamp Act in the province, he remained for much of the summer. He partook of cures in the reinvigorating baths of the place and drinking the waters in the pump-room, learned to his content that, although the Proprietor had sanctioned means of forwarding sheets of the new tax stamps to Philadelphia and procedure in collecting the imposition there, Mr. Penn had carefully avoided having anything to do with the appointment of a collector for Pennsylvania, was gratified that the odium of choosing that agent had been left to Mr. Franklin. He was cheered to realize that in 1765, the Ministry would concede nothing more to the representative of the truculent Pennsylvania Assembly than a chance to embroil himself with folk in the province among whom the Stamp Tax was bound to be unpopular. He doubted that the politician Ben's present insinuation of himself into concurrence with the measure of Parliament would bring him prosperity in his own designs later. He suspected that the appointee to the collectorship, Mr. John Hughes, would find himself in a hornet's nest when he attempted to carry out his official duties in Philadelphia. Away from forum, marketplace, and pulpit, he relaxed, entered into an affable relationship with his landlord and host, Mr. Speed, and from time to time paid his respects to Miss Graeme, come also to Bristol for the cure, and to her hostess, dear Miss Finch, to whom on his own coming he had brought the compliments of Lady Juliana and her niece, Miss Freame. Back to him, more and more came his health, and by August, his heart was quickening sensitively to thoughts of his church and the city of his adoption.

Already, responding to an old wish of Mr. Peters, the Proprietor had forwarded to Mr. John Penn the charter incorporating Christ Church and St. Peter's. In the Rector of the United Churches was the will not only to resume his calling but to increase and further the values made possible to those two sanctuaries and congregations by the new favor of the authentic Governors of Pennsylvania. Health and enlarged usefulness, what more than those could a priest desire? Holding on to that thought made easier the farewells for which he returned to Liverpool, and, even after parting again from his sister, Mrs. Statham, he returned to London in mid-August to close his affairs once more in England. A third time, Thomas Penn welcomed and cared for him. There were last talks at Stoke with the family and the last views of the children. There were arrangements for his voyage. There was a last formality with His Lordship of London.

On September 16, 1765, twenty-three years after Bishop Gibson had refused to rehabilitate Richard Peters in his function, Bishop Richard Terrick admitted him to the proper ecclesiastic declaration. There was no Latin diploma of ordination now to be recorded. Yet there was a forthright Anglo-Saxon quality in the set words of the two certificates which were given to the applicant. One declared over the candidate's name that he would "conform to the Liturgy of the Church of England, as it is by law now established." The other, over the Bishop's name and seal, licensed Richard Peters "to perform the office of priest in the United Churches of Christ and St. Peter's in the City of Philadelphia." Further than that, it pledged the reauthorized priest to conformity to all the authorities, usages, canons, and constitutions of the Church of England as by Parliament established. In the Rector who took the vows on that solemn day was no thought that ever again he would challenge, as he tried to forget he had in 1741 foolishly attempted to question, the right of the Bishop of London to preside over the spiritual destinies of any congregation in the American Colonial Church.

Indeed, the candidate, who three weeks later had sailed from Gravesend and out upon the Atlantic, was glad he carried with him on shipboard memories of a perfected reconciliation with that sacred institution in England, from the full measure of whose peace he had been sadly estranged for almost a lifetime. Remembering that new fact in his experience, he grieved less to be separated now from his relatives in Liverpool and his friends at Spring Gardens or Stoke House. From these, he knew he was bearing many letters, official and private, to Philadelphia, and he enjoyed knowing that through his delivery of them in the province, he would be one further link between the mother country and America. Yet none of the papers he bore with him gave him greater personal happiness than two letters which he had received last May while at Mr. Speed's and ever since treasured. One was from Lady Juliana and the other from Miss Freame.

Lady Juliana Penn, at the town house in Westminster and Stoke, had shared with him her pleasure in religion and the love of her children. Her letter was full of pious kindness and sweet family life. He thought tenderly of her account of her two boys' diet and their playfulness when their tiny faces and hands were marked with spots not yet recognized in May when she wrote as smallpox. He cherished her womanly solicitude for the health of her three friends at Bristol—Miss Finch, Miss Graeme, and himself—and the compliments the latter two ladies had written of himself to his good hostess in London.

As for Philadelphia Hannah Freame, granddaughter of old Mr. William Penn, she was Lady Juliana in another person. She lived for her aunt and Mr. Penn's children, and she knew she had in the Reverend Mr. Peters, one who sympathized with her in her affection for merry John and Granville. Unaffectedly, she wrote of their hours abed, their sleeping and waking, their amusement with toys and their good humor. He cherished everything in her letter—not omitting a gossipy reference to the shocking affair and trial of a Lord Byron whose family remained quite too unconcerned by the matter. He appreciated her affection to Miss Graeme. He was proud that her letter had offered him the option between a "Madonna and Child" and a figure of "Cicero," drawn for him by dear Miss Freame herself, and the subject to be set, when he chose, upon vellum. He would hang his choice of the good young woman's handiwork in the best possible position for it in his Philadelphia study. It should always be a symbol to him of dear friendships in England. Aboard ship, he felt that he was being spared to carry new love of God's Kingdom to America.

XIX

Last Excursion

In February 1742, Thomas Penn wrote to Richard Peters of his satisfaction with everything in a recent treaty with the Indians except the obligation to pay half of the cost of entertainment of the achems with whom the terms had been arranged. His mind, he admitted, was troubled because the Pennsylvania Assembly had not met the charges in full. But his letter during the same month conveyed approval to the Provincial Secretary for proposing to sound the Indians on the subject of another purchase, and Mr. Penn remarked frankly, "I should be glad to purchase Wyoming with the lands below on Susquehanna first."

Some twelve years later, in the summer of 1754, the Proprietor's faithful servant and friend was again very much aware of the existence of thousands of acres of fertile land lying along the North Branch of the Susquehanna, extending northwards toward New York, northeastwards toward the Delaware River and New Jersey, and stretching thence in the direction of the great West Branch of the same river, beyond which lay forest and mountain lands of immeasurable magnitude. Shamokin, at the point of the two forks of Susquehanna, was the gateway between Philadelphia and Onondaga, the key always to the friendship between the children of Onas and the Six Nations. And Mr. Secretary Peters was especially aware of those beautiful, unploughed, and desirable lands in that particular summer because of two treaties to which signatures had been put in July.

One of these two treaties, made in open council with Indians during the famous Congress of Albany, conveyed to Pennsylvania lands west of the Susquehanna and southwest from the Kittochtinny Hills to the southern boundary of the province—a tract as large as old Lancaster County and York and Cumberland Counties all put together, and inclusive of all those valleys from which squatters had been ejected by Mr. Peters, invested with the authority of Pennsylvania law, in 1750. The second treaty, which was rather more privately made, although negotiated between a great group of New England folk of a freeholding type and twelve or more chiefs of the Iroquois, purported to convey an even greater tract of country lying upon the Susquehanna and situate between the 41st and 42nd degrees of latitude, to the members of the Susquehanna Company, an organization embracing several hundred citizens of the Colony of Connecticut.

The first treaty, dated July 6, 1754, included agreements very precious to the Six Nations. Although the rulers of these consented to forego the territory southwards from the Blue Hills toward Maryland, they retained all their lands at Shamokin and Wyoming. In many a solemn clause, they declared:

> We reserve them for our hunting grounds and for the residence of such Indians as in this time of war shall remove from among the French and choose to live there. We have appointed John Shikellamy to take care of them. He is our representative and agent there; he has our orders not to suffer either Onas' people or New England people to settle those lands. And, if any shall presume to do it, we have directed him to complain to Onas, whether it shall be his own people or men from other Provinces, and to insist on their being turned off. If he shall fail in his application, we will come ourselves and turn them off. Nobody shall have this land.

Rather differently, the second treaty, under the first date of July 11, transmitted all this same Wyoming territory, with millions of acres more, from the Iroquois to the numerous members of the Susquehanna Company in Connecticut. One clause in it observed that its purpose was to contribute to the safety of the Six Nations and their defense against the unjust encroachments and insults of the French and of Indians in alliance with these by encouraging their English brethren from New England to plant and settle in a nearer neighborhood. Mr. Peters did not, in the summer of 1754, know the separate phrases of this document, but he was fully conscious of its existence and danger and the personality of its negotiator.

John Henry Lydius, trader and agent, once the trusted friend of Sir William Johnson, often enough that dignitary's rival in Indian affairs, and latterly his enemy, had managed the business for Connecticut—a colony which Mr. Peters very well knew was claiming now to have been granted by royal charter from Charles II in 1662 certain western lands which stretched as far as the South Seas, and which—as, unhappily, when they were mapped from the northern boundary of the New England province, they lay between the 41st and 42od degrees of latitude—coincided with territories afterward bestowed upon William Penn by a second charter from the same monarch in 1681. Both the Secretary of Pennsylvania and Mr. Lydius knew equally well that before 1750, there had been no intent among the citizens and officials of the New England province to effect any colonization west of the Hudson or the Delaware. Likewise, the two men did not severally miss the fact that the clauses of the two treaties conflicted with each other, and both were conscious that—whether or not there had been any practice of duplicity on the part of either of them at Albany during the Congress—a goodly number of Indian chieftains had signed both the deeds. Mr. Peters troubled himself to find out so far as he could just what ones of the sachems who in open council had been responsive to him and to Mr. Weiser had also been wax to the touch of the manipulator for the New England company of freemen. He realized sensitively that there would be inquiries in due season from Mr. Penn, and he was confident that the Proprietor would not choose to let the Wyoming lands slip through his fingers into the grasp of any band of Yankee intruders.

Indeed, after 1754, apart from Ben Franklin, Richard Peters regarded John Henry Lydius as the greatest villain in Colonial America, and in a decade of Pennsylvania history, the Secretary of the Province and the later Rector of Christ Church was not indifferent to whatever evils might fall on the fortunes of the Penns through the malefactions of Lydius. He became watchful in America, as the Proprietor became watchful in London, and he remained alert whether Robert Hunter Morris, William Denny, James Hamilton, or Mr. John Penn held office at Philadelphia as Deputy Governor. The years passed slowly.

In September 1760, he listened to the Delaware Teedyuscung's fears that people from New England were about to intrude in Wyoming and to the appeals of that king that Pennsylvania send a smart protest to the Government in Connecticut lest an Indian war grow out of the rashness of the intruders coming from the New England colony.

In February 1761, he affixed the seal of Pennsylvania to a proclamation of Governor Hamilton ordering the New Englanders out of Wyoming and enjoining all the sheriffs, magistrates, peace officers, and private subjects of George III in the Province of Pennsylvania to aid in keeping out or expelling marauders upon the premises of the Penns and of the wards of the Six Nations.

In November of 1763, he meditated sternly on the woe that the rash folk of Connecticut had brought on themselves from the Indians and on those scenes of the massacre in Wyoming, which the Paxton Rangers had come upon in horror. Always, he knew of representations against the New Englanders being made to the Prime Minister, the Lords of Trade, or the Crown from Sir William

Johnson in America or Mr. Penn in London. He was not unmindful, when he arrived at the Spring Gardens house of the Proprietor in the autumn of 1764, that one Eliphalet Dyer, an attorney from Connecticut, had been for many months in England trafficking with the Connecticut Colonial Agent, Richard Jackson, to secure the interest of the Ministry to the pretensions of the Susquehanna Company.

When, in 1765, he returned to America, he apprehended that his ward in government, Mr. John Penn, would have to keep a sharp eye on Yankees, the rights of the Indians in their Susquehanna hunting grounds, and the beautiful lands of Wyoming. Well, too, did he realize what hopes Mr. Thomas Penn entertained for the further advancement of the province over which he had inherited responsibility from his good father. When the year 1766 came, however, and the Rector of Christ Church and St. Peter's spared time from his flock and the College for more secular affairs, it was not to Wyoming that his attention was primarily devoted. Then, rather, the unpopularity of the Stamp Tax in Philadelphia was a source of care to him, and the unresponsiveness of John Penn to the assistance in business which he had promised the Governor's uncle he would render came as a grief. He was concerned that James Tilghman, whom he had been thinking of for the Land Office, had risked losing favor with the Proprietor by becoming the spokesman of the multitude in Philadelphia who forced the Stamp Distributor, Mr. Hughes, to resign his office and yet was pleased when Thomas Penn wrote later from England that Parliament had repealed the offensive Act of 1765. He disliked the unsettled attitude of the people in America, and too often, he was himself ill in body. Before he sailed from England, he had left with his friend, the Proprietor, instructions for the purchase and shipping of a chariot. Letters between him and Mr. Penn for a number of months bore the burden of that transaction. He looked forward to having a coach who should both fit the dignity of his position and make movement around the city more comfortable for his weakened body.

More, in truth, than it should have done, the material world burdened him in 1766 and 1767, and had it not been that during new illnesses, he had the sympathy and solicitude of many associates, his spirit would have at moments utterly quailed. His active mind, however, was always as interested in treatments as it was in physical symptoms. For, although Dr. Graeme was ' ever faithful in his attendance, Richard Peters studied his case thoroughly and never failed to esteem all the remedies which his less professional friends suggested.

Correspondents far and near interested themselves, summer and autumn, in his unhappily renewed experience of gravel. In August, Thomas Penn wrote from London, glad that the chariot had arrived in Philadelphia and that that vehicle would reduce the need of walking for Mr. Peters, but at the same time, urgent that the invalid do horseback riding whenever possible. Of as great service as he was to people, the Proprietor sincerely enjoined the Rector of Christ Church to adopt every measure for regaining his health and prolonging his life. The eminent Quaker, Dr. John Fothergill, forwarded from England instructions for the treatment of his disorder. Gentle William Bull of South Carolina wrote hoping the sufferer's physicians might find proper palliatives but offered consolation more this time as a Christian than as either humanist or leech. He quoted the proud Epicurean philosophy of Horace: *det vitam, det opes, aequum mi animum ipse parabo,* but advised resignation to God's will as the most effective procedure for Mr. Peters to follow. Less spiritual in his counsel, the traveler Samuel Powell sent on from England a "Treatise" containing Dr. Chittick's secret for dissolving *calculi* in the human body, yet at the same time warned his Philadelphia friend that he must not only expect to be considerably reduced by taking the medicines involved but to find that possibly in his case they might not avail.

Dr. Graeme was as helpful as anyone when he admitted by letter from Graeme Park that the patient "could lisp a medical case like an adept in the profession." If that proficiency had come "from dire experience," at least, that good doctor conceded, Mr. Peters gave "an intelligible and satisfactory account of the effects of carrot tea upon his constitution." He even surmised from the afflicted man's success with that beverage that the results would be analogous in other cases. For the invalid was satisfied in the autumn of 1766 that he had found the *lixivium,* which was most potent to dissolve the stone that was troubling him. He would not let Thomas Graeme's apprehensions, lest carrot top tea act too forcibly on his lax and superinduce other forms of languor, deter him from use of his now trusted solvent. Moreover, when in the early summer of 1767, he was congratulated by Mr. Thomas Penn on his steady progress toward health and informed in the same letter that the Paris Court Calendar for the year was recommending wild carrot tea for the gravel, he felt vindicated as both sufferer and self-physician. He believed, as now his good friend Samuel Auchmuty in New York believed, that he had been delivered "out of the hand of the enemy" and "cured of his painful disorder."

But, as rigorous as the battle against ill health was for him in 1766 and 1767, Richard Peters did not let the ambitions or designs of other men lose interest. If he had become more practiced in his *materia medica,* he remained just as much as ever absorbed in his *materia humana.* Although both he and the

Proprietor had often been disappointed by Mr. John Penn's incapacity for business, there was no chagrin in Mr. Peters' heart when his quasi-ward in provincial government came to arrange with the Rector of Christ Church for his marriage to Miss Ann Allen. Indeed, when on May 31, 1766, Richard Peters performed the ceremony that united in holy wedlock the daughter of his friend, Chief Justice William Allen, with the Lieutenant Governor of Pennsylvania, he forgot all points save that he was doing a service, not only under the blessing of God but for a Family whose value to society in America was only second to that of King George III. Every new tie between the Church of England and the Penns rejoiced him. It was a matter of some indifference to him—as it was not to Dr. Auchmuty in New York or Dr. Chandler in Elizabethtown—that the Church and the Ministers of His Majesty's Government at home were turning deaf ears to appeals from the colonies to have an American bishop appointed. He had latterly seen no great objections to having divinity students sent to England for ordination. He was not convinced that the Colonial Church needed to have a bishop of its own and in its midst in order to prosper. But it meant much to him that his churches in Philadelphia should now have their charter from Thomas and Richard Penn, and the spring during which Richard's older son married was made the happier for Mr. Peters by his work with his churchwardens upon an address of thanks to the Proprietors for the felicities of incorporation. The Bishop of London might remain the only proper authority to license rectors of Christ Church, that sacred institution now drew from the heirs of old William Penn its privileges to prosper materially.

Less pleasant to contemplate was another arrangement that was worked out in the summer of 1766 by the Proprietor. Ever since John Penn had been Acting Governor for the Family, Mr. William Peters, as Secretary of the Pennsylvania Land Office, had had watchful eyes turned upon him. When Richard Peters was in London, he had had to be closeted several times upon the subject of a peculating brother with Mr. Thomas Penn. Several Philadelphians had preferred charges of malversation against William. Mr. Penn did not wish to grieve his friend, the good Rector of Christ Church and the old Secretary of the Province; Mr. Peters wished neither to belie his brother nor to exculpate an offender against Pennsylvania and its Proprietors. Misappropriation of fees might not be overlooked. The regard of a man for his brother was not lightly to be abandoned. Two years after John Penn's suspicions had been aroused, William Peters suffered to resign from the Land Office. The master of Belmont and the master of Stoke House worked out amiably the difficulties which had risen. Having retired, William Peters diplomatically assured Mr. Penn that he would thereafter be content to remain in the province only if it should continue under the Proprietors' government. Having had Mr. James Tilghman installed in his Land Office, Thomas Penn engaged the supplanted ex-Secretary to be his lawyer in several matters of business and graciously undertook to purchase and ship from England an engine with its complete equipment of pipes to be used on William Peters' American estate. Affably, the two men bowed themselves out of official connection with each other, and the Reverend Mr. Richard Peters was relieved at witnessing amenities between his patron and his kinsman. It was not the first occasion on which he had to be complacent to, rather than proud of, his brother. But there were such things as claims of blood, and Richard Peters' best-loved friends were the children of William.

Correspondence with Thomas Penn animated him as always, and he shared in the Proprietor's affections and designs as much as he lived in his own. He felt Mr. Penn's grief at the loss of his ten-year-old daughter, Louisa Hannah, in the early summer of 1766. He admired with him the faithful four months of nursing which Lady Juliana devoted night and day to her suffering child. He was delighted with the messages of remembrance from English friends sent in the Proprietor's letters. As a trustee of the institution, he was highly grateful to Mr. Penn for the gift of a pair of globes, with Mr. Adams' book on the use of them, to the Academy. He deplored his friend's indisposition for a time with a siege of the gout. He was glad for him that the repeal of the Stamp Act had come, that William Pitt had been restored to the head of the Ministry and made Earl of Chatham, and that in his cabinet in 1766 was Lord Shelburne, a minister always cordial to Thomas Penn's interests. He was concerned that the Proprietor should take so much thought on the subject of the freight for his chariot. Mr. Penn had wished to prepay all such charges, but Mr. Barclay had advised him of new regulations for better controlling English ship owners and protecting American importers, which made prepayment inadvisable. His apologies for his seeming, but certainly not meant, discourtesy came for many months after the owner of the vehicle was being borne in it to his sermons at Christ Church, and Mr. Peters consistently argued the lack of all cause for them—just as he thanked Mr. Penn for his consideration in paying for a consignment of two new wigs shipped to the Rector on the same vessel with his coach.

He approved in the spring of 1767 the Proprietor's decision not for the present to encourage Dr. Morgan's proposals for erecting a College of Physicians in Philadelphia, agreeing that it was very early for such an establishment. He deeply appreciated Thomas Penn's good offices to William Peters' English son Jemmy when that hapless young surgeon came to London looking for employment. Nothing was available in any house there, but an opportunity to go to the East Indies presented itself, and to £100, raised for his passage and equipment by Richard Statham and Ralph Peters of Liverpool, the Proprietor added a generous allowance of his own which enabled Jemmy to board a ship for Madura. The delicate and almost anonymous mode of Mr. Penn's benefaction, Richard Peters realized, was as much of a compliment to himself as to his volatile nephew. Quite as pleased was he when the Proprietor offered a gift of £50 currency to induce Thomas Barton to remain with his charge in Lancaster rather than accept a call into Maryland. He esteemed his friend's sympathy on his feeling obliged to add a Wednesday lecture to the ecclesiastical duties of his Sundays. He listened with quiet forbearance to Chief Justice Allen's account, in the summer of 1767, of a letter from Thomas Penn apprising that the English Ministers had quite too much on the *tapis* to concern themselves with the appointment of an American bishop. He did not deplore the prediction that, should the altogether unlikely happen and such a prelate be determined on, Dr. William Smith would not be chosen for the office—as being quite too active a man anyway.

Especially he rejoiced at the news from the Proprietor that, when everyone in England "was much out of humor with the Americans," Pennsylvanians were regularly excepted from such odium, being "looked upon as the only good and dutiful children" in the colonies. For he knew no harm had been done to the province when, in 1765, the good Presbyterians of Philadelphia had added their support to that of the Churchmen of the city in helping keep it, despite Franklin and the Quakers, under Proprietary government. He felt complimented when, in the autumn of 1767, Lady Frances Coningsby transmitted to him through Lady Juliana and Mr. Penn certain powders reputed to have helped the Archbishop of Canterbury and other English folk in their struggles against gravel. But most of all, he felt a secular zest in himself when he knew that Thomas Penn was carrying on promising negotiations in London in the interest of a natural boundary that Sir William Johnson could settle with the Indians and laboring at the same time to secure a grant of land from the Crown to that distinguished Indian agent in New York Province. The seeds of a new mission and exploit seemed to be planting. He was sure he was still capable of collaborating with the Proprietor in the interest of the Family and Pennsylvania.

And, in fact, in 1768, he collaborated effectively. Versatile as ever, in the early months of that year, he solved both to his own and Mr. Penn's satisfaction the problem of a transfer in offices which, mishandled, might have eventuated into affronts. Richard Hockley, suffering from eye strain and eager to be relieved of the responsibilities of the Receiver-Generalship, cast about mentally to find some less exacting function for himself and thought he saw the possibility of it in the position of Naval Officer for the Port of Philadelphia, a source of emoluments long previously held by Dr. Graeme. A letter to Thomas Penn made known Mr. Hockley's wish to resign from his more arduous appointment and to be considered for the duties of the naval office. The Proprietor faced a dilemma. Always, he had treated Richard Hockley as his ward and afforded him every opportunity of material advancement in Pennsylvania. But Thomas Graeme was a gentle old man, the father of a lady whom Lady Juliana and Miss Freame greatly esteemed, and a person who enjoyed the particular regard of Lord Mansfield. He dared not be lightly dismissed to the accommodation of a favorite.

So Thomas Penn thought a plan through and addressed Mr. Peters. He would let the Receiver-Generalship go to Mr. Edmund Physick, appoint Richard Hockley auditor of his accounts with a salary of £200 a year, allow him another £100, all in currency, let him aspire to present possession of Dr. Graeme's function, and for the time retain the great seal. Meantime, Mr. Penn would write a cordial letter to the Doctor upon other matters, and it should be Richard Peters' design to approach the Naval Officer upon the business with some delicacy.

The intermediary accepted his commission without demur. He could see no difficulty in informing Dr. Graeme that it was his patron's wish to let him continue to have the fees of his position and the name of it while another gentleman practiced the authority of the appointment and a clerk performed its labors. Coincidentally, in early May, the Reverend Mr. Peters was suffering from what he described sadly as "a most violent, cold, cough, fever and pain of the breast, with continual catarrh and phlegm." The seizure had fallen on him, as he lamented, upon "Good Friday morning owing to a most cruel washing of his church." Thomas Graeme had to visit him twice daily, and the confidant of Thomas Penn, hean warm toward his kindly physician, decided to speak while his influenza still prevailed. He brought forward the amiable suggestions of the benefactor in London, and a letter, written with promptitude afterward, pictured the results:

> I have opened all to the Doctor relating to Mr. Hockley. He directly burst into a rapture of joy at your generous treatment of him. He said it was all right. It was what gave him pleasure. I read that pan of your letter to him wherein you say you will be security to him. He cried: "This is

too much; let Mr. Penn do what he pleases; he knows my commission is during the pleasure of his Governors. And they might and would, perhaps, have turned me out of it had it not been for the Proprietors." And this is the present state of every dependent. When Mr. Hockley has his commission, any Governor may turn him out. This is a pity, where the Proprietors have a personal regard, that they do not give this commission themselves and make it during good behavior. Then the poor old gentleman's heart exulted and at the same time showed that it might happen that what you intended for Mr. Hockley may do him little or no good but put him out of a certain mode of living, which he might now go into with his son, to the precarious dependence on the humor of a Governor. Excuse my giving these hints; they arose so naturally in the heart of the old gentleman that I could not, out of regard to him and Mr. Hockley, avoid mentioning them just as they arose. Everything is settled between Dr. Graeme and Mr. Hockley; the present person (Mr. Phyle) who executes the office is to do it under Mr. Hockley on a small allowance agreed upon.

In brief, Richard Peters wrote of the adjustment of the income of the naval officer as long before he had written of James Logan's gift of a library to Philadelphia. For a lifetime, he had accepted his cue: Whoever might be the donor of riches or the exhibitor of gentle breeding and kindliness in Pennsylvania, all blessedness there must seem to flow from the elder Proprietor. Right citizens in the province must exult in the benefactions of Thomas Penn.

But it was not only in minor mundane diplomacies during a spell of influenza that the Rector of Christ Church was to avail in 1 768. That year had an autumn as well as a spring, and it had an autumn for which Mr. Penn had diligently prepared overseas in England. For, although more than a quarter of a century had passed since 1742, the oldest surviving of William Penn's sons had neither forgotten the Wyoming lands on Susquehanna nor what, despite Connecticut, might be of interest to the Family. During many months, he busied himself with correspondence and visits to his friends in the Ministry of England. His letters and his offices designed obviously the advantage of Sir William Johnson, yet in him always were ulterior aims of his own. Sir William had been not only His Majesty's most acceptable Indian agent in America. He had served as a general of distinction in the late war. Rewards were in order for him as for other retired officers. Mr. Penn was glad to become his New York friend's sponsor with the Crown.

On September 12, 1767, he was glad he could write that the King had referred Johnson's case to the Attorney-General. A grant of land had been ordered to be passed, in the customary way of grants to half-pay officers, although Thomas Penn had to confide that "His Majesty and his Ministers do not choose to give away the fees of the Governor and other Officers and say they do not think it becomes you to ask it." Did Sir William wish him to take out the grant for him and to pay the fees involved? In the same letter, he promised that, when the Ministry came to town in November, he would make an application for his pay as Johnson had acted under the King's, not a Governor's commission, and would hope to succeed. He could not predict certain favorable results but would do everything possible for his friend's service. He sent his best thanks to him for having induced the Indians to let the surveyors run the Pennsylvania-Maryland line.

A communication to Governor John Penn three months later signified increasing faith in the Proprietor that his affairs were prospering. He had breakfasted with Lady Shelburne, managed to dine with His Lordship, and had spent most of a December day with that Minister. Although he had the mortification of knowing orders with regard to the English-Indian boundary, which Sir William Johnson had been negotiating for three years, were not to be immediately forthcoming, he had been most "seriously promised" they should go by the next packet. Important papers had been left with Shelburne. The next point was to press matters further with Johnson. He was writing, he said, to urge that gentleman "to get as much land for us between the West Branch of Susquehanna as the Indians will consent, and prevent any further dealings between the Six Nations and the people of Connecticut by their obliging themselves when they remove to sell it only to us." He advised his nephew that the proposal was one "of great importance, not only to our immediate profit but to prevent any troublesome and expensive litigations."

On the same December 12, 1767, he addressed Sir William Johnson directly and at length upon the two items of concern:

> I can truly assure you that I have been an importunate solicitor, both on account of your grant and that of the Indian boundary. I was with Lord Shelburne and Lord Clare about them last week and came to town on Thursday, expecting the orders about the boundary would have been despatched by this packet, but after a long conference I had with the first, I find it will not go till the next. I had just received a letter from Mr. Croghan and from Mr. Allen pressing the necessity of it very strongly

and very speedily, which I gave Lord Shelburne copies of to lay before the Council, and I really believe it will be done by next packets.

Lord Shelburne desired I would express his regard for you and his desire to carry into execution what you recommend. He also gave all the assistance he could with regard to your land, and we hope to get a grant under the Great Seal here on an acknowledgment of a bear skin or some such reservation, which will supersede all fees at New York. Of this, I shall write to you further by the next packet.

I have to desire you will use your best endeavors with the Indians to grant us the land, as high as they can be bought to agree to, between the West Branch of the Susquehanna and the Delaware, to prevent all possibility of the people from Connecticut giving us any more trouble there, and that they will covenant when they incline to sell the rest, that they will sell it only to us, as they have always done. I hope to write you fully by the next packet.

"In the meantime," Mr. Penn concluded, he was "with much regard" Sir William's "most obedient and most humble servant." January of 1768 brought changes in the Ministry. Lord Hillsborough, who was a stranger to the Penns, was appointed to the new office of Secretary of State for America, and the Proprietor of the province regretted the prospective loss of an intimate from the helm of colonial affairs in England. But his earlier assiduity was rewarded, and before Lord Shelburne surrendered his old portfolio and became mere Southern Secretary of State, that Minister, to Mr. Penn's very great pleasure, got orders off to both General Gage and Sir William Johnson. Hillsborough did not have, for the present, to be waited for. Gage and Johnson would have a free hand to consult the governors of the several American provinces and arrange to have the line of Pennsylvania established as much to the satisfaction of those executives as the Six Nations would consent to. Again, Thomas Penn wrote to his nephew and Sir William, not neglecting now to make it clear that he was hoping for more than the Susquehanna lands and had his eye on a great southwestward stretch of territory extending to—but not beyond—the Ohio River.

The Rector of Christ Church left, to be sure, the rigors of preparation for the new Indian treaty to his patron in London, but he failed neither in exchange of compliments with his friend nor with Johnson. At much the same time as Thomas Penn was writing from England to the Colonial Indian Agent, that gentleman was warning Mr. Peters of difficulties ahead with the Iroquois, who at the moment were profoundly mistrustful of all the whites, whether in

Virginia, Pennsylvania, or New York. But he was pleased that Governor John Penn and his commissioners were satisfied with his previous endeavors for the interests of Pennsylvania, and he assured Richard Peters that his influence, so far as was consistent, would still be exercised to such ends. With Johnson so amenable, Thomas Penn might well write of his gratitude to the former Secretary of the Province for his aid to the Lieutenant Governor in Indian affairs. His estimate was correct: "Your assistance will be of more service than that of any other person." And perhaps it was not inadvised that he should add to Mr. Peters: "I am much rejoiced that you are in so good spirits."

But the now anticipated treaty was slow in maturing. John Penn wrote on May 22 to his uncle that Johnson was to meet with the Indians in July and that a competent and instructed person would then be sent from Pennsylvania to get the best possible boundary. Yet the Proprietor would see, in the letter enclosed by his nephew from Sir William, that the Government of Connecticut were sending an agent to England to solicit a grant at Wyoming. Expectations dared not be sanguine, however. The Governor could, during that month, only promise that if the Six Nations sold the Wyoming land to the Penns, it should be surveyed at once. Then, in the summer of 1768, an illness befell Johnson and took him to New England for treatment and a sustained recuperation. Autumn came before word could be sent to Thomas Penn by his nephew that the time of the conference was at hand.

On September 12, John Penn wrote from New York to his uncle that he was on his way to Fort Stanwix, at the head of the Mohawk River, where Sir William Johnson would meet with the Indians on the 20th. Traveling with the Governor were Messrs. Chew, Tilghman, and Peters. He had set off from Philadelphia reluctantly and admitted he had come only because his commissioners had made it clear they would not undertake the expedition without him.

His somewhat truculent letter contained, however, three reassuring statements. The commission was hoping to get a better line than the English Secretary of State had suggested for Pennsylvania. Mr. Croghan had pointed out the injurious features of that suggestion and been especially eager to have Richard Peters, "as a person well acquainted with Indian affairs," attend the treaty. The group of Pennsylvanians "were going to exert themselves to the utmost for the Proprietor's interest."

The last promise could hardly be said later to have been kept, for the exertions of John Penn and Ben Chew did not prove dynamic ones in the successful Purchase of Fort Stanwix. Indeed, in mid-October, before the treaty had materialized, Governor Penn, always impatient of any protracted business, turned back toward Philadelphia with Mr. Chew and left the enterprise in the experienced hands of Richard Peters and Sir William. Those two men could remember easily enough the hints that George Croghan had given. Moreover, they were not agents to give up because the Senecas, the Cayugas, and the Onondagoes were tardy in coming or because "the Wishin Indians," as Mr. John Penn named them, "were unwilling to come at all."

On November 5, their purpose was accomplished, the Deed of Fort Stanwix was signed, and the "New Purchase" was made. That it was acquired in the absence of Connecticut and New England commissioners caused neither the former Secretary of Pennsylvania and constant servant of the Penns nor the widely reputed colonial Indian agent misgiving of its success. Mr. Peters had the satisfaction of knowing that Wyoming had been at last bought for the Penns. The Six Nations would say no more, as they had declared at Albany in 1754, "Nobody shall have that land." But, more than that, to the Family would belong a new domain as great in extent as all the lands they had bought from the Indians from William Penn's time forward. Far to the north of the old counties of Philadelphia, Chester, Bucks, Berks, and Lancaster, a block of land running up to the forty-second degree of latitude and vast as they had been purchased. Far to the southwest and west of York and Cumberland Counties, and large as those, another block had been added to the province. The two friends of Thomas Penn and enemies of Connecticut could exult in their achievement with the Six Nations. All that remained, it seemed, was to have the Proprietors send from time to time to Onondaga through Sir William Johnson the further unpaid installments of the purchase price of £10,000.

At length, the Reverend Mr. Richard Peters was free to return with his steady-going business associate, Secretary James Tilghman of the Land Office, and his nephew, Richard Peters, Jr., who had joined him during the treaty, to Philadelphia. On the way were other long journeys on horseback, a brief visit with Sir William at Johnson Hall, with its Indian hostess and Indian and half-Indian scions, a sojourn with the Reverend Samuel Auchmuty in New York City to talk of that good man's new parsonage, of plans for church lotteries, of men fit and men unfit to be in orders, of the Colleges of New York and Philadelphia, of prospective or non-prospective American bishops, of new missions to be suggested to the Venerable Society for promoting the Church of England among the Six Nations. For government and religion, Mr. Peters hoped to keep hand in hand.

Indeed, the Rector of Christ Church felt the responsibilities of his spiritual office long before he got back to his parish. Letters from two of his aides had pursued him while on his secular exploit. On October 14, William Smith dispatched a warning to him. Mr. Duche, he advised, had employed "one Porter," the "most insignificant of all creatures" and reputedly "once a tailor in Bucks," to preach for two Sundays in Mr. Peters' pulpit and already a mercurial party in the congregation were for having Porter appointed to an assistantship in the church—despite his adherence "to certain exceptionable and doubtful, if not hurtful, tenets." Four days later, Jacob Duche, who admitted that he was himself "a little jealous" of the absent priest's affections, other persons having had more letters from his superior than he, wrote in a far different tenor. He explained that the Reverend Mr. Porter, on his arrival in Philadelphia by ship, had come directly to the writer's house, wishing Mr. Duche to accompany him on a prompt visit to pay his respects to the Rector of the United Churches. The latter being away from the city and his return not expected for some time, the assistant had shown courtesy to the stranger, invited him to take lodgings with him, and asked him to preach for him. Mr. Porter had now delivered three sermons, delighting many people with his public performances. Indeed, Mr. Duche had been "pressed very much by some of the most respectable among them" to invite the new clergyman to continue in Philadelphia until Mr. Peters' return. A number of good folks wanted the congregation to have the opportunity to study Mr. Porter's qualifications for an assistantship to their Rector.

In early December of 1768, Richard Peters was back in Philadelphia and in excellent spirits. If Governor John Penn was now assuming credit for successful collaboration with Johnson in effecting the "New Purchase," the former Secretary of the Province allowed himself no occasion to repine. He had been in the saddle once more and in the stir of affairs. Business and the long rides had acted like tonics. Carrot top tea and *lixivium* powders had been supplanted by exercise and interest. His gravel had disappeared. He was a well man again. At home, his friends gathered round him with congratulation both for his services to the Proprietor and his recovery of health. At church, he resumed his preaching with new energy. From England, he was ready to receive the thanks of good Mr. Thomas Penn.

He was ready for the new year, and 1769 began happily for him. Sir William Johnson's compliments followed in letters from that dignitary, who rejoiced in Mr. Peters' friendship and would always devote his best endeavors to the interest of the Proprietor of Pennsylvania. The Indian Agent was pleased that Mr. Tilghman was collecting funds for the payments to the Six Nations and that these were so soon to be forthcoming. He was glad that the Rector already had in mind two young men who would take orders and become missionaries to the Mohawks at Schenectady. He would always be delighted to have "your agreeable correspondence." Samuel Auchmuty's Christmas greetings from New York brought deep comfort, and Mr. Peters appreciated much his New York brother's wish "that both you and I may hereafter, in a better world, avail ourselves of the mirth and satisfaction of that blessed Redeemer, whose birth we now commemorate." Moreover, gracious communications from Thomas Penn did not fail him.

That gentleman wrote from England his gratitude that Richard Peters, although "in a weakly state of health," had so generously devoted himself to the Proprietary interest. He was convinced that the affair could not have been in "more able or knowing hands." Mr. Peters' observations on the Treaty of 1754 had been very much to the purpose. Mr. Penn had hoped that the Indians would see the equity of their being left in possession of the lands west of the Allegheny Mountains—a privilege not scrupulously secured to them by their treaty with Lydius and the Susquehanna Company. The Proprietor felt great pleasure that his friend had continued in better health during his journey and at the conference. Mr. Peters had laid him "under great obligations" by his services at Fort Stanwix. Those obligations could be met only by the friendship which Mr. Penn would always wish to show him in every possible fashion. That the whole enterprise had agreed with last year's invalid gave joy to all the Family. Everyone under Thomas Penn's "roof" hoped sincerely that their Philadelphia friend might long continue in the good state of health that he had now attained.

So the Rector of the United Churches rejoiced. He had availed for the Penns. He might now avail for Christ's Kingdom. He was willing now to let the Proprietor in England reward Mr. George Croghan and Sir William Johnson for their labors preliminary to and at Fort Stanwix by soliciting grants of land to them from the Crown. He was content that John Penn should further plans for laying out five thousand acres about Pittsburgh, including the town, and believed, like the Proprietor, that that community would "become considerable in time." He was gratified that warrants could be issued for the taking up of land at Shamokin and in Wyoming and surveyors be designated to act in those places. But he no longer expected to manage main transactions for the Pennsylvania Land Office. He had himself parish and friends now to serve in the function of priest.

Indeed, he did not look further into the secular seeds of time, and he had no prevision in January 1769 of the harvests of blood for which planting had been made in the "New Purchase of 1768." Others than he would campaign and settle, struggle and die on the long-favorite hunting grounds of the Indians in the "Pennymite" Wars so swift to follow between Pennsylvania and Connecticut Yankee rival settlers. The black shadows of the Massacre of July 4, 1778, were a full decade away. The Rector of the United Churches of Christ and St. Peter's in Philadelphia gave himself anew to religion. He did not know what further implications of stark and on-Christian tragedy lay in the beautiful Wyoming that he had bought for the Penns.

XX

Sans Dieu Rien

If an angel, hypothetically visiting Philadelphia in the eighteenth century, would have been sure of experiencing detraction there and been certainly charged with living too gay a life, or one quite "exceeding the points of honor, virtue, or modesty," it was hardly to be expected that Richard Peters, mere mortal, should always continue free of detractors. Indeed, however clear might be his conscience and however unaware of who might be speaking to his discredit, his mind might remain, his conduct or character came at times into censure. Human, rather than angelic, his reputation on occasion bore spots.

Isaac Norris was not of his admirers in May 1741, as he sat writing to Robert Charles, then Secretary to the Province, and irony crept into the Quaker's letter.

> The Parson A. Cummings [he said] died the 19th of last month and was buried the 22d, universally lamented. And, as he lingered for some time without any probability of recovery, P---- made all possible interest to have succeeded him, and in order to it formed an election of churchwardens much out of the usual manner. But, after the Parson's death found, even those who liked him as a companion would not vote for him as a Parson, and there was no probability of success, so that he did not put up. But he is on a committee for writing to the Bp of London to send them one of the BP's own naming. He may possibly endeavor to make an interest for himself there, which would set our Church into much confusion-but thou wilt hear more on this head from other hands.

If Norris had his doubts about Mr. Peters' clerical ambition before the Reverend Mr. Cummings was fully ready for burying, fifteen years later, the sons of Nicholas Scull, SurveyorGeneral of Pennsylvania, who had been brought up in their father's profession and served as his subordinates, kept restive eyes on the

Secretary of the Land Office. James and Edward Scull, in letters to their sire, scored Richard Peters for ubiquitousness. Edward resented his condescension, condemned his mercurial issuance of warrants for lands definitely known to be in dispute, rated his meddlings, questioned the honesty of his transactions, and discounted his mental powers. Nor did he hesitate to accredit all the Sculls for experiencing far more fatigue of body and mind than Mr. Peters in serving province and Proprietors.

Yet the younger surveyor's estimate, attaching itself to modes of Richard Peters in business, was hardly more caustic than a comment that sprang from George Roberts in 1763. In a November letter to Samuel Powell, which was facetious enough to come from a cavalier, that young Quaker smiled at all Philadelphia's renewed enthusiasm for Whitefield, feared the evangelist's possible invasion of Friends' Meeting, and instanced with contempt the collapse of two clergymen of the United Churches of Christ and St. Peter's. "The G—dlike Peters and imitating Garrick Duche," he declared, "are turned proselytes to his doctrine." So the amiable Rector, who had only the year before returned to his priestly function, bore an unfortunate odium now, not for so slight a matter as the issuance of two tickets for one piece of land, but for a reputed lapse in his religion.

Laconic, too, on the subject not only of William Peters but of his brother was Edward Shippen, Jr., writing to his father in Lancaster. He candidly rejoiced in 1766 when the master of Belmont was ordered discharged from the Land Office by the Proprietors, and Mr. Tilghman was appointed in his stead. As his captious style put it, the order "not only trips up Snigs but gives a blow to the Cardinal's Interest," and the young lawyer's slur implied that Philadelphians might as mockingly smile down on prelates as it frowned uprighteously on peculators in lay offices. And stern in implications were the comments of Thomas Coombe at the end of the decade during which Richard Peters had visited Stoke. For these came from a young graduate of the College of Philadelphia and a pupil of Dr. William Smith who had gone to England for ordination into the church. It would, indeed, have been one thing for Richard Peters to know after the Treaty of Fort Stanwix—if he had known—that lay minds had questioned his powers and his integrity. To know that a second clerical mind censured would have been quite another matter and harder to bear. Moreover, Thomas Coombe's remarks to his father on the Philadelphia Rector, though unredeemed by their constancy, were lashing ones.

The young candidate for orders not only doubted the sincerity of Mr. Peters' promises of aid to him in finding favor in England, but he suspected the genuineness of his sponsor's reasons for not having him engaged early to assist at Christ Church. Moreover, he not only questioned Mr. Peters' interest in his friend William White, but he insinuated in letters to Thomas Coombe, Esquire, that he did not dare to write what he really thought of the Rector for fear of having his epistles unsealed on shipboard and read by the Pennsylvania passengers. Action from the priest of Christ Church, he thought, might speak better than words.

Once, he even let his irony bristle into a written opinion. He asked his parent to convey his compliments to Mr. Peters on a printed sermon by that divine which Mr. Thomas Penn had handed him in London. He averred, "The author would scarcely forgive me should I say that I do not comprehend it." And for final piquancy, he quoted from a scholar with whom he had been recently talking: "Sublimity, when applied to sermons, is but another name for learned nonsense."

Yet, whatever the world, lay or clerical, might think of his capabilities and behavior, the Reverend Mr. Richard Peters carried a serene mind with him from the 1760s into the 1770s, and, on the whole, he had a goodly experience.

Many things in 1769 gave him a sense both of well-doing within his efforts and of sympathetic recognition from fellow laborers and friends. He had admired Thomas Barton ever since that graduate of Trinity College had come from Ireland to begin his Christian ministry in America at the College in Philadelphia. He was glad to know he was now well established and beloved in the parish of St. James' at Lancaster. To none better, away from the capital city, could he have trusted for guidance his errant nephew, poor slow-minded Billy, older brother to the incomparable Dicky, and problem both for his uncle and his father, William Peters. To have the good minister standing *in loco parentis* to the scapegrace, whether or no there were occasional lapses from faithful church attendance in the country to spells of drinking, renewed in Richard Peters his affection for the younger clergyman and added further cause for a correspondence in which, despite periodic unhappy motives, he delighted. Always agreeable, too, was it to have messages from Samuel Auchmuty. Like the New York priest of Trinity Church, he was certain just what cleric should not be in orders, and he appreciated his good brother's ready responses to any discussion of parish needs, problems, and regulations sensitively. Like him, he hailed with exaltation every sign of advancement of the Church of England in America through pamphlet, sermon, lottery, or mission.

But it was through the dedication of the new Lutheran Church of Zion, rather than within the sacred boundaries of his parish and church, that the

Reverend Mr. Peters felt in June 1769 both his breadth of mind as a Christian and his acceptance in Pennsylvania as a divine. At the instance of the ministers and the congregation of the parent Lutheran group in St. Michael's, the Rector of Christ Church was prevailed on to participate in the ceremonies, and, having inclined to their wish, he delivered a sermon so much to their satisfaction that they both urged the printing of it and arranged for a translation into German by the Reverend Henry Melchior Muhlenberg.

For his text, he drew on Luke 5:13 and 14:

> And suddenly, there was with the angel a multitude of the heavenly hosts praising God and saying Glory to God in the Highest, and on earth peace, good-will towards men.

But, although both his extensions of thought and his phrases were new, he felt constrained by no need to change either his old modes of procedure or his tenets of mind. Exegetically he divided and subdivided, parceled and reparceled. Initially, he joyed in the fact that Lutheran and Episcopalian could be worshiping together, that theirs were sister churches, and that they were all Christians and members of the body of Christ. He was glad that their prayers breathed "one and the same primitive Apostolic piety" and "the same impartial universal Love." He admitted his preference for the Church of England but vowed his general love for all Protestant churches and his particular regard for the Evangelical Church of the Lutherans of St. Michael's and Zion. What, most of all, he did was to look into "the Temple" of the angels' hearts to see what it was that stirred in the breasts of the heavenly host that made them praise God. Preeminently, he wished to explain "in what posture they stood" toward the Divine.

So he interpreted it in three main headings: first, the true reason and motive for angelic worship; second, the attitude of the angels' hearts; and third, the fact that what was in their breasts has also been made possible in man's through Christ's incarnation. Chiefly, he exhorted his hearers (and later his readers) to call forth the imputed powers of their human hearts "into the same spiritual and heavenly exercise."

> Let them attend to the posture of the angels.
>> If they looked towards God, there was the Triune Majesty of Love-if towards one another, there it was in full communication springing forth as the glance of a firmament without them, and within them taking a

particular seat in every one of their hearts, and bringing with it their natural bodies of glory—if they looked towards the earth, the same streams of happiness were spreading themselves all over its surface, gliding at the same time into every human heart, that felt the power of its redemption.

Let them remember that as all died in Adam, so "in Christ should all be made alive."

Nothing, in brief, in his dedicatory sermon, as Richard Peters himself knew, was uncharacteristic of his mental posture in religion. And, if he was pleased with his composition and the printing and translating of it, he was not averse to having its praises sung by perusers. Congratulations on the quality and wisdom of its text, in fact, contributed much to the cheer of spirit which clung to him through the remainder of 1769 and generally throughout 1 770.

There were, of course, more secular causes for pleasure. He was glad he could be chief advocate of and executive for incorporation within the Colonial Church, collecting and dispensing means of support for the widows and orphans of deceased clergymen. It was satisfying to know that, at length, Thomas Penn had secured to Sir William Johnson his grant of land from the Crown. Richard Peters was pleased not only with the encomiums that now came to him from the Proprietor on his handling of the treaty in New York but with Mr. Penn's statement of his conviction that the purchase price, though "pretty large," was not "exorbitant." He felt complimented that the same gracious benefactor had procured for Richard Peters, Jr., a commission as Register in the Court of Vice-Admiralty at Philadelphia and that his nephew's career in the officialdom of the province had been so initiated.

He enjoyed likewise letters which came from members of the Peters family in Liverpool. His brother, who was visiting with his son Ralph, wrote enthusiastically both of his daughter-in-law Elizabeth and of the notable folk who gathered round her when members of the connection, including William, had been taking the waters at Buxton. A most agreeable company had gathered at that Derbyshire resort. The Duchess of Athol, now become the wife of Lord Adam Gordon—a peer whose visit to Philadelphia Richard Peters would remember—had signalized Elizabeth with her attentions. William Peters himself had esteemed a new acquaintanceship with Lord and Lady Vernon and with several barristers and their ladies among the guests at the spa. In most pleasant society, he had made excursions to Chatsworth, to Matlock, and to Lord Scarsdale's fine seat in the county noted for its ducal residences. Even from Liverpool in May 1769, William could write encouragingly: Sister Statham was much improved in health. Although a letter written by Ralph Peters a week later did not sustain that statement of his father, remarking rather that Aunt Statham was having new hectic symptoms, the communication from that good nephew gave his uncle in Pennsylvania gratification. Elizabeth Peters had been much helped at Buxton, Ralph's daughter, and hers was growing into "a fine prating girl," his wife and he were busily restoring the old Peters country estate of Platbridge.

If two months later, William Peters was to write out of a greatly changed attitude, the good Rector of Christ Church refused to let himself be too deeply troubled. He was conscious he had served his brother and his brother's family well. The improvident William had gone to England with little money and "scarce a shirt," as he said, "to his back." He had adeptly borrowed and then had affably shared in the amenities of Buxton. Presently, there succeeded a time in Liverpool when the welcome became thin. Richard Peters smiled knowingly when he read from his brother's second letter a new estimate of Ralph's wife. For he could understand well enough why Elizabeth should tire of her father-in-law, and he could not quite fall in with William's condemnation of her for having "such high notions of family and fortune." It was more comfortable, he realized, not to intervene too directly in the disputes of either families or commonwealths. Witness the position of Mr. Penn, who had but recently counseled Secretary Tilghman it would be best to get military aid from the General of His Majesty's Forces in America to drive the Connecticut folk out of Wyoming and doubted the wisdom of having Pennsylvania companies perform that act before Connecticut had time to explain whether their settlers had gone in with the approval of Government. As for William Peters, his brother knew he had a faculty for landing right-side-up after almost any altercation.

So Richard Peters continued thinking benevolently. In fact, he felt he enjoyed in the autumn of 1769 not only "a happy situation," as William Bull of South Carolina termed it in an October letter on the subject of the sermon to the Lutherans, but what that friendly correspondent called "a state of catholic and evangelical charity." It was a satisfaction also to know how generously the good Carolinian was stirring himself to find both stipends and spiritual cures for two clerics whom the Rector of Christ Church had advised going into the southern province. Moreover, three letters that came to him in the first week of January 1770 brought pleasure. Samuel Johnston, the sponsor for the mission church at York, praised a supply who had been sent there and at the same time bespoke Mr. Peters' interest in his son Charles, a bashful pupil now studying at the Academy whom the clergyman might encourage both in his English and Latin. One Andrew Goranyon of Wiccacoa, hitherto a stranger, wrote simple laudations of both the English and the German versions of the printed sermon of last June and prayed humbly that "compositions of equal edifying strength" might attain the ends they intended. And good Mr. John Porter, to whose preaching at Christ Church in 1768 William Smith had taken such exception, and who before that time had released himself from the shackles of Calvinism to become a Churchman, wrote of the inspiriting success he was having with congregations at Bush River, Maryland. There, he was preaching to audiences of different societies, boldly asserting that God is found in every church, constantly declaring "that true church communion altogether consists in union to Christ."

As the new year advanced, Richard Peters' comfortableness of mind remained with him. The death of Hannah Statham in February brought sorrow from England. But Elizabeth Peters' account of the sad event manifested just that serene tone that a true Christian might desire in a letter of bereavement and consolation. All of Elizabeth's husband's family had done their duty to their mother and aunt in the last sickness. Mrs. Statham had assured her niece by marriage "how happy she was in her family" and, after bearing her illness with uncommon resignation and fortitude, had "perfectly resigned herself to the will of God."

So her brother in Philadelphia resolutely kept his thoughts turned away from grief and allowed his sister's translation only to inspire him to patience and a renewal of attachment to his kinsmen. He followed with interest his brother William's efforts to find a business in England in which to establish his youngest American son, Thomas, as an apprentice. When to that purpose the proper brewer had been contracted with in Bristol, Richard Peters was prompt to write to his friends in that English city in order to have Tommy sponsored in his new life by such good folk as William Cruger and John Speed, as the guardianship of Thomas Barton had been drawn round Billy Peters in Lancaster County, Pennsylvania. Further, he commissioned young Mr. White, in Britain for his ordination, to purchase a watch as a gift to Tommy from his uncle after the youth arrived from America.

In June, he wrote to his brother on the subject of their sister's death. Hannah, he insisted piously, was with them now no less than before. He exhorted William to wait like him for the appointed time. They would all meet again where none could feel any more sorrow. They would have their "mutual sympathies in the same manner angels have them." "God's love in Christ would spread over their hearts. The streams would overflow with the mothers' hearts, and there would be an eternal effluence from the true fountain and an eternal mingling of the streams of love with and in and through the hearts of each other."

Yet Richard Peters did not confine this letter of 1770 to a plenitude of spiritual hope. Rather, he added a forthright account to William of his material condition and a clear statement of measures which he intended to take to see that his estate should be left to his brother and his brother's children. Moreover, he closed with pledges of affection for William and his heirs and the remark that he was informing them of what he had written to their father.

That he was bent on generosity, every word frankly attested. No selfishness marred his communication. But in the message of consolation from the Rector of Christ Church to wayward William Peters, the coil of mortality was still fastened. Its writer had not forgotten either the text or the manner of his sermon to the Lutherans. Pride of phrase commanded his spirit no less than loyalty in blood kinship. Even as he wrote, he was remembering the praise recently come to him from Thomas Penn on his performance at the opening of the Church of Zion. The Proprietor, by letter of March 14 from London, had welcomed with joy the printed copy of Mr. Peters' text and wished "heartily that the catholic spirit recommended by it might spread throughout all professions" of Christianity and make all Christians into good neighbors.

So the spiritual head of the two United Churches of Philadelphia disposed himself benignly to what life should next have in store for him.

What it most personally offered in the twelve months that succeeded June of 1770 was the sense of attachment and of use in himself, which he found in the loyal affections and ambitions of his young clerical friends and his several blood nephews. He had reached his sixty-seventh year, but the future of the Church was precious to him, and it was like an elixir to have the admiration and confidence of youthful aspirants to the priesthood. He followed with absorption the Reverend Mr. Auchmuty's designs to keep Sir William Johnson's Indian allies provided with religious instruction, became deeply interested in Mr. John Stuart—believed by his New York sponsor to be surpassingly qualified "to preach the glad tidings of salvation to poor heathen," corresponded with the zealous candidate, and rejoiced when he had got Mr. Stuart to England and his ordination by episcopal hands. Presently, he knew with great satisfaction that the young missionary, with £70 a year and the usual allowance of books as a stipend, was furthering successfully the sacred work of the Venerable Society among the Mohawks.

Yet more intimately personal was his interest in two young graduates in classics and divinity from the College of Philadelphia. William White and Francis Hopkinson had shone among the pupils of Francis Alison and Dr. William Smith. Now they were in England seeking admission to holy orders, and both kept writing with respect at once cordial and delicate to the Rector of Christ Church and Trustee of the College. Mr. White, by reason of his many obligations to him, ranked Mr. Peters among his best friends. He carried out business commissions for him. He coincided with him in his view that the Bishop of London was "that polite and condescending man" whom Mr. Peters had described him to be. He regretted, however, that His Lordship was of the opinion that Mr. White was rather too young to be given either deacon's or priest's orders at present. He would follow the Bishop's advice and not do indiscriminate preaching in England, but unfortunately, as he had to be much in London, he could hardly follow the great prelate's advice to go for further study just now at the universities. He hoped Mr. Peters was continuing in his good state of health.

Francis Hopkinson wrote with the same modest deference, acknowledging many favors, but his first letter was rather more explicit in manner. It told candidly of the illness of the Bishop of London and of how the Bishop of Norwich had substituted for him in ordaining the young cleric from Philadelphia on December 23, 1770, at St. James's Chapel. Immediately afterward, Mr. Hopkinson had been offered a curacy in Hertfordshire, but he had declined the charge on the advice of the Bishop of Worcester, who wished him to lose no opportunity of improving his mind by being left in the country. He knew of no other appointment likely to offer for the time, but he would wait patiently and school himself to the maxim of Tacitus: *Fortunam inter dubia, Virtutem inter certa, numerare.* Nothing would make him repine at the dispensation of a good Providence. Indeed, Richard Peters could not but approve of the graceful combination of learning and piety in the sentences of his *protégé*. Scholarliness, poetic disposition, and saintliness—all seemed to blend in with the spirit of Mr. Hopkinson. The old priest in Pennsylvania was more than pleased that the young religious wanted not only to share his Latin with him but was sending his experienced friend a copy of Dr. Kennicott's *Historical Account of the Collation of Hebrew Manuscripts of the Old Testament,* "a work of great labor and expense to the author and much esteemed in England." He was glad, too, for the fervent prayer of his friend's son and friend that Mr. Peters might be preserved in health and happiness "to be a support to the church and friend to virtue."

Altogether, he was delighted with his two youthful wards in religion, and he would allow himself no displeasure when a letter on the subject of them came from whimsical Thomas Coombe. That young priest, sent from the College several years earlier and ordained in England, now wrote from London tardy acknowledgment to Mr. Peters. He had enjoyed the reunion with his old friends and fellow students, Mr. White and Mr. Hopkinson. These two had both been ordained three weeks before by the Bishop of Norwich, His Lordship of London being "indisposed" at the time. Mr. White read prayers in the afternoon of the day of his ordination; Mr. Hopkinson had not yet appeared "in the desk." Mr. Coombe had been visited six months ago by Mr. William Peters, who looked to be in very good health. Mr. Coombe anticipated war with both Spain and France. Politics in Paris was a current subject of great interest. "The removal of the Duke de Choiseul was entirely owing to the influence of the King's mistress." If Mr. Coombe was late in acknowledging Mr. Peters' many civilities in Philadelphia, he begged Mr. Peters to believe his "silence had proceeded from nothing in which want of respect had had the least share."

The Rector of the United Churches read Thomas Coombe's letter meditatively. Perhaps he had been wrong in suspecting a lack of regard for himself in that young cleric, news of whose popularity in the pulpit had been coming back from England. Human nature was often more dilatory than it was malicious. If Mr. Coombe had been tardy in writing, so, too, had Richard Peters been given to procrastinating. Only a few weeks earlier had he got round to writing his congratulations and good wishes to Philadelphia Hannah Freame, who had married and become Lady Dartry almost a year ago. And, after all, the volatile Thomas had written just the sort of news which Mr. Peters wished to have of his cherished William White, from whom in March 1771, no message on his ordination had come directly. It was always well to meet any apprehended disrespect with condescension. The mellowing priest thought indulgently of Mr. Coombe.

The year 1770 had been rich for him. Among its late gifts had come the degree of Doctor of Divinity from Oxford. Through Mr. John Montgomery as personal messenger, a young minister returning to America to assume a living in Maryland, the great English University forwarded its diploma of honor, and the recipient took great joy not only in the distinction but in the voices of approval which spoke in his parish. The doctorate was both acme and index to happiness. No words of felicitation ever pleased the Rector of the United Churches more than the phrases sent early in 1771 by Myles Cooper from King's College, New York. That amiable professor rejoiced that the honor had been conferred "by the most upright, learned, and religious society upon earth." Unqualifiedly, he pronounced Oxford the most notable "support of both religion and loyalty throughout the British Empire." The mood of exaltation stayed on in the Reverend Dr. Richard Peters. Toward all things, he was disposed happily.

If he grieved for the present death of Mr. Richard Penn, younger of the two Proprietaries of Pennsylvania, he was pleased that Thomas Penn should now have determined to have Richard Penn, Jr., replace his brother John for a time as Lieutenant Governor of the Province. He was happy, too, that another scion had been born into the Family. Lady Dartry had given birth to a son, an infant who might one day inherit his paternal grandfather's title of Viscount Cremorne. Everything pointed pleasantly. Lady Dartry would write him, he hoped, telling of her joy at being a mother. There would be further duties in his parish which he was going to be well enough to perform. There would still be the love of his young friends in England and of the younger members of his family connection. And in due season, all these things abundantly were.

William White and Francis Hopkinson addressed him again. Richard Statham and Ralph Peters in England, and Richard Peters, Jr., in Philadelphia—all were dutifully responsive to their uncle. Lady Dartry wrote thanking him for his congratulations on her "very peculiarly happy lot," sending Lord Dartry's best compliments to Mr. Peters and wishing she might show her friend in person the fine little child with which she had been blest. The congregation of Christ Church and St. Peter's took pride in the mentor who preached from the two pulpits. Francis Hopkinson's letters told of their author's ambitions to this American parish or that, of his indifference to this charge, of his sense of obligation to the Philadelphia clergyman. With simple forthrightness, they evinced his piety of spirit. They were made elegant by an apt quotation from the Latin tongue. Their writer could say truly with the Old Bachelor in Menander:

> *Etsi id molestum, atque alienum a vita mea*
> *Videtur, si vos tantopere istuc voltis, fiat.*
> —*Terent. Adelph.*

Nothing should seem baneful, nothing alien, in his life if God willed it. Richard Peters admired the young scholar's aptness in employing an aphorism from comedy to express the right attitude of mind for a Christian.

William White acknowledged obliging and affectionate letters from the Reverend Dr. Peters. He told of his travels in England, of new friends there, of associations both learned and polite. He warned the Rector of Christ Church not to let his good flow of spirits make him overrate his strength and reminded him that country air was his best remedy.

He had visited Tommy Peters in Bristol. He had passed three weeks at Bath and, while there, had often talked with the Bishop of London in the Pump-Room, who had inquired very particularly for Dr. Peters' health. More than that, he had established connections with old friends of the Pennsylvania priest in Oxford. Although invited to beds in both Magdalen and Worcester Colleges and settled with an English companion in Worcester, he spent pleasant hours at Wadham. Indeed, Mr. Costard, Vicar at Twickenham, who had been a fellow in that college when Richard Peters was enrolled there and remembered his former pupil with great pleasure, had been Mr. White's sponsor and introduced him to Mr. Swinton, another of Dr. Peters' associates also at Wadham, and today "one of the curiosities of the University." Through Mr. Costard, he also had the advantage of meeting with the famous Dr. Kennicott. That great scholar had affably described the ten years of his labor collating the Hebrew manuscripts, and, to give his friend in Philadelphia a sense of the work; the young visitor was sending a copy of the savant's proposals for its effectuation.

William White was, in fact, enchanted with Oxford during his two weeks sojourn. He visited every college, every chapel, every library, and every garden in the University and delighted in them all. But in other respects, he was moving modestly in England. He was following the injunction of the Rector of Christ Church not to do excessive preaching, even though he desired to do more public speaking if only to overcome his native backwardness.

His letters, of course, were wanting in both the religious spirit and the Latinity of Francis Hopkinson, as their reader well perceived. But the warm friendliness of them delighted Richard Peters. He liked greetings through the youthful writer from old associates in England; he liked extending the greetings of the son of Colonel Thomas White to friends in Philadelphia. Altogether, he reflected, this callow aspirant to the priesthood was just the person to purchase for him in London the new doctoral robe to which the degree from Oxford now entitled the Rector of Christ Church. Nothing pleased him more than having his young friend assume that obligation, and there was further happy correspondence between the two men until Mr. White had secured and shipped to Dr. Peters the proper prunella gown and cassock with silk sash. For that consignment, the addressee could remunerate, as he chose, Mr. White's father in Philadelphia or the son in England. William rejoiced that Dr. Peters continued in better health. He was always his affectionate and obliged friend.

Yet grateful as the tokens of esteem from the two young clerics in England were to their mentor, they were not more welcome to Richard Peters than contemporary expressions of regard from his nephews. If Billy Peters still continued a problem for his uncle and the Reverend Mr. Barton, Dicky was everything that a secular ward should be. When the aging minister had set before Richard, Jr. the intended disposition of his estate, that kinsman responded most affectionately, writing:

I declare before God, I had rather you enjoyed your life and health than that by the loss of either, I should gain ten times more than you can possibly give me. I most heartily thank you for the proofs of your regard you have lately particularly shown me. But, without them, your constant kindnesses to me since my infancy perfectly convinced me of your great affection to me.

The bread which the uncle had cast upon the waters seemed now to be returning in increased measure. Yet Dicky's letter was more than dutiful. It came from a responsible person and man. The older Richard Peters approved fully an added comment from his nephew: "I have long seen that the situation of our family will make it necessary for me to attend to their affairs, and I shall always look upon myself as bound to do it whenever it is in my power." The uncle could feel convinced that into other hands than his own, and capable hands, was to be committed to the care of the American branch of the Peters of Platbridge and Liverpool. He was glad he had always shown faith in Dicky.

The comfort that the Rector of Christ Church could draw from his nephews in England was, however, of more spiritual persuasion. Richard Statham could write with neither the ingenuous amiability of William White nor the scholarly charm of Francis Hopkinson. But that young barrister straightwardly and assuringly announced his intentions:

> It shall, at the same time, be my constant care to retain such a grateful sense of the Divine Goodness and of our entire dependence upon Him for every blessing we enjoy as ever to remember that we can do nothing of ourselves and that it is only through the merits of our Redeemer that we must look for happiness in this world and that which is to come.

His uncle felt, as he read the young man's words, that Hannah Statham had not died but only gone before. Her attitude survived in her son.

But it was William Peters' English son Ralph who wrote at once most personally and most devoutly. That heir to his grandfather in Liverpool and in charge of the good aunts who had reared him had learned much of business from a hard childhood and laborious youth. Yet he had escaped the coils of materialism and preserved his soul. His Uncle Richard treasured tenderly the words of a letter from Raphy, which reached him in the last months of 1771:

> It is the foremost of my most sanguine wishes that I might be able to obtain that Christian resignation which you describe to have to the

Divine Will as to your stay on or removal from this world. I strive to let the things of the world sit easy with me and not to let covetousness or ambition get hold of me. The conquest over these, I hope, is a step toward it. My hearty prayers and endeavors shall not be wanting for aid towards attaining it, and I am not without my hopes of succeeding in some degree. But whether I shall be able to do it to that eminent height you are so happy to do, I cannot be without my fears.

On the whole, the reader of his three nephews' letters could not think dismally of the family to which he belonged. His brother William had been culpable, no doubt, for many a dereliction, and William's son, Billy, in Pennsylvania, was much of an oaf. But by and large, the Peters had been and were fine stock. The Rector of Christ Church permitted himself moments of thinking well of his breed. He meditated at times on the arms which the family bore and which so often he used in sealing his letters. Surely, he told himself, the crest of the coat, with its two lions' heads ringed and set back to back, stood for restraint and rugged mutual support. The rose in the bar superior, he knew, was a symbol of substantial wealth and respect. The two cinquefoils on its bend dexter were vaunts of perfection; the two eschallops in its field represented pilgrim-like piety. All were devices to accredit a Christian.

Yet it was the motto of the coat that Richard Peters liked to believe he esteemed most. *Sans Dieu Rien* were the words. He knew that they meant that man must not expect to achieve anything without God's help, and he trusted that in his labors and performances, he had had just such Heavenly aid. Nor did he forget the assurance of the Psalmist: "His truth shall be thy shield and buckler."

It was as good a translation of the motto as any. And in it, he felt, could be something of the posture of the angels.

XXI

After Indian Summer

After 1771, true autumn and winter became the portion of Richard Peters. He met them often with equanimity, failing neither in courage nor cheer. But he knew that seasons of illusion were to be past rather than future experiences with him. He was no longer to have unmitigated physical health. The deficiencies of the flesh came back in 1772, and although he did not constantly suffer from either his lax or the gravel, intermittent periods of weakness and pain taxed him with an ever-increasing certitude of return. He was no more a well and vigorous man. He had his chariot to take him from his Walnut Street residence to ecclesiastical and pastoral duties or the houses of his friends. He had his robes to increase the dignity of his pulpit as he stood preaching at Christ Church or St. Peter's. He had the affections of his parishioners and friends to administer to him in his illnesses, although old Dr. Graeme's death in September 1772 came to him as a true sorrow. There were still labors to be performed for the advancement of religion. There were still meetings of the Council of Pennsylvania to be attended for furthering or protecting the interests of the province. He could still offer service to the Family—service more important, he told himself, than even his conduct of the marriage ceremony at Christ Church when Lieutenant Governor Richard Penn took Mary Masters of Philadelphia to be his bride. For, although never unwilling to be a part of the personal lives of all the connections of the Proprietaries, he wished unfailingly to buttress the political strength of his old masters.

Yet he realized the sterner winds of late autumn and winter were at hand. He could not do as he had done. He was not going to reach the ripe age of eighty-four as Thomas Graeme had reached it. There would be no more journeys to faraway points like Fort Stanwix. His exploits would be in his study, in the pulpit, at the Council table, and in the affairs of his brother's children. His luxuries and his ambitions both grew into needs.

After Indian Summer

He gave himself, then, on the one hand, to memories, on the other to passive rather than active cooperation with clericals and statesmen. Except in his parish, he no longer assumed leadership.

In his heart, he kept charity of spirit. If a young Philadelphian had begotten a child out of wedlock and then quarreled with his paramour, more than the ear of Richard Peters was inclined to the unhappy story. Generously, he stood between George Clymer and a discarded mistress, armed with counsel for both of the sinners and serving as an intermediary for funds allowed by the man for the care of his illegitimate offspring. To Isabella Kearney, who had borne a little girl to an absconding lover, he was the means of reconciliation with her outraged family, and his purse was opened to the needs of the unfortunate young mother and her infant, as sad letters acknowledged. More near to his family circle was the elopement of Polly Peters with a plain Mr. Smith, and forbearing Uncle Richard not only brought peace between the offending bride and her angry mother, Mary Brientnall Peters but induced her father in England not to exclude Polly from his will. As best an old man could, he eased the ways of sinners and lovers, and he did not wholly forget the beam that was once in his own eye.

Yet he admitted to himself that other offices of kindness and religion gave him more pleasure. There was a more certain honor in directing use of the funds which good laymen were now allowing to the widows and orphans of Church of England clergy, in supervising the supply of ministers from all the denominations of Philadelphia to preach at Sunday forenoon services to the inmates of the Bettering House, in inspiriting missionaries of the church stationed at far distant points, in encouraging friendship between Episcopacy and Protestantism in Sweden, in corresponding with gentlemen like William Byrd of Westover in Virginia on the subject of ministers for the church in their parts, in settling—in his function as Rector of Christ Church and chief administrator of the incorporation which it had gained by its charter—of the estate of good Dr. John Kearsley, that noble old communicant who had just died, leaving his property for the endowment of a hospital and home for impoverished gentlewomen belonging to the Church of England.

Yet, if in such works, Dr. Peters found his richest rewards, other less arduous elements in his experience brought amiable satisfaction. He took great pleasure in the reports of William Smith's success in the southern colonies in raising funds for the College of Philadelphia, as well as that learned man's finding new pupils for its professors. He followed with interest Dr. John Morgan's efforts and prospectuses for having a college of physic founded in Pennsylvania and supported as an American institution by other of the provinces, and was glad that Governor Richard Penn and former Governor James Hamilton were both proponents. He found it a delight to subscribe to and to further the circulation of printed sermons, letters on family worship, and pamphlets of religious instruction by Churchmen. He enjoyed the exchange of civilities with Swedish visitors, exchange of letters with William Bull, Thomas Barton, Samuel Auchmuty, and latterly with Dr. Thomas Bradbury Chandler, Rector of St. John's at Elizabethtown, New Jersey, and the doughty advocate of bishops to reside in America. He was happy to be chosen by Mr. Thomas Penn to be the transmitter, late in 1772, of the Proprietor's gift to the College of a set of the Works of Dr. Skelton, an author whose life the donor could praise as being "of one piece with his writings." He felt, not unpleasantly, the flush of an old personal conceit in himself when John Andrews, missionary at York, wrote to express gratitude through him to Mrs. Richard Penn and her mother, Mrs. Masters, for kindnesses to the mission and the added compliments on the long acknowledged acceptance of his benevolent friend among gentlewomen. It was like having facetious John Carter write again: "The ladies would not repine at their confinement if they were so happy as to be under the same roof with so enlivening a friend as Dr. Peters."

Yet in 1773 and 1774, the Rector of the United Churches understood well enough that the days of new ambition had ended for him-that last autumn and chill winter were fixed, too, on his own physical life. Sad testimonials to the limitations of the flesh were the annual printed records of illnesses, deaths, and burials in the congregations of Christ Church and St. Peter's, which he included resolutely among his papers. He was conscious not only of how many died of smallpox, "teeth and worms," or sore throat but of what numerous parishioners were carried off by "decay" and "old age"—forty-two of them, in fact, between the December of the one year and that of its successor.

Earlier, Richard Peters had had every advantage that the bounty of the Penns could afford him. Latterly, Providence had permitted him grace in the holy offices of the church. But now, not merely signs of dissolution in mankind were about him. The structure of human society also was being transformed. In America and the province, ways and men kept ever-changing. Talk of the fallacy of taxation without representation increased everywhere, and resistance to the successive modes of taxing that the English Parliament applied became more menacingly open. The levy on tea had led to frank insurrection in Massachusetts. Universal indignation from Virginia to New England greeted the

Parliamentary Act to close the Port of Boston in redress. Congresses from all the colonies were meeting in Philadelphia to consider ways of responding to what they deemed the arbitrary encroachments of the Mother Country. More particularly, in territory bought by Richard Peters and John Penn for Pennsylvania at Fort Stanwix in 1768—despite the protests of Governor to Governor, despite litigation in England, and despite minor armies sent from Philadelphia and Northampton County to displace them—Connecticut intruders held and cultivated the fairest of the Wyoming fields. In the province itself, the Assembly grew more powerful daily; Ben Franklin occupied his saddle more firmly than ever. All was as though the erstwhile Secretary to the Commonwealth belonged to a past epoch.

So, whether or no he knew occasional honors and pleasure, apprehension clung to Dr. Peters, and personal sorrow weighed in upon him. A first paralytic stroke befell Thomas Penn, and for his old friend in England, the Philadelphia clergyman suffered greatly. At home, Richard Hockley developed a malignant growth which tortured and corrupted his back into one monstrous suppurating sore, and Richard Peters attended with the last votives of affection an intimate who on many an occasion had been nurse to himself. Then, when death came to that invalid, again, he was the scribe, now writing to Lady Juliana, as once he had written of Nanny Hockley to the Proprietor in 1745. And once more, his mind was sadly absorbed in the dreary symptoms of mortal decay.

Yet his letter of September 1774 was neither all lament for Mr. Hockley nor all unconscious revelation of his pains and fears. In it was frank insistence that he could not do otherwise than write as he did of Mr. Penn's long beloved ward since, as he said to Lady Juliana, he owed everything that he had to her husband's good Family. His message was but one more attempt at returning thanks to a benefactor. Obviously, he wished both to bear solace to the Proprietor of Pennsylvania and to have it from him. When Lady Juliana's reply came, he read her words with great eagerness. She spoke of the grief of all the circle of the Penns at Stoke; like a Christian, she wrote of the comfort of knowing that the dead man had now been relieved of the last illnesses of his body. She said she "knew few things would hurt Mr. Penn more than the death of poor Mr. Hockley." She narrated that when she told him, "he shed tears and repeated what I have always heard him say that he loved Dick as a child." She added that he had his fourteen-year-old son John Penn solemnly called to him and that he bade his heir "love and befriend any descendants of that good man's."

Momentarily, as the Rector of Christ Church read, he wondered whether the daughter of the Earl of Pomfret had ever heard the whispers which sometimes drifted around Philadelphia as to who had been the real father of Dicky Hockley. But he was prompt to put that thought from him as one that might be offensive to his best friends on earth.

In March 1775, Thomas Penn himself died, and in the year that followed, grief-stricken and invalid Dr. Richard Peters remained very sorrowful and anxious. Through months of it, as a good Christian and Churchman, he must tread careful paths of diplomacy. In the catastrophic times, it was as necessary to keep congregations strong in their faith in religion as it was to save men from the errors of political treason. Loath as he was to celebrate days set aside by the Continental Congress for "fasting, prayer, and humiliation through all the colonies," he would not risk disinclining his parish from hearkening to the ways of celestial wisdom. At Christ Church, then, and St. Peter's, and in all the churches of the province, arrangements were made for suitable observation and preaching preparatory to and on the Day of Fast, July 20, 1775. That concession made to the wishes of the laity, Mr. Peters and all his aides—William Smith, Jacob Duche, Thomas Coombe, William Stringer, and William White—on June 30, forwarded a memorial by the hand of the Honorable Richard Penn to the Bishop of London, explaining an act which, however it might be misjudged in England, was performed in their hope of preserving peace and harmony within their flocks. Four days later, the troubled Rector wrote to the Secretary of the Venerable Society, expressing his hope that the Bishop would receive "with the tenderness of a father" the reasons for the conduct of the ministers in Pennsylvania. The "calamitous state of their church on account of the unnatural war which is carrying on in their very bowels" must be the excuse on which their plea for favor rested. They dared not alienate from religion the numerous uniformed patriots who worshiped in their sanctuaries.

To these epistolary activities, Richard Peters gave with all the energy he could. But he was ill and tried. A flux had tormented him much in the last years. Carrot-top tea had lost all its powers of relief. The numerous cures for the flux and the bloody flux which he painstakingly recorded in his list of "receits," whether or no they had cured the Duchess of Northumberland or helped Governor John Penn, availed the copyist for no enduring season.

Bodily suffering did not, however, sum up his total private concern. His favorite nephew, Dicky Peters, had become a leader among the new Military Associators of Philadelphia and was actually heading a company of young patriots who had organized themselves to resist any attempt of Great Britain to interfere with the liberties and independence of America. And there was no stopping this red-blooded, full-souled Richard Peters, Jr.! The generations of men were metamorphosing. "*Mutabile mutandis,*" thought the invalid uncle. In September 1775, in his failing health, he found cause for resigning from his rectorship. To his faithful assistant, Jacob Duche, who some weeks earlier in July had preached so acceptably in the Old Church to the whole body of Continental Congress, he relinquished the chief responsibilities of the sanctuary and parish. In the same month, for the last time, he attended the Council, the old provincial body whose authority had now, like that of the Lieutenant Governor, dwindled before the new revolutionary Committee of Safety, which Franklin headed and the Assembly inspired.

Yet the aging cleric did not cease altogether from interest in the world. Temporalities occupied him for some time further. With an old shrewdness, he studied the lands he owned in many parts of Pennsylvania and corresponded with surveyors on the subject of his holdings. Had the persons who had taken these remained on them? Had they disposed of their improvements to others and decamped? What was the present condition of each parcel? And what are the full rights of Richard Peters, chief owner, there? And if he inquired studiously for his interests, he requested information quite as zealously as to the lands of the Proprietors. Moreover, he made ready for dissolution with a mind entirely practical. His sister-in-law, Mary; William Peters' wife; his nieces, Mary Smith and Elizabeth Peters; his great nephew, Richard Peters Smith; his godson, Thomas Barton's son of Lancaster; his friends, Jacob Duche and Francis Hopkinson; his nephews, William, Thomas, and the recalcitrant Richard Peters, Jr.—must all be provided for by a proper testament.

Another thing, too, was necessary. The cheerful Dicky was in love with Sally Robinson and talked of marrying her. His uncle remembered certain blots which had become too evident in the past of the Peters family; to the roster of them, Dicky must not be allowed to add any new mistakes. On the May day in 1776, when the retired Reverend Dr. Richard Peters signed his will, he signed a settlement of £2,000 Pennsylvania money upon his best-esteemed nephew. The sum could be had by Dicky as soon as he completed his intended marriage; only in consideration of secure completion of that could he have it after his uncle's death. To the document which confirmed the gift and its conditions, the grantor affixed the seal and arms of the Peters family with a distinct impress.

Thus, although he overlooked his English nephews and nieces entirely in his final testament, the ways of grace and business were combined in the last actions of Richard Peters. For Dicky he made honorable wedlock certain, fortune, as certain as he could. In the paths of love and affection, he held himself constant. If old suspicions of Israel Pemberton and Ben Franklin persisted in his dying thoughts, or febrile contempt for the Assembly of the Province remained, just as integral endured his loyalties to Thomas, John, and Richard Penn. On July 4, 1776, the bell at the Pennsylvania State House, which had hung and rung over so many years of Richard Peters' work, pealed out the message of national independence for the United States of America. Six days later, the retired Secretary of the Province and Rector of Philadelphia surrendered his spirit into the care of Providence.

On the 11th of the month, his will was proved at the Courthouse, and on the same day in Christ Church, his body was lowered into an aisle vault overlooked by the pulpit from which during forty years it had been his envy, his ambition, and his pride to preach.

In adjacent tombs lay the ashes of Archibald Cummings, Robert Jenney, and Jane Elizabeth Falconier Assheton Cummings Jenney, and but a few yards away in another grave, those of Robert Assheton, first of the three husbands of that lady. Like Richard Peters, all these ministers and communicants of the Church of England in Pennsylvania awaited in peace the sound of the trumpet and, at the Last Day, the judgment of Heaven.

Yet no Philadelphia newspaper in July of 1776 recorded either the death of the late ex-Rector of Christ Church and St. Peter's and former Secretary of the Province or the ceremonies held at his interment within those sacred precincts where so long he had devised, counseled, and guided.

Acknowledgments

In Shaping this biography of Richard Peters, the author owes much to contemporary scholars and students of eighteenth-century Pennsylvania—to persons who have lived with men and women of the old province not as visitors among ghosts or shades but as familiars with neighbors and friends (or political adversaries). To Dr. Julian P. Boyd, are due thanks for my first introduction to Richard Peters as an animate personality. Of the constant help in tracking documents and allusions which was afforded me by the late Charles Berwind Montgomery and of his genial fellowship in the understanding of men and events, no sufficient acknowledgments can now be set down. I am in debt to Dr. Paul A. W. Wallace for an ever-deepening sense of the Provincial Secretary's ease and variety. Mrs. Evelyn Abrahams Benson has particularly obliged me by her throwing light upon Thomas Cresap and general relations between Colonial Maryland and Pennsylvania. Through Miss Jessica C. Ferguson and Miss Nell B. Stevens of the Pennsylvania State Library, Dr. Henry W. Shoemaker, Miss Ethel Sporck, Mrs. Dorothy G. Lynch, and Miss Byrle F. MacPherson of the Pennsylvania State Department of Archives, Miss Cathadne H. Miller and Miss Sara Ruth Bond of the Historical Society of Pennsylvania—I have had not only access to folders, files, and tomes of an older day but sympathy and understanding which of ten made my quest of material a full delight.

To the Taft Foundation of the University of Cincinnati, my obligation is especially great for a grant-in-aid, which made it more possible for me the visits and sojourns in Harrisburg and Philadelphia while I pursued my research.

Sources

Printed Works

In tracing the career of Richard Peters and his associations with men of his century, I have, of course, resorted to a goodly number of printed texts: sources as various as Benjamin Franklin's *Autobiography*, Burke's *Peerage*, *The Dictionary of American Biography* (20 Vols., 1928–36), Edward L. Clark's *A Record of the Inscriptions on the Tablets and Grave-Stones in the Burial-Grounds of Christ Church, Philadelphia* (1864), Benjamin Dorr's *A Historical Account of Christ Church, Philadelphia, from its Foundation, A.D., 1695 to A.D., 1841* (1841), George H. Morgan's *Annals of Harrisburg* (Harrisburg, 1858), William Henry Egle's *History of the Counties of Dauphin and Lebanon, in the Commonwealth of Pennsylvania* (Philadelphia, 1883), Charles P. Keith's *The Provincial Councillors of Pennsylvania* (Trenton, 1883), Howard Malcolm Jenkins' *The Family of William Penn* (Philadelphia and London, 1899), and Nellie Peters Black's *Richard Peters: His Ancestors and Descendants* (Atlanta, 1904). But my dependence upon these has been discriminating and only occasional rather than constant, as it has also been with such items as Frank M. Etting's *An Historical Account of the Old State House of Pennsylvania* (Boston, 1876), Charles Miner's *History of Wyoming* (Philadelphia, 1845), the genealogical tables of Arthur Pound's *The Penns of Pennsylvania and England* (New York, 1932), and with inclusions in periodicals like the selections from the "Diary" of David Fisher *(Pennsylva11ia Magazine,* Vol. 17) and R. Stewart-Brown's article "An account of the Oil Painting 'Liverpool in 1680' with notes on the Peters Family of Platbridge and Liverpool" *(Transactions of the Historic Society of Lancashire and Cheshire,* 1908).

Much more assiduously have I consulted and depended upon authoritative printed public and ecclesiastic records, as well as upon texts and pamphlets published in Pennsylvania in Peters' day. My adherence has been faithful, at times almost to the extent of blindness, to such official publications as the *Pennsylvania Colonial Records* (Vols. 1–10) and *Pennsylvania Archives* (Series 1, Vols. 1–2, and Series 8, Vol. 5), and to collections like *The Susquehanna Company Papers*

Sources

(Julian P. Boyd, Editor, Wyoming Historical and Geological Society, 4 Vols., 1930–33) and *Historical Collections Relating to the American Colonial Church* (Vol. 2, Pennsylvania, William Stevens Perry, Editor, 1871).

I have moreover drawn closely upon pamphlets, like Benjamin Franklin's *Plain Truth by a Tradesman of Philadelphia* (1747) and William Smith's *A Brief State of the Province of Pennsylvania* (md edition, London, 1755, reprinted for J. Sabin, New York, 1865), and upon three discourses released by Richard Peters himself: *The Two Last Sermons Preached at Christ Church in Philadelphia, July 3, 1731, A Sermon on Education* (B. Franklin and D. Hall printers, Philadelphia, 1751), and *A Sermon Preached in the New Lutheran Church of Zion, 26 June, 1769*.

One mimeographed source I employed was the *Papers of Colonel Henry Bouquet* (Pennsylvania Historical Commission, Harrisburg, 1940–41).

Manuscripts

The spirit and the substance of the biography, with its interpretation of Richard Peters and his times and his contemporaries, have, however, depended most of all upon manuscript sources.

These have ranged from such items as files of "Deeds" and "Tickets" in the Land Office, Pennsylvania State Department of Internal Affairs, Provincial Papers, Pennsylvania State Department of Archives, Harrisburg, and the Report of the Pennsylvania Commissioners at Albany, 1754 (American Philosophical Society, Philadelphia)-to collections and items, possessed by the Historical Society of Pennsylvania, Philadelphia, such as the Society Collection (September 16, 1765), the Dreer Collections of Washington Letters and Revolutionary Generals (I, 38), the Logan Papers (Vol. 4: Letterbooks of James Logan, pp. 415–416), the Journal of Deborah Norris Logan (Vol. 10), James Steele's Letterbook, 1729–1731, the Shewbart Papers, Benjamin Chew's "Diary," and Conrad Weiser's Correspondence (Vol. 2, 1757–1766). Moreover, they have embraced innumerable entries, memoranda, and instances of report or counsel in Thomas Penn's Letters to Richard Peters, 1752–1772, the many volumes of Thomas Penn's Letterbooks and the Penn Manuscripts ("Official Correspondence," "Private Correspondence," "Philadelphia Land Grants," "Supplementary," "Saunders Coates"), volumes 1–8 of the Peters Papers, and Richard Peters' Letterbooks. And included among them, too, were Richard Peters' "Diary Book, 1762," which tells with equal verve of chitchat with ladies and parishioners, of tiffs with other Philadelphians, and texts for sermons in the year of its author's resumption of his clerical calling in Christ Church, and the Latin certificates of ordination treasured from the days of his early priesthood.

Personalia

These, together with all references to Richard Peters and William Peters in their family life and social circles, as well as references to Nanny and Richard Hockley, wards of Thomas Penn, have been definitely based on manuscript sources, in letterbooks and correspondence of the Peterses and the Penns, and elsewhere. The matter of William Peters' second marriage and the christening of his first two American children on the day of that event is confirmed by the Records (Baptisms and Marriages) of Trinity Protestant Episcopal Church, of Oxford, Philadelphia County, as shelved by the Genealogical Society of Pennsylvania, Philadelphia.

Clerical Ambitions

The clerical ambitions of Richard Peters and his associations with the Academy and College of Philadelphia are presented on the basis of similar authority. Peters' correspondence in 1741 with Ferdinando John Paris, legal agent of Thomas Penn, when he hoped for Mr. Paris' intercession with the Bishop of London to secure him the living of Christ Church, made vacant by Archibald Cummings' death, is to be found in the Penn Manuscripts ("Philadelphia Land Grants," "Supplementary," and "Saunders Coates").

Secretarial Activities

Peters' duties as Secretary in the Land Office, as Secretary to the Pennsylvania Provincial Council, and as member of the latter board, as written of in the biography, are based upon his correspondence generally with Thomas Penn, upon Council Books, upon the Peters Papers and Letterbooks, and Provincial Papers. His attendance upon the surveyors of the Pennsylvania-Maryland line in 1739, his connections with the Marsh Run affair in 1745, his associations with the campaign and defeat of General Braddock, his opinions of the Delaware Chief Teedyuscung, and his participation in the "New Purchase" at Fort Stanwix in 1768 are mainly founded upon the latter volumes and documents.

Index

Aaron, a Mohawk, 115
Academy and College of Philadelphia, 1, 173, 245, 251, 259, 268
Address to the King, 88
Albany, 71, 88, 89–90, 94, 125, 166, 215, 227, 229, 240, 267
Albany Commissioners, 72–73
Alexander, William, Lord Stirling, 201
Alison, Dr. Francis, 145, 195, 198–99, 203, 211, 223, 251
Allen, William, vii, 20, 62, 94, 109, 137, 232
Allen, Mrs. William, 56
American Colonial Church, 1, 225, 267
Andrews, Rev. John, 260
Argo, 122
Armstrong, Colonel John, 147–49, 213
Assaraquoa (Governor of Virginia), 69–70, 78
Assembly of Pennsylvania, 131, 143, 153, 171, 264
Assheton, Robert, 264
"Association," 96, 102
"Association Paper, The," 100, 104
Auchmuty, Samuel, 231–32, 240, 242, 246, 251, 260
Aughwick, 117, 127, 149, 152
Augusta Regiment, 183

Backhouse, Rev. Richard, 40–45
Baird, Patrick, 61
Baltimore, 26
Baltimore County, 108
Baltimore, Lord, 25–28, 36, 69, 106–107, 117, 169, 209
Barclay, Mr., 42, 48–49, 51, 233
Barclay's *Apology*, 98
Barton, Rev. Thomas, 167, 173, 203, 208–209, 234, 246, 250, 255, 260, 263
Bath, 1, 103, 224, 255
Battery, 97, 104, 109, 129, 209
Baynor, George, 166–67
Bealer, Rev. Mr., 57, 61
Bearcroft, Philip, 48–49
Behme, Pastor, 61
Belcher, Gov. Jonathan, 166
Belmont, 126, 232, 245

Berks County, 210, 214, 217, 240
Beverly, William, 69, 72
Big Cove, 117
Big Juniata, 116–17
Bishop of London, 4–5, 11–13, 17–18, 33–35, 37, 39–40, 42–44, 48–50, 52–54, 61, 64, 201, 205, 220, 225, 232, 252, 254, 262, 268. *See also* Gibson, Edmund, and Terrick, Richard.
Blue Hills, 116, 179, 228. *See also* Kittochtinny Hills.
Blunston, Samuel, 106
Board of Trade, 65, 222
Board of War, 2
Bombay Hook, 92, 96
Bootle, Mr., 8
"Borromean Islands," 65
Bouquet, Colonel Henry, 186–95, 205, 213, 218–19, 267
Bownes, Obadiah, 45
Braddock, General Edward, 139–40, 150–69
Bradford, Andrew, 20
Braywick, 171
Brief State of the Province of Pennsylvania, A, 130, 267
Bristol, England, 10, 19, 45, 224–26, 250, 254
Bucks County, 20, 101, 179, 221, 240–41
Bull, William, 231, 249
Burd, Colonel James, 147–51, 165, 191
Burton, Colonel, 163–64
Bush Hill, 19, 22, 86, 105, 139, 172, 199, 267
Buxton, 248–49
Byrd, William, 259

Cabins burnt, 106–19
Cahoon, George, 116
Callowhill, Hannah (Mrs. William Penn), 57
Canada, 79, 87–89, 144, 166, 202
Canassatego, 62, 69–74, 78
Canterbury, Archbishop of, 1, 123–25, 145, 205, 220, 222, 234. *See also* Secker, Thomas.
Cape Breton, 78–79, 84, 88, 104, 143
Carlisle, 148, 151, 159, 162, 172, 176–77, 208, 213, 215, 219

Cartagena, 77
Carter, John, 260
Catawbas, 25, 68–69, 77–79, 150
Cayugas, 68, 78, 95, 110, 240
Chamberlaine, Samuel, 26–29
Chambers, John, 71, 116
Chancellor's sail loft, 99
Chandler, Dr. Thomas Bradbury, 232, 260
"Chapel of ease" (St. Peter's Church), 110
Chariot, 230–33, 254
Charles II, 19, 80, 228
Charles Edward, Prince, 86
Charles, Robert, 16, 38, 244
Charter of Pennsylvania, 19, 80
Chartier, Peter, 77, 79
Cherokees, 68, 70, 77, 190
Chesapeake, 84
Chester, 40–41, 175
Chester County, 25, 27, 34, 101, 159, 240
Chew, Benjamin, 175, 192–94, 203, 219, 239–40, 267
Chippewas, 209
Chittick's "Treatise," 231
Choiseul, Duke de, 253
Christ Church, vii, 1–2, 4, 11–12, 14, 18–19, 23, 32, 34–41, 44–54, 61, 64, 109–110, 129–30, 196–201, 205–209, 219–25, 229–40, 246–68
"Cicero," 96, 216, 226
Clayton, Asher, 210, 214, 216
Clymer, George, 259
Colden, Gov. Cadwallader, 215–16
Coleman, Mr., 98, 111, 175
College of New Jersey, 200
College of Philadelphia. *See* Academy and College.
College of Physicians, 233
Commencement, 198–99, 202–203
Committee of Safety, 263
Conestoga, 211–17, 223
Conestogoes, 106, 211–12
Congress of Albany, 227
Connecticut, 125, 128, 142, 181, 209–210, 223, 228–30, 236–43, 249, 261
Conococheague, 151, 153–54, 173, 219
Constitution of the Mother Country, 124
Continental Congress, 1, 262–263
Coombe, Thomas, 245–46, 253, 262
Cooper, Myles, 253

Costard, Rev. Mr., 255
Council at Onondaga, 115
Council Books, 61, 65, 73, 75–76, 80, 92, 94, 122, 125, 144, 154, 160, 268
Council of Pennsylvania, 87, 157, 160, 258
Court at Kensington, 26
Court at St. James, 74
Court of Rome, 88
Cox, Mrs. Maria, 171
Cremorne, Viscount, 254
Cresap, Thomas, 106–108, 118, 122, 148, 153, 265
Croghan, George, 110, 115–16, 118, 147–50, 165, 194, 237, 239–40, 242
Crow Foot, 151
Culloden, Battle of, 88, 93
Cumberland County, 115, 117, 148, 159, 173, 184, 208
Cummings, Rev. Archibald, 4, 11–13, 17, 23, 32, 34, 41, 55, 64, 200, 264, 268
Curry, Rev. Mr., 38

Dartry, Lady. *See* Freame, Philadelphia Hannah.
Daunt, Knowles, 107–108
De Lancey, Gov. James, 143, 160, 162, 165
Delaware, Forks of the, 63, 178
Delawares, 62–63, 77–78, 95, 110, 135, 172–73, 178–81, 209–210, 219
Denny, Gov. William, 2–3, 173–95, 229
Depositions, 92–93
Derby, James Stanley, Earl of, 6, 8, 13, 16, 32, 67, 109, 221
Diahogo, 178, 181–82
"Dialogue on Peace, A," 202
Dinwiddie, Governor, 149, 153
Diocese of London, 50, 52
Dixon, Jeremiah, 209
Doctor of Divinity, 5, 253
Dove, Mr., 194
Drummossie Moor, 86–90
Duche, Rev. Jacob, 175, 198–204, 220–22, 241, 245, 262–63
Dunbar, Colonel Thomas, 142, 161–70
Dunlop, Andrew, 122
Dyer, Eliphalet, 230

Eastburn, Benjamin, 26–30, 179
Easton, 159, 192, 194

Index

Easton, Treaty of, vii, 174, 177–91
Easton Neston, 121
Elder, Rev. John, 167, 210, 216
Elliss, Nany, 56
Elliss, Mrs., 56
Elphinston, Mr., 127
Episcopacy, 61, 259
Episcopal colonists, 4
Erastianism, 53
Evans, Peter, 12–13, 33, 37–38, 41–43, 84
Evans, William, 84
Ewing, Rev. John, 211, 217–18, 223

Fairfax, Colonel, 188
Fairfax, Lord, 122, 188
Falconier, Jane Elizabeth, 55, 264
Family. *See* Proprietary Family.
Fermor, Thomas, Earl of Pomfret, 121
Finch, Miss, 225–26
Finley, John, 116
Finley, Dr. Samuel, 200
Fire Companies, 99, 109
Five Nations, 24, 216
"Fleet" marriage, 8–9
Forbes, General John, vii, 190–94
Fort Augusta, 182, 184
Fort Cumberland, 147, 150–51, 155–65, 188
Fort Duquesne, 143–44, 152, 158, 161, 166, 170, 191, 193
Fort Stanwix, 239–45, 258, 261, 268
Fort Stanwix, Treaty of, 2
Fothergill, Dr. John, 180, 231
France, 77, 104, 109, 125, 180, 202, 205, 210, 253
Francis, Tench, 123
Francis, Mrs. Tench, 204
Frank pledge, 195
Franklin, Benjamin, vii, 6, 14, 20–23, 32, 59–60, 67, 95–99, 104, 109–13, 119–27, 133, 149–53, 156–58, 167, 170–78, 188–89, 195, 218, 222–24, 229, 234, 261, 263–64, 267
Franklin, William, 156, 200
Freame, Margaret (Mrs. Thomas Freame), 55–56, 65,
Freame, Philadelphia Hannah, afterwards Lady Danry, 223, 226, 253–54
Freame, Thomas, 55
Fredericktown, 156

French and Indian War, 6
French and Indians, 174
Friendly Association, 173, 182, 191
Friends, 17, 39, 191. *See also* Quakers.
Friends Meeting-Place, Jordans, 222
Frontenac, 158
Fulham Palace, 45

Gage, General, 214–15, 238,
Gale, Levin, 26–29, 71, 108
Galloway, George, 116
Galloway, John, 15
Galloway, John (of Maryland), 202
Galloway, Mrs. John, 202
Galloway, William, 116
Ganside, Mrs. *See* Peters, Nelly.
George I, 50, 121
George II, 29, 53, 68, 74, 77, 86, 88, 107–108, 186
George III, 202, 220, 224, 229, 232
German, 61, 71, 96, 146, 247, 250
Gibson, Edmund, Bishop of London, 14, 20, 33, 35, 38, 41, 43, 46–52, 84, 196, 225
Gibson, James, 217, 219
Gooch, Gov. William, 71–78, 88–89
Gookin, Gov. Charles, 12, 54
Goranyon, Andrew, 249
Gordon, Gov. Patrick, 22, 106, 248
Graeme, Elizabeth, 220–21, 225–26
Graeme, Dr. Thomas, 20, 34, 71, 75, 92, 95, 168, 172, 198–99, 220, 230–31, 235–36, 258
Graeme, Mrs. Thomas, 200
Graeme Park, 19–20, 168, 231
Gray's Inn, 21
Great Crossing, 159, 161
Great Meadows, 159, 167, 170
Growden, Lawrence, 25–30
Gunter's chain, 28

Half-King, 127. *See also* Tanacharisson.
Halifax, Earl of, 177
Halkett, Sir Peter, 142, 161–63, 168
Halkett, Captain, 190
Hamilton, Andrew, vii, 10–13, 19–22, 32, 43, 56–57, 60, 67, 86–87, 94, 102, 104, 112, 114
Hamilton, Gov. James, 86–87, 90, 94, 102, 104–105, 109–14, 118, 125, 127, 135,

139, 146, 171–72, 175–78, 188, 190, 195, 197–99, 203–205, 211, 229, 260
Harris' Ferry (*also* Harrisburg), 2, 167, 172, 216, 265
Harris, John, 167, 172, 216
Hart, James, 92
Heap, George, 128–29
Henry the Mohawk, 128
Hiddleston, David, 116–17
"High Dutch," 81
Highlanders, 87–88
Hillsborough, Lord, 238
Historical Account of the Collation, etc., 252
Hockley, Nanny, 65, 83–84, 261, 268
Hockley, Richard, Sr., 65, 83, 170–72, 199, 223, 234–36, 261, 268
Hockley, Richard, Jr., 67, 83, 262
Hockley, Samuel, 83
Hogg, Captain, 159, 161, 165
Hoops, Adam, 147
Hooswick, Thomas, 81–82
Hopkinson, Rev. Francis, 98, 111, 203, 251–56, 263
Howie, Rev. Alexander, 43–44
Hughes, John, 175, 224, 230

Independent Company, 161
Indian lands, 71, 115, 119
Indian policies, 24
Inglis, Rev. Charles, 56, 203
Inner Temple, 8
Innes, Colonel James, 160, 165–66
Iroquois (Six Nations), vii, 60–80, 95, 115–16, 125–126, 143–44, 166, 172, 174, 178–82, 192–94, 209, 213–16, 227–30, 237–41

Jackson, Richard, 230
Jacobitish tendencies, 86
James II, 96
Jenney, Rev. Robert, 54–55, 63, 67, 196–97, 264
Jennings, Edmund, 69, 73
Jersey Commissioners, 27
Jersey Indians, 178
Jersey Market, 57–58, 216
Johnson Hall, 240
Johnson, Sir William, 144, 165, 172, 178, 181, 188, 194, 209, 214–15, 219, 223, 228–30, 234–42, 248, 251

Johnston, Samuel, 249
Jones, Robert, 203
Juniata lands, 60, 63, 116–17, 122, 181
Junto, 21–22, 109

Kearney, Isabella, 259
Kearsley, Dr. John, 19, 33, 37, 39, 41–44, 259
Keimer, Samuel, 20
Keith, Sir William, 20, 130, 220
Kendall, Benjamin, 215
Kennicott, Dr., 252, 255
Kent County, 21
King George's War, 1, 104, 109
King, Tom, 192
King's College, 253 *See also* College of New York.
Kinsey, John, 64, 94
Kittochtinny Hills, 30, 126, 179, 227. *See also* Blue Hills.
Knowsley Palace, 8–9, 20, 221

Ladd, John, 26
Lambeth Palace, 222
Lancaster County, 107–108, 134, 210–11, 215, 218, 227, 250
Lancaster, Treaty of, vii, 74–76
Land Office of Pennsylvania, 35, 51, 106
Langhorne, Jeremiah, 13, 64
Lardner, Lynford, 65, 91, 94, 101, 171
Lathom Chapel, 8, 22
Lawrence, Thomas, 25, 33–34, 38, 57, 77, 100
Lee, Thomas, 69–76, 110, 175
Leyden, University of, 3, 7–10, 14, 120
Library Association, 21–23, 109
Liston, Edmund, 92, 96
Little Conolloways, 117
Little Cove, 117
Little Meadows, 159, 163
Liverpool, 3, 7–13, 31, 38, 60, 63, 65, 189, 204–206, 220–26, 234, 248–49, 256, 266
Logan, James, vii, 11, 16–25, 62, 68, 75, 91, 96, 103, 112, 114, 126, 132, 236, 267
Logstown, 110
London, Bishop of, 4, 7, 11–18, 33–54, 61, 64, 201, 205, 220, 225, 232, 252, 254, 262, 268. *See also* Gibson, Edmund, and Terrick, Richard.
Lord of the Manor, 80
Lords of Trade, 35, 125, 223, 229

Lottery, 57, 145, 246
Loudoun, Lord, 176–77, 181, 186, 188
Lower Counties, 33, 39, 157
Loyal Hannen, 93
Lutheran Church, Easton, 192
Lutheran Church of Zion, 246, 267
Lutherans, 3, 61, 246, 249, 251
Lycon, Andrew, 116–17
Lydius, John Henry, 128, 223, 228–29, 242

Macclenachan, Rev. William, 197
"Madonna and Child," 226
Magdalen College, 255
Manor of Mask, 80–82, 115
Manors, 24, 60, 63, 80
Marsh Creek, 80–84, 115
Marshall, Edward, 179
Martin, Bernard, 93
Martin, David, 111–14
Martin, Colonel Josiah, 123, 126
Mary of London, 93
Maryland-Pennsylvania line, 29, 80
Mason, Charles, 209, 223
Meadows, The, 126, 150
Military chest, 162
Mingoes, 209
Mitchell, Captain, 58
Mohawks, 68, 110, 242, 251
Mohicans, 110, 178, 181
Monongahela, 159, 162–63, 167
Montgomery, Rev. John, 253
Montour, Andrew, 78–79, 110, 115, 149, 152, 165
Moore, Dr. Thomas, 37–38, 42
Moravians, 3, 19, 57, 177, 211
Morgan, Evan, 13, 34, 200
Morgan, Dr. John, 233, 259
Morris, Betsy, 56
Morris, Captain Roger, 163
Morris, Gov. Lewis, 89
Morris, Gov. Robert Hunter, 127–28, 142–73, 228
Morrisania, 127
Mount Vernon, 188
Muhlenberg, Rev. Henry Melchior, 247
Murray, William, 215

Nanticooks, 181
Neshaminy Creek, 179

New Buildings, 99, 204
New doctoral robe, a, 255
New England, 78, 84, 104, 126, 142, 147, 210, 228–29, 239–40, 260
"New Purchase," 240–41. *See* Fort Stanwix, Treaty of.
New York, 22, 68, 71–72, 77, 97–98, 123, 125–27, 143, 160, 162, 165–66, 188, 190, 215–16, 220, 227, 231–42, 245, 248, 251, 253, 266–67
Newcastle, 34, 39–41, 43, 92, 182, 202
Newcastle County, 101, 129
Newcastle, Duke of, 77, 87, 89
Newcastle, an Indian, 181
Niagara, 144, 158, 166
Nicodemus, 178
Norris, Isaac, 125, 174–75, 212, 215, 244
Northampton County, 174, 177, 179, 260
Northwest Passage, 122
Norwich, Bishop of, 252–53

Ogle, Governor, 28
Ohio, vii, 79, 95, 110, 115, 126, 150, 190, 206, 209, 218–19
Ohio Indians, 115
Ohio River, 127, 149, 166, 193, 238
Olompias, King, 77–78, 95
Onas (William Penn or his representative), 24, 69, 74, 77–78, 118, 126, 227–28
Oneidas, 25, 68, 78, 94, 110
Onondaga, 70–73, 77–80, 115, 227, 240
Onondagoes, 25, 68, 110, 128, 240
Orders in Council, 29–30
Orme, Captain Robert, 154–65, 169
Ormskirke, Lancashire, 196
Orytagh, 179
Oxford, Philadelphia County, 34, 43, 67, 268
Oxford, University of, 3, 5, 7–8, 20, 23, 120, 253–55

Palatinate Germans, 19, 92
Palmer, Anthony, 75, 90–91, 94, 97, 100
Pamela, 56
Paris, Ferdinando John, 35–52, 102–103, 231, 253
Parliament, 87, 130, 144, 166, 175, 223–25, 230, 260–61
Parsons, William, 81–82
Path Valley, 117

Paxton, 95, 172, 210–13, 223
Paxton "Boys," 210–12, 215, 218–19
Paxton Meeting House, 167, 210
Paxton Rangers, 211, 229
"Peace Address," 207. *See* Address to the King.
Peepy, Jo, 178, 180
Pemberton, Israel, 57–60, 173, 177–78, 180, 182, 190–93, 219, 263
Penn, Granville, 223, 226
Penn, John, Proprietor, 90, 94–95, 121, 125, 128–29, 171–72, 205–206, 209–20, 225, 229–32, 237, 239–40, 242, 261
Penn, Gov. John, 239, 241, 262
Penn, John (son of T. Penn), 261
Penn, Lady Juliana Fermor, 121
Penn, Juliana, 226
Penn, Louisa, 233
Penn, Richard, Proprietor, 25, 64, 91, 101, 111, 114, 125, 129, 171–72, 195, 214, 232, 253, 262, 264
Penn, Gov. Richard, 258, 260
Penn, Mrs. Richard, 260
Penn, Sophia, 223
Penn, Springett, 20
Penn, Thomas, 4, 11–12, 16–17, 20–21, 27, 32, 35, 37–41, 47, 49, 52–75, 80–87, 93–104, 109–30, 137, 146, 157, 159, 170–81, 188–95, 205–207, 220–42, 246, 248, 251, 253, 260–62, 267–68
Penn, Admiral William, 62
Penn, William, Founder of Pennsylvania, 19–26, 49, 53, 55, 57, 62, 69, 86, 91, 172, 188, 222, 226, 228, 232, 236, 240
Pennsbury, 20
Penn's Creek, 167
Pennsylvania Gazette, 20, 59, 147, 207, 209
"Pennymite" Wars, 243
Pepperell, Sir William, 89, 131, 144
Perspective view, 120, 124, 128, 130–31
Philadelphia County, 43, 268
Phillips, Rev. Francis, 12, 54
Physick, Edmund, 177, 235
Pitt, William, Earl of Chatham, 233
Plain Truth, 95–96, 101, 109, 218, 267
Platbridge, 7, 249, 256, 266
Plumsted, Clement, 10–11, 84
Pomfret, Earl of. 121, 123, 190, 261. *See* Fermor, Thomas.
Pontiac, 208, 213

Poor Richard's Almanack, 20
Popish citizens, 130
Port of Philadelphia, 92–93, 235
Porter, Rev. John, 241, 250
Powell, Samuel, 231, 245
Pownall, Thomas, 176–77
Presbyterians, 3, 6, 109, 130, 145, 202, 214, 216–18, 223–24, 234
Prince of Wales, 207
Princeton, 200
Privateers, 68, 84, 93, 96, 98, 101, 104
"Proposals Relating to the Education of Youth," 111
Proprietary Family, 11, 60, 121, 177, 189
Proprietary party, 58, 223
Proprietors of Pennsylvania, 17, 106, 116–17, 126, 129
Protestant Episcopal Church of America, 1
Province Island, 212, 214

Quaker majority, 89
Quakers, 6, 13, 98–99, 109, 130–31, 170, 173–82, 191–93, 211, 214, 217, 219, 234

Reading, 159, 182, 184
Reading, Rev. Philip, 199
Rector of the Academy, 111
Register of the Admiralty, 2, 68, 189
Release of the Delawares, 180
Roberts, George, 245
Robinson, Sally, 263
Roman Catholics, 146, 170
Romans, 85
Ross, Rev. Aeneas, 52–55
Ross, Rev. George, 40–45
Ross, John, 44, 197
Royal Americans, 215
"Rules of War," 104
Rutherford, John, 149, 168–69

St. Clair, General Sir John, 87–89, 147–53, 156, 161, 163, 190
St. James' Chapel, London, 252
St. Lawrence River, 77, 88, 165–66
St. Michael's Church, 247
St. Peter's Church, 1, 196–201, 205, 219–20, 224–25, 230, 243, 245, 254, 258, 260, 262. *See also* Christ Church and the United Churches.

Index

Salisbury Plains, 173
"Sans Dieu Rien," 244–57
Sauer, Christopher, 146
"Scalp acts," 209
Scarborough, 221
Scarroyady, 144, 152
Scotch-Irish, 19, 81, 108, 117, 210–11, 214, 216–17
Scull, Nicholas, 124, 129–30, 179, 244–45
Secker, Thomas, Archbishop of Canterbury, 123–24, 145, 205, 220, 222, 234
Seeley, Mr., 214
Senecas, 25, 68, 78, 110, 128, 240
Shamokin, 77–79, 95, 115, 126, 181–82, 227–28, 242
Sharpe, Gov. Horatio, 142, 153, 159–60, 198
Shawnees, 77, 79, 110, 178, 181, 209, 219
Sheehays, 211
Sherman's Creek, 117
Shewbart, John, 83–84, 267
Shewbart, Mary, 83–84
Shikellamy, 78–79, 95, 115, 117
Shikellamy, John, 126, 142, 228
Shippen, Edward, Sr. (aka Ned), 58–59, 98, 140, 159, 185, 198, 212–13
Shippen, Edward, Jr., 245
Shippen, Joseph, 13, 34, 209
Shippensburg, 117, 149, 151–53, 158, 165, 208
Shirley, Gov. Sir William, 77–78, 88–89, 131, 142–43, 147–48, 162–63, 166–68, 172
Shirley, William, Jr., 148, 150–61, 163, 169
Six Nations, vii, 60–62, 68–79, 95, 115–16, 125–26, 143–44, 166, 172–82, 192–94, 209, 213–16, 227–29, 237–41
Skelton's Works, 260
Slough's inn yard, 212
Smith, Matthew, 212, 217, 219
Smith, Richard Peters, 263
Smith, Samuel, 108
Smith, Provost William, 123–26, 141, 145–46, 158–59, 194–95, 199, 202–207, 220, 223, 234, 241, 245, 250–51, 259, 262, 267
Smout, Justice, 82
Socrates, 85
South Carolina, 187, 190, 231, 249
Southern Indians, 149–50
Spain, 77, 109, 202, 253
Spaniards, 88, 92–93

Spanish prisoners, 92
Spanish privateers, 84, 96, 98, 104
Spanish War, 77
Spectator, 21, 192
Speed, John, 224–26, 250
Spotswood, Governor, 71
Spring Gardens, 223–226, 230
Stamp Act, 224, 233
Stanley, Charles, 8–10, 32, 221
Stanley, Sir Edward (11th Earl of Derby), 32
Stanley, Mistress, 9, 13
Stanwix, Colonel, 187
State House ("Independence Hall"), 3, 19–20, 22, 100, 112, 129–30, 197–98, 264
Statham, Richard, 205–206, 221, 223, 234, 254, 256
Statham, Mrs. William, 204, 206, 221, 225, 248–50, 256. *See* Peters, Hannah.
Stedman, Alexander, 199–200, 204
Steel, James, 55–56
Stenton, 19, 23, 25
Stewart, Lazarus, 210, 212
Stirling, Lord. *See* Alexander, William.
Stoke, 222–26, 232, 245, 261
Stringer, Rev. William, 262
Stuart, James, the Pretender, 87
Stuart, Rev. John, 251
Sturgeon, Rev. William, 196–201, 204, 220
Susquehanna Company, 228, 230, 242, 266
Susquehanna Indians, 190
Susquehanna lands, 125, 128, 238
Sussex County, 129, 157
Swaine, Charles, 154, 158, 164–65
Swedish visitors, 260
Swinton, Mr., 255

Tachanoontia, the Black Prince, 69, 79
Taghneckadorrus, 95
Tanacharisson, 127. *See also* Half-King.
Tarachawagon. 70, 74, 78, 115. *See also* Weiser, Conrad.
Teedyuscung, vii, 135, 174, 177–82, 188–92, 229, 268
"Temple" of the Angels' hearts, 247
Tennant, Rev. Gilbert, 111, 211
Ten Nations, 181, 191–92
Terrick, Richard, Bishop of London, 225
Thomas, Gov. George, 25, 29–30, 35, 41, 52, 56, 61, 68–72, 75–76, 86–91, 128, 131

Tilghman, James, 230, 233, 239–41, 245, 249
Tittany, Moses, 180
Tocarryhogan (Lord Baltimore or his representative), 69, 78
Treaty of 1754, 242
Trinity Church, New York, 246
Trinity Church, Oxford, 67
Trinity College, 246
Tulleken, Captain, 186
Tulpehocken, 18, 79, 84, 159
"Tunbridge acquaintance," 169
Tuscarora Path, 117
Tuscaroras, 25, 68, 78, 117
Twightwees, 95, 115, 150

Union Flag (Union Jack), 110
United Churches of Christ and St. Peter's, 1, 197, 221, 225, 243, 245. *See also* Christ Church.
University of Edinburgh, 213

Vandergucht, 129
Venerable Society for the Propagation of the Gospel in Foreign Parts, 9, 13, 35, 39, 48–49, 54, 146, 158, 167, 173, 196, 240, 251, 262
Vice-Admiralty Courts, 76
Vidal, Stephen, 13, 34
Virginia, 10, 21, 25, 68–79, 84, 88, 93, 98, 110, 118, 122, 127, 136, 142–45, 149, 152–53, 161, 166, 188, 190, 239, 259–60
Virginia Company, 110, 161

Wadham College, 8
Wagons for Braddock, 149–61
Walking Purchase, 179–80
Warrant and Patent Books, 71, 222
Washington, George, viii, 126, 131, 136, 150, 163, 165, 188, 267
Weiser, Benjamin, 194
Weiser, Conrad, 24, 60–63, 68–79, 84–85, 90, 92, 95, 110, 114–17, 127–28, 138, 172, 174, 179–85, 192, 194, 209, 229, 267
Weiser's Battalion, 182
Westminster College, 7, 13, 120
Westover, 259
Wetherholt, Captain, 183
White, Colonel Thomas, 199, 255
White, Bishop William, 1–3, 6, 116, 136, 246, 251, 253–56, 262
Whitefield, George, 34–44, 61, 108–109, 111, 119, 138, 245
Whitefieldian Charity School, 119
Whitefieldianism, 109
Whitefieldians, 40, 43, 61, 111
Whitehall, 46, 48, 51, 77, 87–88, 122
Whitsunday communion, 203
Wiccacoa (Battery), 104, 109, 129, 249
Williamsburg, 78–79, 142–43
Willis, Richard, Bishop of Winchester,
Will's Creek,
Wilson, Thomas,
Winchester, Richard Willis, Bishop of, 196
"Wishin Indians," 240
Wolfe, General James, 195
Woman at Westminster, the, 13
Worcester College, 255
Wyandots, 110, 208
Wyoming, 60, 63, 126, 128, 142, 181, 184, 209–210, 227–30, 236, 239–43, 249, 261, 266–67

York, Archbishop of, 1
York County, 110, 114, 156, 167, 227, 240
York Town (York, Pennsylvania), 110–11, 114, 146, 158, 249, 260
Youghiogheny, 146, 151
Young's *Night Thoughts*, 63

Zane, Isaac, 192
Zenger, John Peter, 22
Zinzendorf, Count Nicolaus, 57, 61

About the Author

Hubertis Maurice Cummings (1884–1963) was a 1907 graduate of Princeton University, member of Phi Beta Kappa, and long-time professor of English at the University of Cincinnati. He was the son of Homer Hamilton Cummings and Sarah Cowden Cummings. Hubertis was a historian, essayist, and poet, and the author of several books including: *The Mason and Dixon Line: Story for a Bicentenary, 1763–1963*; and *Richard Peters, Provincial Secretary and Cleric, 1704–1776*. Cummings lived for many years at a fine home at 2331 Market Street in Camp Hill, Pennsylvania. He was born and died in Harrisburg, Pennsylvania. He was cremated and then buried at Paxtang.

www.ingramcontent.com/pod-product-compliance
Lightning Source LLC
Chambersburg PA
CBHW01195l150426
43195CB00019B/2894